The Lord Who Heals You

Discovering God's will

and ways for receiving

healing through the

stories of the Bible.

Pastor Kate Forsyth

Ark House Press
arkhousepress.com

© 2025 Pastor Kate Forsyth

All rights reserved. Apart from any fair dealing for the purpose of study, research, criticism, or review, as permitted under the Copyright Act, no part may be reproduced by any process without written permission.

All scripture is taken from the New Spirit Filled Life Bible, New King James version, Jack Hayford, executive editor. Published by Thomas Nelson Inc, Nashville, USA 2002.

Cataloguing in Publication Data:
Title: The Lord Who Heals You
ISBN: 978-1-7638801-7-7 (pbk)
Subjects: REL006160   RELIGION / Biblical Reference / General;   REL077000 RELIGION / Faith; MED034000 MEDICAL / Healing;

Design by initiateagency.com

CONTENTS

Preface..ix
Introduction..xi
1 God's Character- 'The Lord Who Heals You'......................1
2 God Is Good...7
3 God Is Merciful..15
4 God's Will And Provision For Healing..............................20
5 God's Will And Provision For Healing (Part 2).................29
6 Forgiven And Healed Together...35
7 God Is Willing..41
8 Healing Is The Children's Bread.......................................49
9 As Your Soul Prospers..57
10 It's All In Your Perspective...64
11 God's Perspective Brings His Power.................................71
12 A Spirit Of Wisdom And Revelation................................79
13 Seeing The Impossible Become Possible..........................86
14 Believe That You Receive (Part 1)....................................92
15 Believe Before You Receive (Part 2)...............................102
16 I Believe; Help My Unbelief...110
17 The Hindrance Of Unbelief..115
18 Arise In Faith...124

19	Do Not Be Afraid, Only Believe	133
20	Faith That Touches God	140
21	The Honour Of God	148
22	Just Say The Word	154
23	Power In The Name Of Jesus	162
24	Healing In Communion	170
25	What About Job?	178
26	Pauls' Thorn	187
27	Idols Around Healing	194
28	Free Indeed	206
29	Where The Spirit Of The Lord Is	213
30	Turning From Darkness To Light	222
31	Forgiven To Forgive	234
32	Spiritual Warfare	242
33	He Restores My Soul	250
34	The Implanted Word Which Is Able To Save Your Soul	259
35	The Lord's Prayer For Healing	270
36	Freely You Have Received Freely Give	278
37	The Works That I Do You Will Do Also	290
38	Ministering Healing	304
Conclusion		317
References		319
About the Author		321

ENDORSEMENTS

'I wholeheartedly recommend this much-needed book for those seeking healing. Kate has been one of our most dedicated and impactful healing ministers during the 36 years she and her husband, Richard, have been part of our church.

They led our healing service for 10 years and witnessed miracles during those sessions, including cancer healings, restored eyesight and hearing, recovery from diabetes, internal organ diseases, and multiple back injuries. Many childbirth complications were also resolved.

With a devotional of the same name on YouBible, with 28000 subscribers, Kate teaches us how to stand in faith, manage disappointment and discouragement, and not give in to theories people propose when healing doesn't occur immediately.

Kate also shares the healing principles employed by Jesus in the numerous accounts of healing found in the Gospels, which can effortlessly be applied to your own circumstances.

The book concludes by sharing ways you also can bring healing to others.

Pastor Phil Pringle, *C3 Church Global Founder and Leader*

I have known Ps Kate for several decades - both as a colleague on our team at SYD and also a valued friend. Alongside her husband Richard, together they have led our healing services on Sunday - as well as praying over several men & women offsite in homes, hospitals and on altar calls.

Kate's heart to minister healing prayer and clear biblical teaching comes from both her own testimony of personal miracles and studying God's Word as the foundation for not only herself, but for others to receive healing and maintain it. Her powerful ministry (though she is a quiet soul) is in her fruit.

So I highly commend this book to you the reader. May the power of the work of the cross and Kate's revelation of it in these pages, release many more precious souls into both salvation and freedom from disease and bondage.

Pastor Chris Pringle, C3 Church Global Co-Founder and Leader

Healing was at the centre of the ministry of Jesus Christ and I believe it should be a central part of what we do now as His representatives – the church. Ps Kate Forsyth is someone who lives and breathes this ministry. Her latest book, **The Lord Who Heals You**, will help you to experience the healing power of God personally, as well as equipping you to lay hands on the sick and see them recover. Kate has been a member of the C3 movement for over 35 years and after experiencing a profound and miraculous healing herself, has taught and ministered healing for many years. Her revelation around the finished work of the cross, the power of scripture and the work of the Holy Spirit will empower you to step into the healing power of Jesus Christ.

Pastor John Pearce, C3 Church Global Executive Director

WITH MUCH GRATITUDE

My eternal gratitude is first and foremost to God - the Father, Jesus and the Holy Spirit - who not only showed His miraculous healing grace to myself and my family, but to so many others who we have seen healed over the years. These many healings included those experienced through the healing service that my husband, Richard and I ran at C3 Church, Oxford Falls location in Sydney and through the many years of teaching in the C3 Bible College there. I also acknowledge that the following messages are those given to me by the Holy Spirit from times in His presence and are certainly not of my own wisdom or understanding. I am so appreciative that He would share His Word with me, as of course He also does for you, for He is no respecter of persons.

I am so thankful to my husband Richard, my children Annalise and Michael and daughter-in-law Tonia for their support and encouragement and for being such good 'sounding boards' for many discussions on healing and the Scriptures. You are the most beautiful and wonderful family - I love you and am so grateful for you.

I am thankful for the support and encouragement of many friends, with special mention to Jenny Holman and Wendy Gilbert. Thanks for the encouragement, prayer support and partnership in ministry of members of our former healing service team - I can't mention all but special mention to Jean and Jim McFarlane, Heather Bush, Jude and Bruce Allen, Shareena and Albert Visvalingam.

Thank you to Dr Phil Pringle and Pastor Chris Pringle the C3 Church Global Founders and Leaders, and Pastor John Pearce, C3 Church Global Executive Director, who provided endorsements for this book. I salute your love for God and unwavering commitment to Jesus and the ministry of His healing grace. You encourage and inspire me in every way.

Thank so much to Heather Bush, Jean McFarlane, Wendy Gilbert and Richard Forsyth for their valuable support in editing and proof-reading for me. I am very grateful to you all.

Finally, but certainly not least, I would like to express my profound gratitude to Dr Phil Pringle, along with Pastor Chris Pringle, and Pastoral Executives Pat and Amanda Antcliff, who have supported us over the years, believed in us, and enabled us to grow by releasing us into the many opportunities we have experienced in church life over the last 35 years. I could never be in this position without your faith filled, inspiring and encouraging leadership and I am very thankful for you.

Kate Forsyth

PREFACE

To those of you looking to receive healing, I want to encourage you that our God truly is the 'The Lord who heals you' and that you have great hope in Him. For those doing this study to build your faith; to be someone who ministers healing to others, I applaud you, for this is a ministry dear to the heart of Jesus.

I myself, had a season of having to look to the Lord for a miracle when I suffered a debilitating disease thirty-five years ago at the time of writing, asthma, immune insufficiency, with constant illness, and a diagnosis of not being able to have children. The Lord was faithful to His character and His Word, and today I am healed, walk in great health and am blessed with two beautiful (now adult) children.

Since that time, in teaching and ministering healing, I have seen healings and miracles of a whole range of conditions - including cancers, vision loss, hearing loss, infertility, internal organ diseases, backpain, knee and other joint issues, and pain in its many manifestations.

God has promised to be our Healer and has made full provision for this in the death and resurrection of our Lord Jesus Christ. A combination of the ministry of the Holy Spirit and the power of the Word of God releases that divine healing to us today.

THE LORD WHO HEALS YOU

I could share a plethora of stories from my own and others' lives but, in this book, I wanted to bring out the stories that the Holy Spirit inspired for recording in the Bible; the ones He wanted us to glean from. Out of the great multitude of healings that would have occurred in Jesus' and other's ministries in the Bible, what is it about the few detailed stories recorded that we need to see, learn from and apply to our own lives?

I want to encourage you as you go on this study of the healing Scriptures to really delve into the Word of God, allow it to sink in and change you, and stay the course for the whole study. I would also suggest doing the chapters in order as I have designed this study so that each chapter builds upon teachings from the previous chapters.

Let me pray for you as you begin: "Dear Father, I thank you for this reader who is coming to study Your Word in a deeper way, reaching out to You for Your healing grace. May the healing grace and divine life that flows from Jesus and the finished work of the Cross of Calvary fill them now, remove all sickness, disease and pain as 'by His stripes they were healed' and may Your anointing rest upon them to release Your healing to others, in Jesus' mighty and wonderful name. Amen."

Bless you

Kate Forsyth

INTRODUCTION

This book is designed to take you on a journey through many Scriptures on healing to help you discover, acknowledge and, I pray, receive the healing that God made possible through Jesus' work at the Cross of Calvary. The Scriptures are from the New King James version of the Bible unless stated otherwise (with a numerical link to their reference).

I realise that, for many of you, this can be a challenging topic as, so often in life, our experience doesn't reflect what the Scriptures are promising or what many believers tell us we should be living in. It can not only be challenging, but discouraging and hurtful at times. While I can't take away all your challenges, I hope to remove the discouragement and pressure that many sick believers can feel and to help you find a place in the Rest of God's grace where His healing can come to you.

One Scripture I like to bounce off regularly to explain the challenge that we face between what is promised and what we currently might be experiencing is Hebrews 10:14.

Hebrews 10:14 *For by one offering He has perfected forever those who are being sanctified.*

On one hand, God has perfected forever those who are walking with Him, and on the other hand, it is written to those who are <u>being</u> (that is, still in the process of being) sanctified. When we choose to accept God's free gift of salvation, made possible through Jesus' offering of Himself as a sacrifice in our place, for our sins, we are declared to have the righteousness of God in Him (2 Corinthians 5:21). However, we don't display perfect righteousness that day, or any day after, even though we have received a perfect salvation and forgiveness. We will walk out the process of sanctification, where we progressively become more like Christ and progressively experience what God has already given us.

When we sin and come to God to receive forgiveness, we understand that it has been provided (1 John 1:9) and we receive it freely. We don't come with doubt as to whether it's God's will to forgive us, or wonder if the answer is "no" nor do we entertain thoughts as to whether God brought the sin or wants it left in our lives to teach us something. We know it is done and to question it in that way would be to dishonour God and His perfect gift. So, why do Christians so often approach healing this way when it is part of the same salvation?

When we sin, we don't say "Well that salvation prayer didn't work because I'm not perfect". No, we understand there is a process of us living it out. We find some sins go at that point of receiving Christ; most of the sanctification process is worked out through prayer and applying the Word of God and some sins, even for the greatest of Christians, are still there at the end. Does that mean that Jesus didn't pay the price for those sins? Of course not. Does that mean that the person doesn't have enough faith when they have faithfully walked with God all those days, trusting in Him? Of course they have faith. Some areas remain a mystery - and so it is with healing.

INTRODUCTION

There are two sides that we have to negotiate in our Christian life - the absolute truth of what God has said and our circumstances or experience. God has declared who He is, what He has done for us, His will and His power that is available to bring that to pass as absolutes- but we are still in a process of laying hold of it and experiencing it. We experience His promises and power a bit at a time and change little by little. Some breakthroughs happen instantly (we love those ones!) and some are over a process over time.

> **2 Corinthians 3:18 NIV**[2] *And we all, who with unveiled faces contemplate the Lord's glory, are being transformed into His image with ever-increasing glory, which comes from the Lord, who is the Spirit.*

God always declares the end from the beginning and, as we believe and trust Him with that truth that He speaks to us, we connect to the power of God. This power is essential to take us on the journey to experiencing the promise - for none of this change can occur through our works and none of it occurs without the power of God. Eventually, we become and have, who and what, He declared us to be and have, at the beginning.

God declares He is the Healer and that through Jesus' work on the Cross of Calvary we are healed. As we believe it and build that truth into us, start to see ourselves that way, we connect with God and the power of His Spirit at a deeper and deeper level, through faith. This enables us to progress in experiencing His healing grace. If we wait for circumstances to line up before we believe or we 'dull down' the truth, then there is no power to take us toward the promise.

So, we must be able to firmly hold God's truth and face our experience at the same time, without changing the truth or denying our circumstances. There have often been two responses in the Body of Christ that mess this up, where believers either try and dampen down truth or 'hype up' experience.

The first response, to dampen down the truth, is so that it is not so challenging or so that circumstances can be explained. This is the source of many religious teachings such as "Healing is not for all', "God is trying to teach you something through this sickness", "It's not for you yet" or "Even Paul had a thorn in the flesh". It is good to note that these first three responses (and many others that will be addressed later) are not validated by Scripture and Paul's thorn, so often used out of context to relate to sickness, will be discussed later in its correct context. If we allow these false teachings to creep into our beliefs, they cause us to disconnect from the power of God that is essential to receiving the healing that God has for us. The power of God is revealed when we connect our faith to truth and not to "What if it doesn't happen" or "It may not be for you".

The second response is where some 'hype up' their experience, perhaps trying to look like their version of a 'great faith' person, not recognising that you can have faith and imperfect circumstances at the same time. These people talk in such a way that denies the circumstance and are often harsh toward those who suffer as 'not having enough faith'. Our experiences are real and, at times really tough, and we don't have to pretend otherwise but we do need to, in the midst of the circumstance, direct our attention and faith to God's truth that has all the power to change our experience.

If you are on this journey to receive healing or are supporting another, it is important to note that a person's faith is not measured by their circumstances. The person who gets healed quickly doesn't necessarily have more faith than the one 'on a journey'. Faith is only measured by the heart's response to truth, of which only God can be the Judge. Don't become the judge of another's faith level because of what they are going through. We are not to be harsh, accusing people of not having enough faith, but rather,

INTRODUCTION

encouraging them in the grace of God. We are to encourage people in the character, mercy and promises of God and recognise that truth must always be expressed through love.

However, we also need to realise that God's power will not reveal itself when we indulge in complaining, hold to religious arguments that contradict God's Word or use someone's experience to challenge the truth of His Word. The argument "What about so-and-so's experience?" is not a valid challenge to the truth of God's Word, because their circumstance does not dictate God's character, His will and finished work in Christ or the measure of power that He has made available to us.

So, faith can at times appear 'extreme' because it requires believing an absolute truth while, at the same time, navigating a current experience that may look very different. We are not in denial but believing that God and what He has done for us, is enough to bring change to our experience. I feel for all who are struggling in the area of their health and do not dismiss the hardship of that challenge. However, in the following studies, I will be presenting the unchangeable truths of God's Word, His absolutes, because that is where we all need to connect our faith; that is where the power of God operates from.

Kate Forsyth

1

GOD'S CHARACTER- 'THE LORD WHO HEALS YOU'

Exodus 15:26 *and said, "If you diligently heed the voice of the LORD your God and do what is right in His sight, give ear to His commandments and keep all His statutes, I will put none of the diseases on you which I have brought on the Egyptians. For I am the LORD who heals you."*

Often as we face sickness, disability or life's challenges, they can bring limitations to our lives that seem insurmountable and it can at times seem unrealistic to be believing for them to change. However, the salvation that comes through Jesus Christ, the inherent power in God's Word and the work of the Holy Spirit can change not only us, but the circumstances that we face.

Matthew 7:24-27 [24] *"Therefore whoever hears these sayings of Mine, and does them, I will liken him to a wise man who built his house on the rock:* [25] *and the rain descended, the*

> *floods came, and the winds blew and beat on that house; and it did not fall, for it was founded on the rock.*
>
> [26] *"But everyone who hears these sayings of Mine, and does not do them, will be like a foolish man who built his house on the sand:* [27] *and the rain descended, the floods came, and the winds blew and beat on that house; and it fell. And great was its fall."*

If we get our foundations right, we may go through the storms of life, but we will come out the other side stronger and God always brings you out with blessing and a story of His miraculous grace.

In Richard's and my experience, our lives have been strengthened because of various trials – although, it certainly didn't feel like it at the time! This is because of what God has done in us, the miracles He has done and the blessing that He brought us out into. However, every time it required that our foundations be right and if they weren't, to be adjusted, before that happened.

There are three basic foundations to build your faith on with God's Word that will bring you through challenges and into blessing, and these are God's character, God's will and God's perspective. These three foundations anchor our souls in truth through the storms and position us for the power of God to change things. As believers, we need to have a deep, immovable conviction in these three areas to be those who have steadfast faith, not only in our own challenges, but in ministering God's power to others.

We are starting by looking at the first of these foundations, the one that must be laid first, and that is God's perfect, unchanging and reliable character.

God is who He says He is. This sounds obvious but if we don't have this foundation right, it distorts everything else.

Paul writes in 1 Corinthians 3:10,11, '*[10]According to the grace of God which was given to me, as a wise master builder I have laid the foundation, and another builds on it. But let each one take heed how he builds on it. [11]For no other foundation can anyone lay than that which is laid, which is Jesus Christ.*'

God is good, which means He is always good even if good things aren't happening to you. It robs you of your confidence and faith, to go to God if you think He is behind what is happening to you, rather than the One who loves you, has mercy on you, wants to help you and give you His grace to overcome.

God is the Healer, even if someone is not getting healed at this moment. So, we can still honour and worship Him for being our Healer, whether we are experiencing it or not. Our circumstances don't dictate His character.

Malachi 3:6 *"For I am the Lord; I do not change".*

Hebrews 13:8 *Jesus Christ is the same yesterday, today and forever.*

When we choose to believe in His character, despite whatever is going on, to trust Him and declare that to Him and over our circumstances, things start to shift. On my healing journey, there was a time when it looked like things weren't changing and I came to a point where I said to God, "Whether I get healed or not, I will still believe and honour You as my Healer to my dying day". For me, this was one of many breakthrough moments and a turning point in progressing towards being healed.

In Exodus 15: 26, God reveals Himself to the Hebrew people as 'the Lord who heals you'.

Exodus 15:22-26 [22] *So Moses brought Israel from the Red Sea; then they went out into the Wilderness of Shur. And they went three days in the wilderness and found no water.* [23] *Now when they came to Marah, they could not drink the waters of Marah, for they were bitter. Therefore the name of it was called Marah.* [24] *And the people complained against Moses, saying, "What shall we drink?"* [25] *So he cried out to the LORD, and the LORD showed him a tree. When he cast it into the waters, the waters were made sweet.*

There He made a statute and an ordinance for them, and there He tested them,

[26] *and said, "If you diligently heed the voice of the LORD your God and do what is right in His sight, give ear to His commandments and keep all His statutes, I will put none of the diseases on you which I have brought on the Egyptians. For I am the LORD who heals you."*

The people are complaining which is a natural reaction to tiredness. I can imagine that if we walked for days, were thirsty and came to these bitter pools the feelings that we also would have, of weariness, disappointment, maybe even anger, but the people are letting the situation dictate their response. Healing doesn't come with God responding to our natural reactions or complaining, but when we respond to God's supernatural answer.

God's response is for Moses to throw a tree into the water. The tree is a type or prophetic picture of the Cross (1 Peter 2:24 *'who Himself bore ours sins in His own body on the tree that we having died to sins might live for righteousness, by whose stripes you were healed'*). God's response is always to put Jesus and His redemptive work into the situation, and in this case, the waters are healed. That this is an example of healing for us is seen in verse 26 when the Lord uses this situation to reveal Himself as the Healer to His people.

"I am the Lord who heals you" in the Hebrew is 'Jehovah Rapha'. The names of the Lord starting with Jehovah, in the Old Testament, are called His redemptive names. Through them, God revealed to His people what He was going to restore to them, that had originally been lost in the Fall, in this case health. The word 'rapha' means 'to cure, heal, repair, mend, restore health'[3]. It is used in the Bible for the healing of physical sickness.

God is not saying that we must keep His word perfectly in order to be healed. His healing comes as we respond to His truth - a truth that is revealed through Jesus and the Scriptures. When we 'give ear' to what He says above that of others; and when we respond to the prompting of the Holy Spirit 'diligently heeding His voice' we will find that He has made healing fully available to us, and that He will lead us into it.

So, we start with recognising and honouring God for who He is, Jehovah Rapha, the Healer. He is worthy of worship and honour for who He is and what He has done, independent of whether we are experiencing healing or not.

We need our first foundation firmly laid, that God is who He says He is and is worthy of honour for this, irrespective of our circumstances. We need to hold firmly to the truth of who He is in all seasons of life. This rooting of ourselves in truth, not only anchors our soul but starts connecting us to 'the Lord who heals'.

Reading:

- Exodus 15:22-27
- Jeremiah 17:14
- Genesis 20:17
- 2 Chronicles 30:20
- Psalm 89:34
- Hebrews 6:13-20

Thought for the day: God says "I am the Lord who heals you".

Reflection: Write down any insights or revelations that you have had as you reflect on God's character.
_____
_____
_____

How do you see God in your current (or even past) circumstance(s)? Is how you see Him to be, reflected by how He reveals Himself in the Scriptures?
_____
_____
_____

Write down three Scriptures below that declare God's character e.g., He is love, He is the Healer, He is merciful and kind- and start to see Him that way in your own life - rebuild any cracks in this first and very important foundation.

Scripture 1:

Scripture 2:

Scripture 3:

2
GOD IS GOOD

Psalm 27:13 *I would have lost heart, unless I had believed, That I would see the goodness of the LORD In the land of the living.*

God is good! However, He is not always presented that way, even in the church. There are teachings in some circles that would suggest that God would withhold healing, favour some with it and not others or even dare to go as far as to say that He would put sickness on someone to teach them something. Such false portrayals, so inconsistent with His nature and Word, rob people of heart, literally courage, and faith. We gain heart when we believe and it is hard to believe and trust someone if you don't know them to be good and trustworthy - but God is good!

John 10:10 *The thief does not come except to steal, and to kill, and to destroy. I have come that they may have life, and that they may have it more abundantly.*

The thief that Jesus refers to in this teaching is not the devil as is so often quoted, even though that is his job description. The thief here actually refers to religious leaders and their teachings, that were not shepherding people in God's ways. If you believe religious teaching that is based on man's reasonings and traditions, rather than truth, it hinders you receiving healing. This kind of teaching steals, kills and destroys all that God has for you and yes, allows the enemy, portrayed as the wolf in this chapter, to attack.

God is not withholding healing from us but false believing about God and His willingness to heal us, can hinder us receiving healing. Jesus came to give you 'life' - Himself - more abundantly. If I could put a definition on the healing power of God, it would be 'His life'.

So often it is religious traditions that are hindering believers receiving their healing. The church has developed so many reasons why healing didn't happen, but they don't align with the teachings of Scripture. In Matthew 15:6, Jesus said the traditions of man make the Word of God of no effect. When we accept religious traditions that contradict the Word of God, we hinder ourselves receiving the healing that God has for us.

Some teach that healings and miracles have passed away but Hebrews 13:8 says *Jesus Christ is the same yesterday, today, and forever.* He healed yesterday, He heals today and He will continue to heal.

> **Matthew 9:35,36** *Then Jesus went about all the cities and villages, teaching in their synagogues, preaching the gospel of the kingdom, and healing every sickness and every disease among the people. But when He saw the multitudes, He was moved with compassion for them, because they were weary and scattered, like sheep having no shepherd.*

Luke 4:40 *When the sun was setting, all those who had any that were sick with various diseases brought them to Him; and He laid His hands on every one of them and healed them.*

Some would believe that God gave or allowed sickness to teach you something or that sometimes the answer is "no". God can't operate against His own will and He has revealed in the Word that He is good, He is the Healer, that it is His will to heal His people and that the work of the Cross makes the answer "yes". Jesus, the revealed will of God, healed all who came to Him and never once put sickness on anyone. To say that God would make someone sick is slander to His character. It would be evil to put cancer on your child to teach them a lesson. Scripture says that God is love, His mercy endures forever and 'He is the Lord who heals you'.

Acts 10:38 *how God anointed Jesus of Nazareth with the Holy Spirit and with power, who went about doing good and healing all who were oppressed by the devil, for God was with Him.*

Jesus' ministry reveals the nature of God; that He is good, merciful, loving and compassionate. In the following passage from John 9, Jesus is in the process of removing Himself and His disciples from a situation where people want to kill Him, and yet, in compassion, He stops to heal a blind man whom others had judged.

John 9:1-3 [1]*Now as Jesus passed by, He saw a man who was blind from birth.*

[2] *And His disciples asked Him, saying, "Rabbi, who sinned, this man or his parents, that he was born blind?"* [3] *Jesus*

> *answered, "Neither this man nor his parents sinned, but that the works of God should be revealed in him".*

Having seen a man blind from birth, Jesus' disciples ask Him, *"Rabbi, who sinned, this man or his parents, that he was born blind?"* How many believers who have struggled with illness have felt the condemnation of religious thinking, or even beliefs of other religions, that their suffering or disability must be due to something they have done, or that they mustn't be doing something right.

This man has had a long-term affliction and as time goes on with a long-term condition, questions can arise, such as, "If God wanted to heal me, I would be healed by now"; "Maybe I don't have enough faith" or "Maybe I've done something wrong". Doubts, condemnation, and unbelief from within, or from others, can creep in and create a mindset or belief system that doesn't align with what God wants to do in a person's life.

Often people's interpretation of God's will comes through trying to reason as to why people suffer, and it can result in a belief so contrary to God's actual will. Even with Jesus, God in the flesh, the religious people concluded that God was judging Him because He suffered, but He took it all upon Himself so that we could be freed from it. Human reasoning doesn't come up with the correct interpretation of God and His will but, rather, He and His will are revealed through Jesus and the Bible.

Even the disciples who have been with Jesus ask, out of the religious thinking of the time, if that poor man was being punished for sin - in other words, that God is harsh and judgemental. The leaders of the synagogue later respond to the man out of that harsh, judgmental attitude. We reflect what we believe about God. However, if we understand that God is love, merciful and good, then that should not only impact us, but shift our expectation of what He wants to do in us.

Jesus' response is, *"neither this man nor his parents sinned, but that the works of God should be revealed in him."*

The word 'revealed' means 'that what has been hidden before should be made known or demonstrated' - in this case, healing. For us, healing has been made available before through the work of the Cross but now, by the Holy Spirit, it should be made known and demonstrated in the physical realm. God doesn't bring sickness or disability in order to display His works, but if they occur, then He desires His healing and redemptive work to be revealed and experienced.

The Message Bible[4] puts verse 3 as - *Jesus said, "You're asking the wrong question. You're looking for someone to blame. There is no such cause-effect here. Look instead for what God can do."*

> **John 9:6-7** [6] *When He had said these things, He spat on the ground and made clay with the saliva; and He anointed the eyes of the blind man with the clay.* [7] *And He said to him, "Go, wash in the Pool of Siloam" (which is translated, Sent). So he went and washed, and came back seeing.*

Jesus puts a mixture of clay and saliva on the man's eyes which is very messy! It's good to think here, "If Jesus wanted to come in and mess things up a bit to shift me into a place of healing, would I be happy for Him to do it?" This is not saying He would ever shame anyone, because we never see, in the Bible, Jesus shame anyone, but He does sometimes stir things up a bit.

In sickness, one can get stuck and adapt to the situation and sometimes God has to shift a person, making them move in response to Him so they get 'unstuck', aligned with His purpose and thus, bringing the release of healing.

For this blind man, he would have thought that God had judged him; he was stuck in a restricted lifestyle, but there in front of him was God in the flesh, full of compassion, not judgement, but just wanting to stir things up a bit so that a shift would take place.

So, do we just want Him to do His works 'tidily', keeping us dignified, or will we let Him have His way on how He wants to bring the healing? He could have 'done it tidily' if He wanted to. Jesus did many healings on the spot and without the mud in the eye method.

Jesus makes the man walk to the pool to wash (there and back about 1300 -1500m), when He could have just healed him on the spot. He deliberately makes the man break the man-made religious rule of how far he could walk on the Sabbath (1000 - 1200m). Jesus likes to mess up man-made religious traditions. Religious traditions that don't reveal God accurately are not holy or sacred. Jesus is Holy and His Word is sacred, and we want to be responding to Him.

The man's step of faith is not so much about finding the pool while he is still blind, and potentially with no help from others because they feared the response of the religious leaders. The big step of faith is being prepared to step out of everything he has known before, previously held beliefs about God, religious traditions taught to him, risking rejection and the judgement of the religious leaders to receive what Jesus really wants to reveal and give to him. Sometimes people can believe things strongly through religious culture that according to Jesus and the Word of God are incorrect.

At this point, all the man knows is that this random Man has come up, seen him when others didn't, shown him love and compassion when others didn't and has now asked him to do something that disobeys the law of the culture. He has to put everything on the line to respond to Jesus while, in the context of the passage, not really knowing anything about Him. The revelation of who Jesus is was to come in a later conversation in the story. I believe that it was an encounter with the love of God that shifted Him and it's my prayer that you will also encounter His transforming and compelling love. The man responds and the result is a miraculous healing.

It's important that we see Jesus for who He really is and not see Him through the eyes of religious tradition that so often doubts and judges. Believe in the goodness of God who heals all. Respond to His Word knowing that He is trustworthy and that He is good.

Reading:

- John 10:7-10
- John 9:1-7
- Acts 10:38
- Matthew 12:9-15
- Luke 14:1-6

Thought for the day: God is always good and His plans for you are good. Jesus is the same yesterday, today and forever.

Reflection: Write down any insights or revelations that you have had as you reflect on God's goodness.

_____
_____
_____
_____
_____
_____
_____
_____
_____
_____
_____

Write down three Scriptures below that declare God's goodness.

Scripture 1:

Scripture 2:

Scripture 3:

3
GOD IS MERCIFUL

Luke 17:13-14 [13]*And they lifted up their voices and said, "Jesus, Master, have mercy on us!"* [14]*So when He saw them, He said to them, "Go, show yourselves to the priests." And so it was that as they went, they were cleansed.*

So often in Scripture we find people crying out to Jesus or the Father for mercy and, in the receiving of the miraculous, expressing an understanding that they had received mercy from God. So, what is this quality of mercy and how do we receive it?

Mercy is a tendency or nature to be forgiving and kind towards someone who hasn't earned it and is in need. Mercy is a manifestation of God's unconditional love for us. Compassion is being moved by that feeling of mercy to meet the need - it is not just sympathy or comfort but an action that brings help, change and healing.

Psalm 116:5 *Gracious is the LORD, and righteous; Yes, our God is merciful.*

THE LORD WHO HEALS YOU

Isaiah 54:10 *For the mountains shall depart and the hills be removed, but My kindness shall not depart from you, nor shall My covenant of peace be removed," says the Lord, who has mercy on you.*

Psalm 145:8,9 *⁸ The Lord is gracious and full of compassion, slow to anger and great in mercy. ⁹ The Lord is good to all, and His tender mercies are over all His works.*

Psalm 103:1-5 *¹Bless the LORD, O my soul; and all that is within me, bless His holy name! ² Bless the LORD, O my soul, and forget not all His benefits: ³ Who forgives all your iniquities, Who heals all your diseases, ⁴ Who redeems your life from destruction, Who crowns you with lovingkindness and tender mercies, ⁵ Who satisfies your mouth with good things, So that your youth is renewed like the eagle's.*

David reminds us to not forget the benefits of the Lord - He forgives all our iniquities and heals all our diseases. He redeems (pays the price to restore back) our lives from whatever has brought destruction or harm and pours out upon us kindness and mercy that we never earned nor deserved. He blesses us and restores us. David advises us to come to God remembering His nature and benefits and to bless Him, thank Him and worship Him for them.

Hebrews 4:14-16 NLT ⁵ *¹⁴ So then, since we have a great High Priest who has entered heaven, Jesus the Son of God, let us hold firmly to what we believe. ¹⁵ This High Priest of ours understands our weaknesses, for he faced all of the same testings we do, yet he did not sin. ¹⁶ So let us come boldly to the throne of our gracious God. There we will receive his mercy, and we will find grace to help us when we need it most.*

GOD IS MERCIFUL

We need the mercy of God when we are in need and none of us can earn God's help or healing. God is so gracious and He invites us to come to Him to receive mercy - His forgiveness, kindness and help when we need it, and His grace which is His empowering, miracle working power in our lives through the Holy Spirit. So, the writer of Hebrews shows us to come boldly to God based on what Jesus has done for us and not based on our own performance.

Jesus is travelling one day toward Jerusalem and He is passing through Samaria and Galilee.

> **Luke 17:12-19** *[12] Then as He entered a certain village, there met Him ten men who were lepers, who stood afar off. [13] And they lifted up their voices and said, "Jesus, Master, have mercy on us!"*
>
> *[14] So when He saw them, He said to them, "Go, show yourselves to the priests." And so it was that as they went, they were cleansed.*
>
> *[15] And one of them, when he saw that he was healed, returned, and with a loud voice glorified God, [16] and fell down on his face at His feet, giving Him thanks. And he was a Samaritan.*
>
> *[17] So Jesus answered and said, "Were there not ten cleansed? But where are the nine? [18] Were there not any found who returned to give glory to God except this foreigner?" [19] And He said to him, "Arise, go your way. Your faith has made you well."*

Jesus would have known that only one of the ten lepers in this situation would be grateful and respond to Him, but He still healed them all. This demonstrates that Jesus doesn't heal because we deserve it but based on His mercy. The Samaritan in the story, the 'outsider' who didn't feel worthy, was grateful because he knew it wasn't deserved. It's not about whether you are undeserving, supposedly 'deserving', good, or not so good, but it is based on the fact that Jesus is good and He is the Healer.

What about the other nine? Is it possible that a sense of worthiness can creep into the believer; that can, even unconsciously feel like "I should be healed" because I have been a Christian for years, been good, been seeking God and have served Him. In Luke 17:7-10 Jesus talks about a servant waiting on his master and says that the servant should not expect thanks, because he is just doing what is his duty to do. In light of all that has been done for us, our serving and worship is just a reasonable response, in no way earning for us what has already been freely given.

God will heal, not based on our deserving but upon His grace, received through faith. In Luke 17:5-6 Jesus shares on how even a tiny portion of faith brings results. Often the prayer response to sickness can be out of fear or anxiety, getting masses of people praying, begging God to do something that He has already done, as if He needs convincing to heal. Even though it's essential that we pray, we are healed <u>because of what Jesus has done for us</u> and it's the prayer of faith that heals the sick.

Faith is not entitled, not works (or lack of works), not begging but rather a response to seeing who Jesus is, seeing the mercy and goodness of God in Him and what He has done that causes one to believe and respond to Him (works of faith).

As healing is based totally on Him and is His free gift, it is available to all: new believer, mature believer and unbeliever. It's a free, fully paid for and undeserved gift!

Our response is to humbly receive it and give God the praise due to Him.

Reading:

- Luke 17:5 -19
- Matthew 14:14
- Matthew 19:2
- Matthew 21:14
- Matthew 15:30,31
- Luke 7:11-15
- Psalm 118:17

Thought for the day: God is always merciful and invites you to come to Him to receive His mercy and grace, the manifestation of which includes healing.

Reflection: Write down any insights or revelations that you have had as you reflect on God's mercy.

_____
_____
_____
_____
_____
_____
_____
_____

Write down three Scriptures below that declare God's mercy.

Scripture 1:

Scripture 2:

Scripture 3:

4
GOD'S WILL AND PROVISION FOR HEALING

Isaiah 53:5 *...and by His stripes we are healed.*

The second foundation that we need to lay in our belief system, after God's character, is God's will, as revealed in Jesus and what He did for us. God wants us to be well and has made full provision for healing through the sacrifice of Jesus.

Most of God's promises are what He has already provided for us; not something He may or may not do; not something we earn if we are good enough, but something already attained for us by Jesus.

2 Corinthians 1:20 *For all the promises of God in Him are Yes, and in Him Amen, to the glory of God through us.*

In Isaiah 52:13 - Isaiah 53:12, the prophet Isaiah, 700 years before it takes place, has a vision of the suffering, sin-bearing Servant, clearly being Jesus (as evidenced in Matthew 8:16,17; John 12:37,38 and Acts 8:30-35).

The picture is of a suffering beyond that experienced by any other man - so clearly not just the horrific physical wounds witnessed by the disciples but extended to a marring of spirit and soul with the filth of mankind.

Isaiah then sees what Jesus would accomplish - the bearing of not only our sins and judgement, but our sicknesses, weaknesses, distresses, grief, sorrows and pains.

He sees that Jesus' sacrifice would bring healing to us and His blood would 'sprinkle' us, alluding to the practice in the temple of the Old Testament, that would purify and separate one unto God. Isaiah 53 is the heart of the gospel!

Isaiah sees Jesus bearing our sins (wrongs, as in actions) and iniquities (wrong inner inclination or perversion from sin) as our substitute, bearing the punishment that would bring us peace, buried with sinners but with the rich (buried in a rich man's grave) and raised up to justify many. In addition, Isaiah also sees something else - that in the same way that Jesus would bear our sins, He would bear sickness and pain on our behalf.

> **Isaiah 53:4,5** [4]*Surely He has borne our griefs and carried our sorrows, yet we esteemed Him stricken, smitten by God and afflicted.* [5]*But He was wounded for our transgressions, He was bruised for our iniquities; the chastisement for our peace was upon Him, and by His stripes we are healed.*

The word 'griefs' in verse 4, according to Young's Concordance[6], is the Hebrew word 'choli' and is correctly translated 'sickness, weakness or pain'. The word 'sorrows' is the Hebrew word 'makob' and is correctly translated as 'pain'. My quotes are from the New King James Bible and contain these corrections in the footnotes. Therefore,

Isaiah 53:4 could read 'Surely He has borne our sicknesses and weaknesses and carried our pains.'

Young's Literal Translation of the Bible[7] puts verses 4 and 5 as, '*⁴Surely our diseases he did bear, and our pains he carried; whereas we did esteem him stricken, smitten of God, and afflicted. ⁵But he was wounded because of our transgressions, he was crushed because of our iniquities; the chastisement of our peace was upon him, and with his stripes we were healed.*'

The Amplified version of the Bible[8], which brings out in parentheses the original intended meaning that was lost in translation, puts it like this:

> ⁴ "*Surely He has borne our griefs (sicknesses, weaknesses and distresses) and carried our sorrows and pains (of punishment), yet we (ignorantly) considered Him stricken, smitten, and afflicted by God (as if with leprosy).*
>
> ⁵ *But He was wounded for our transgressions, He was bruised for our guilt and iniquities; the chastisement (needful to obtain) peace and well-being for us was upon Him, and with the stripes (that wounded) Him we are healed and made whole.*"[3]

In verse 4, the words 'borne' and 'carried' ('nasa' and 'cabal' in the Hebrew), are the same words in verses 11 & 12, to describe Jesus' bearing of our sins as our substitute.

> **Isaiah 53:11,12** ¹¹*He shall see the labour of His soul, and be satisfied. By His knowledge my righteous servant shall justify many, for He shall <u>bear</u> their iniquities.* ¹² *Therefore I will divide Him a portion with the great, and He shall divide the spoil with the strong, because He poured out His soul unto death, and He was numbered with the transgressors, and He <u>bore</u> the sin of many, and made intercession for the transgressors.*

'Cabal' means 'to bear a load'[3], and 'nasa', 'to carry, lift, bear up'[3] and, included in the definition, 'to take away or carry off'. Now in Isaiah 53:11,12 these words speak of Jesus bearing our sins, which He bore as our substitute, entirely removing them from us and dealing with the sin problem in its entirety. So too in verse 4, do these words convey the truth that Jesus bore sickness, weakness and pain as our substitute, removing the load from us.

Many times, in Scripture, we see God transfer from one to another as a substitute, for example, with the sins of Israel being transferred to a goat that was sent away from the people, into the wilderness (Leviticus 16:10,21). We can't physically see the transfer taking place but according to God it is done. In the same way, you might say today, "How could Jesus have borne my sins or sicknesses 2000 years ago?" Rather than try and reason out how He achieved this, understand that when God says He has done the transfer and we identify with what He says, in faith, then God responds with the same power as if the transfer had visibly taken place.

Isaiah 53:5 reads '....*He was bruised for our iniquities......and by His stripes we are healed.*' The word 'stripes' is literally 'bruise' or 'blows that cut in'[3]. Therefore, the same 'bruise' by which Jesus suffered for our sins is the same 'bruise' by which we are healed. Isaiah is bringing out that both our sins and our sicknesses and pains were being borne together, in the vicarious suffering of Christ.

> **Isaiah 53:10** *Yet it pleased the Lord to bruise Him; He has put Him to grief* (literally sickness) *when You made His soul an offering for sin.*
> (inserted words mine)

The Amplified version[8] reads, '*Yet it was the will of the Lord to bruise Him; He has put Him to grief and made Him sick. When You and He made His life an offering for sin...*'

It pleased God, for the bruise or impact of our sickness to be placed upon Jesus, because it meant that we could be completely redeemed from it, and it happened when He was being made an offering for sin. They occurred at the same time.

The wording in the Amplified version[8] of '*when You and He made His life an offering for sin*' highlights the unity of agreement on the plan of salvation between the Father and the Son and the willingness of Jesus to give His life for us. I hear some say that they struggle with a God who would sacrifice His Son, but this was not the case - no one took Jesus' life but He freely, and with great love, gave it for us. In great oppression and suffering, He put up no resistance and 'for the joy that was set before Him, endured the Cross, despising the shame' (Hebrews 12:2).

Isaiah 53:1 says '*Who has believed our report? And to whom has the arm of the Lord been revealed?*' The arm of the Lord, which is the power of God, is revealed to those who believe His report.

When we receive God's salvation, we believe His report that Jesus bore our sins and judgement and was raised from the dead, having thoroughly dealt with them.

Immediately the power of the Holy Spirit comes, bringing forgiveness and connection to the Father in Heaven. In the same way, we are to believe God's report that Jesus bore sickness, weakness and pain on our behalf and was raised from the dead having thoroughly dealt with them. This brings the power of the Holy Spirit who releases the purchased healing to us.

The fact that Jesus bore our sins doesn't mean that we immediately live a perfect life or never sin again. Neither does it mean that we don't have the challenge where, while some things change straight away, some shift at a slower rate as we continue to seek and connect with God at a deeper level, take hold of the Word of God and allow it to change us. So, it is with healing - sometimes there are immediate results and sometimes it may be slower, but can I encourage you to keep believing, keep honouring God and keep applying the finished work of Christ to your life.

It is good to come before the Cross each day. Have you ever stopped to think about Jesus' suffering on your behalf? We can so easily rush in our prayer life, asking for forgiveness or healing, but not slowing down enough for a real transaction to take place between us and Jesus' work of redemption. I often go through Isaiah 53 slowly, with Communion, meditating on what Jesus did.

Still yourself before God, close your eyes and see Jesus. Do you see that suffering? He did that for you so that you could receive God's power to forgive, heal and redeem you. Remember Jesus, alone on that Cross, the magnitude of rejection and betrayal, the sorrow, the extreme pain and the heavy burden of mankind's sins, sicknesses and the curse. Yet, in that moment, was the greatest victory in history and the source of the greatest power of all, available as much today as it was then.

> **Romans 1:4** ....*and declared to be the Son of God with power according to the Spirit of holiness, by the resurrection from the dead.*

God doesn't bring the suffering and pain, but it can be the place where we find the power that Jesus has made available for us, if we will allow it to bring us to the Cross. Don't despise the pain or circumstance that brings you to your knees before Him, that draws you closer and causes you to hunger for His words and thirst for His presence. For in so doing, you will find a life and power that cannot be found any other way. God's purpose in the suffering of Jesus was not that suffering would remain on you, but that you would find resurrection life and power and be able to rise again, in this life and into eternity with Him.

> **Hebrews 2:10,11** *¹⁰For it was fitting for Him, for whom are all things and by whom are all things, in bringing many sons to glory, to make the captain of their salvation perfect through sufferings. ¹¹ For both He who sanctifies and those who are being sanctified are all of one, for which reason He is not ashamed to call them brethren.*

This is not to say that Jesus was deficient in any way or that He Himself needed perfecting. His suffering made Him complete as our Saviour because He took it all in our place. God didn't stay distant and just send some healing or answers from afar because He could. He came so close and identified with us, as One closer than a brother, taking all our suffering upon Himself, and providing so great a salvation.

Hebrews 2:8-10 refers to man's lost dominion and then the coming of Jesus. He now occupies that place of dominion on our behalf with all things under His feet.

Restoration or healing doesn't come with an arrogant assumption of 'this belongs to me', for verse 8 tells us that '*we do not yet see all things put under him*' (referring to mankind and dominion). Verse 9 goes on - '*But now we see Jesus...*' - our Captain, our Champion, as one who fights for another or a nation, as David did on behalf of Israel. Jesus fought and won the fight for us. Restoration and healing come with the recognition that 'this belongs to Jesus' - however, He freely offers it to us as a gift and through opening our heart and submitting to Him, accepting what He did on our behalf, a humble heart receives in faith what has been freely given by grace.

So, are you sick? See that Jesus bore it in your place - it is on Him. Can you see it? See it transferred from you to Him, according to what Scripture tells us. Allow the Holy Spirit to minister to you in that moment and don't rush on. The Holy Spirit does what I call 'the divine transfer', removing the sickness <u>from</u> you and releasing God's healing power <u>to</u> you.

Reading:

- Isaiah 53

Thought for the day: '…and by His stripes we are healed'.

Reflection: Jesus has taken all sickness upon Himself and provided healing for me as a result. What does my life look like in light of this?

_____
_____
_____
_____
_____
_____
_____
_____

Write down any insights or revelations that you have had as you reflect on God's will and provision for you to be healed.

_____
_____
_____
_____
_____
_____
_____

Write down three Scriptures from Isaiah 53 below that reveal what Jesus has done for you.

Scripture 1:

Scripture 2:

Scripture 3:

5

GOD'S WILL AND PROVISION FOR HEALING (part 2)

Matthew 8:16,17 *¹⁶When evening had come they brought to Him many who were demon-possessed. And He cast out the spirits with a word, and healed all who were sick, ¹⁷that it might be fulfilled which was spoken by Isaiah the prophet, saying: "He Himself took our infirmities and bore our sicknesses.*

Jesus and the disciples have had a busy time! They have come down from the mountain where Jesus has given the greatest sermon of all time. Jesus has healed the leper, the Centurion's servant and coming into Peter's house afterwards, laid hands on Peter's mother-in-law and she has been healed of a fever - all with immediate healings. Then evening has come and many more are brought to Him and He heals them all!

In this context, the Holy Spirit, the inspirer of all Scripture, brings the connection with Isaiah's prophecy, and Matthew quotes Isaiah 53:4. He is quoting from the Hebrew, and reveals Isaiah 53:4 as referring to sickness, not grief and sorrow, and it is used in context with Jesus healing the sick. All the sick were healed, in fulfilment of the prophecy that Jesus would bear the sickness of all.

Some will debate that this passage only referred to Jesus' healings on that one day but that would be inconsistent with the reference to Isaiah 53 that speaks of the redemptive work of Jesus at the Cross of Calvary, that applies not for a day, but for all people for all time.

> **Matthew 8:17 AMPC**[8] *He Himself took (in order to carry away) our weaknesses and infirmities and bore away our diseases.*

The Amplified version brings out the essence of Isaiah 53:4,5 with Jesus' removal of sickness and weakness from us, as He bore it on our behalf. As often seen with King David's psalms, the Holy Spirit brings revelation and future prophecy through Scripture, that the writer of the time could not yet have understood.

> **2 Peter 1:20,21** [20] *knowing this first, that no prophecy of Scripture is of any private interpretation,* [21] *for prophecy never came by the will of man, but holy men of God spoke as they were moved by the Holy Spirit.*

Matthew is quoting (Matthew 8:17) Jesus' redemptive work at the Cross as being the reason for everyone being healed - before the time of the Cross!

By way of explanation, I will use Jesus' bearing of sin as an analogy because the way that He dealt with our sins, is the way that He dealt with our sickness. In the Old Testament, sin was atoned for (meaning 'to cover') by the shed blood of an innocent animal but, it wasn't actually fully paid for until Jesus went to the Cross. So, the forgiveness provided prior to the

New Covenant was based on a future payment - the person received it fully, but it was 'on credit'.

Likewise, Matthew 8:17 refers to Jesus' vicarious suffering as being the reason for people being healed, even prior to the Cross. He was to bear and take away their sickness and infirmities (weaknesses), at that stage still a future event - and people were healed in Jesus' earthly ministry on that basis of a future payment. God is the Healer but that healing is due not only to His character, but His will and provision, secured through Jesus' sacrifice for us. So, for us, this means healing is not just something God can do, or does at a whim, but something that He has made a full and secured provision for.

Another passage that draws from Isaiah 53 is 1 Peter 2:24.

> **1 Peter 2:24** *Who Himself bore our sins in His own body on the tree, that we, having died to sins, might live for righteousness - by whose stripes you <u>were</u> healed.*

The same means by which Jesus bore our sins is the same means by which we are healed. Note that this passage is past tense because it was fulfilled on the Cross. In Isaiah 53:5 it reads *'by whose stripes you <u>are</u> healed'*, being in the present tense, because Isaiah is having a vision of what is happening at the time of the Cross. Now Peter writes, *'by whose stripes you <u>were</u> healed'*.

> **Ephesians 2:8** *for by grace you have been saved through faith and that not of yourselves: it is the gift of God, not of works lest any man should boast.*

Salvation in the original Greek text is the word 'sozo' meaning 'to save: deliver, protect, heal, preserve, do well, be or make whole'[3]. Salvation is a package – when you put your faith, attention, focus and trust in Jesus

Christ's sacrifice, healing comes as well as forgiveness, deliverance and eternal life.

Sometimes the word 'sozo' is used for healing (e.g., Matthew 9:22, Mark 10:52), and sometimes for eternal life (e.g., Acts 4:12) because they are both part of the same salvation. The combining of forgiveness of sin and healing so often seen in Scripture is not to suggest that all sickness is a result of an individual's sin, but that it had its original entry point into mankind through sin, both being dealt with through Jesus' sacrifice for us.

So, incorporating the meaning of 'sozo' into the passage in Ephesians 2:8 the translation includes 'For by grace you <u>have been healed</u> through faith'. So once again, the Scriptures describe our salvation, including healing, in the past tense i.e., it has already been done.

John 19:28 says 'Jesus, knowing that all things were now accomplished' and then two verses later 'He said "It is finished"'. Not that it was now all over for Him, but that He had finished all that the Father had given Him to do, which was the accomplishing of all things to completely redeem us from sin and the law of sin and death.

That one day in history changed everything! Every evil thing that came into the world because of sin had its power completely broken that day, and a salvation with full redemption from sin and all of its consequences, including sickness, was made available to all who would receive it.

So often when believers pray for healing, they are pleading with God or trying to persuade Him to heal them, as if God is reluctant to do so. As far as God is concerned, He has already provided healing for us, just as He has already provided forgiveness. He looks back on the Cross of Calvary and sees all of His promises already provided through the sacrifice of Jesus – and all the promises of God are 'yes and amen' in Him (2 Corinthians 1:20).

So, we might say "Well why wasn't I healed when I prayed?". As we believe what He says, build the Word of God into our belief system and

GOD'S WILL AND PROVISION FOR HEALING (PART 2)

allow its inherent power to change us, we start to progress towards full healing. We can't let circumstances dictate what we believe, about what God has given us in Jesus Christ - it brings cracks in the foundation that sabotage the breakthrough that God wants to bring in your life.

Reading:

- Exodus 23:25,26
- Deuteronomy 7:14,15
- Matthew 8:16,17
- 1 Peter 2:24
- John 19:28-30

Thought for the day: God's perspective is that He has already provided healing for you - "It is finished".

Reflection: Write down any insights or revelations that you have had as you reflect on healing being part of the salvation you have received in Christ and as such, given as a free gift.

_____
_____
_____
_____
_____
_____
_____
_____
_____
_____

Write down three Scriptures below that reveal that healing has already been provided i.e., it is 'past tense'.

Scripture 1:

Scripture 2:

Scripture 3:

6

FORGIVEN AND HEALED TOGETHER

Luke 5:17 *Now it happened on a certain day, as He was teaching, that there were Pharisees and teachers of the law sitting by, who had come out of every town of Galilee, Judea, and Jerusalem. <u>And the power of the Lord was present to heal them.</u>*

This following story reveals not only that Jesus sees healing and forgiveness as being available together, but how gracious God is in making healing available, without us having to earn or deserve it. Sickness came into the earth originally through sin, along with a host of other curses. When Jesus died in our place, He didn't just pay the price for our sins but for all of the curse, of which sickness is a part. If sin was revealed to be a link to a 'package' of curses and not an isolated entity, then salvation is so much more a package of the redemption, victory and blessings of God. Hebrews 2:3 advises us to not neglect 'so great a salvation'.

I just want to clarify, that if someone is sick, it is very rarely due to their individual sin, but the result of living in a fallen world in which sickness has had a terrible impact.

Therefore, we are not to be like 'Job's friends' trying to analyse where the suffering came from and accusing the poor sufferer of some hidden sin.

> **Luke 5:17-26** [17] *Now it happened on a certain day, as He was teaching, that there were Pharisees and teachers of the law sitting by, who had come out of every town of Galilee, Judea, and Jerusalem. And the power of the Lord was present to heal them.* [18] *Then behold, men brought on a bed a man who was paralyzed, whom they sought to bring in and lay before Him.* [19] *And when they could not find how they might bring him in, because of the crowd, they went up on the housetop and let him down with his bed through the tiling into the midst before Jesus.*
>
> [20] *When He saw their faith, He said to him, "Man, your sins are forgiven you."* [21] *And the scribes and the Pharisees began to reason, saying, "Who is this who speaks blasphemies? Who can forgive sins but God alone?"* [22] *But when Jesus perceived their thoughts, He answered and said to them, "Why are you reasoning in your hearts?* [23] *Which is easier, to say, 'Your sins are forgiven you,' or to say, 'Rise up and walk'?* [24] *But that you may know that the Son of Man has power on earth to forgive sins"—He said to the man who was paralyzed, "I say to you, arise, take up your bed, and go to your house."*
>
> [25] *Immediately he rose up before them, took up what he had been lying on, and departed to his own house, glorifying God.*

> ²⁶ *And they were all amazed, and they glorified God and were filled with fear, saying, "We have seen strange things today!"*

Jesus is bringing the Word on that day - what a glorious day that must have been! The Word brings faith (Romans 10:17) to receive what God wants to do, and along with the Holy Spirit who moves in perfect union with it, it carries the power of God to do it.

In pastoring, I find that there are people who just want to be prayed for quickly, in a manner that, for them, doesn't really honour God, at a time that suits them and these ones often fail to receive their healing, despite the fact that it is fully provided for.

While God does move supernaturally in so many moments when we pray, and many times without great faith in the one we pray for, it is also important that we are people who build our lives on His Word and allow faith to fill our hearts.

There are so many stories in the New Testament of people who made a sacrifice to be in the presence of Jesus to receive healing and didn't expect God to fit in with them. It is an issue of honouring Him for who He is and what He has done. We will look at a few notable examples in the stories of the Centurion and Jairus, but we also have a great example in this passage in Luke 17 of the sacrifice made by the four faithful friends of the paralysed man. They all knew that only Jesus had what they needed and they laid aside everything else to seek Him.

The story then goes on to say that 'the power of the Lord was present to heal them'. Now it is important to note who is being referred to as 'them'. Just prior to this statement Luke highlights that Pharisees and teachers of law were there. So, 'them' in this story are those who are opposed to Jesus, who have come to criticise Him and hope to 'catch Him out' and accuse Him.

Jesus actually wanted to reveal Himself to them. He didn't reject them; He wasn't withholding healing from them but they didn't receive any healing because they were too busy sitting back critiquing God and not believing or honouring Him.

We don't stand back and critique God like He is a performer, or challenge Him as to why certain things haven't happened. He is God, perfect and good in all His ways, and He doesn't invite us to challenge or critique Him - He calls us to believe Him.

That was the moment for the religious leaders to be healed but they missed it by not believing or giving due honour.

The friends of the paralysed man stand in stark contrast, with their passion to reach Jesus with their friend; that they will do anything, even pull apart someone's roof, to get into the presence of God. Luke notes that 'when Jesus saw their faith', He responded. God moves not on need but in response to faith. Faith receives the grace of God.

Psalm 78:41 records that when Israel questioned and challenged God through unbelief, and dishonoured Him, not remembering His power that they 'limited' Him. Now we can't take anything away from God Himself or make Him weaker in any way by any action of ours, but we can restrict Him moving in our lives and limit what we receive from Him through prideful attitudes like these. This is what prevented the religious leaders receiving healing on that day while the paralysed man received a great miracle.

> **Luke 5:20** *When He saw their faith, He said to him, "Man, your sins are forgiven you".*

Jesus declares forgiveness to the man but in so doing, releases healing as well, because they are part of the same salvation that He has purchased for us. Healing and forgiveness go together. Again, let me clarify that if sickness is still present in your body, it does not mean that you haven't received forgiveness for sins that have been repented of. This is rather to highlight what Jesus is revealing of Himself here.

After discerning the criticism in the hearts of the religious leaders, Jesus states in verse 23, *'Which is easier, to say, 'Your sins are forgiven you,' or to say, 'Rise up and walk'?*

He is declaring that He can say the man is forgiven or He can say that he is healed, because from Jesus' perspective, they both amount to the same thing. They were both to be part of the saving work that He would do.

So, we have already looked at how some healings and breakthroughs are instantaneous, most are received through the receiving and application of the Scriptures along with the ministry of the Holy Spirit, and some remain despite the finished work of the Cross and our faith. Our challenge is to keep believing, keep honouring God for who He is and what He has done, even on the really tough days.

Don't let discouragement or cynicism come on the journey with you and resist challenging God or questioning His goodness and truth in those difficult moments. He loves you; He is still for you; His promises remain for you. God looks at the faith of the heart, not outcomes. Can I encourage you to keep coming, daily, to Him; to honour and worship Him and let His truth continually fill your heart. Let His everlasting love for you and His truth encourage you. Stay positioned for Him to reveal His magnificent salvation to you and bring His healing power.

Reading:

- Luke 5:15-26
- Luke 6:17-19
- Luke 9:11
- Psalm 103

Thought for the day: You have free access to both forgiveness and healing through Jesus and they are received the same way - through simple faith.

Reflection: Write down any insights or revelations that you have had as you reflect on whether you have been questioning or challenging God when you haven't received answer to prayer? If so, how can you change this into a response of trust and faith?

_____
_____
_____
_____
_____
_____
_____
_____
_____
_____
_____
_____
_____
_____
_____
_____
_____
_____
_____

7

GOD IS WILLING

Matthew 8:3 *Then Jesus put out His hand and touched him, saying, "I am willing; be cleansed." Immediately his leprosy was cleansed.*

Matthew 8:1-4 (also in Mark 1:40-44; Luke 5:12-14)
¹ *When He had come down from the mountain, great multitudes followed Him.* ² *And behold, a leper came and worshiped Him, saying, "Lord, if You are willing, You can make me clean."*

³ *Then Jesus put out His hand and touched him, saying, "I am willing; be cleansed." Immediately his leprosy was cleansed.* ⁴ *And Jesus said to him, "See that you tell no one; but go your way, show yourself to the priest, and offer the gift that Moses commanded, as a testimony to them."*

When a leper was diagnosed with their condition, they had to immediately be removed from their family and community and would have to cry out "unclean" if anyone came near them. It was wrongly seen as a symbol of sin and the judgement of God. It would bring ostracism, rejection and shame. There would be grief and sorrow with all that was lost, mental and emotional health challenges, lack with the loss of all earning of income, and a complete absence of hope - as the disease was incurable at the time, resulting in a prolonged decline and death.

It is like a portrayal and embodiment of the curse that sin brought on the Earth, some aspects of which are described in Deuteronomy 28 with the curses of the law. These curses included many sicknesses and afflictions and then Deuteronomy 28:61 goes on to say that it included all the sicknesses not listed there. In addition, there was poverty, broken relationships, calamity and life not going well for a person.

Despite the wording in the chapter that God would bring these things, in context with His nature, other Scriptures and the fact that none of these curses are His will, I believe that they were not a punishment by God for sin but rather, an identification of the impact of sin and what life, outside of alignment to God's ways and provision of atonement, could bring. Jesus has provided complete redemption from everything listed under the curse of the law.

> **Galatians 3:13-14** [13] *Christ has redeemed us from the curse of the law, having become a curse for us (for it is written, "Cursed is everyone who hangs on a tree"),* [14] *that the blessing of Abraham might come upon the Gentiles in Christ Jesus, that we might receive the promise of the Spirit through faith.*

That poor leper was not allowed to approach Jesus or the crowd and yet he comes. It doesn't say how he managed to get himself before Jesus - perhaps he was bold and just came shouting "Leper! Unclean!", with all people, except Jesus, recoiling as he approached. Who knows?

Somehow, he has managed to get to a place where it's just him and Jesus, removing all the distractions and the clutter of the crowd. So, what does one say, when suffering so greatly and having now come before God? Some would complain, others accuse, but not this man. He rightly honours Jesus for who He is and worships Him, despite the worst of circumstances. What a magnificent and sacrificial approach to his God! Our circumstances don't dictate whether we honour God or not. He is always due honour and worship, for He is eternally God and He is eternally good.

Having acknowledged Jesus as God, by worshipping Him, the leper knew that Jesus was able to heal, but in his rejected state, he was not sure how Jesus i.e., God would respond to him. He knows that Jesus would do that healing or miracle for someone else, but would He do it for him?

Jesus demonstrates His immediate acceptance of the man and declares, with no hesitation, that He is willing to heal him. With the understanding that Jesus healed all who came to Him in His earthly ministry and then, in His death and resurrection, made healing available to all, we do not need to come to Him wondering if He will receive us, or if He will be willing to heal us. We can have the full assurance that He is willing. This is not because of who we are, or that we have deserved it, but because of the grace of God. Grace is received through faith and so we need to be fully assured of both God's ability to heal and His willingness to heal.

Jesus touched the leper, against the Law of the Old Covenant. He would be considered to have been defiled by this action and to have taken on the impurity of the leper, making Himself 'unclean'. The curse, however, has no power over Him, and in the same instant, He imparts the healing power of God. This, my friends, is a picture of the Cross. Jesus could have just spoken the words "Be cleansed" "Be healed". His word alone has the power to heal, and many healings were achieved that way. However, He chose to touch the man, to take on his suffering, with it having no power over Jesus, and then release to the man His healing grace.

This points us to the Cross, the moment in history where God, once and for all, provided atonement and redemption (both temporal and eternal). Jesus took the whole package of sin and its consequences by divine transfer. By divine transaction, He released, and continues to release to us, forgiveness, restoration of relationship with God, hope, healing (spirit, soul and body), freedom, restoration of a person's life and eternal life.

Sin separated us from a holy God and Jesus did what no one else could do, in that He took on human form, lived a perfect life and demonstrated God's will for us. He then took upon Himself our sins, judgement, sicknesses, pains and the curse, to provide forgiveness, healing and redemption. This is why we can say that He is the only way to God (John 14:6) and the only hope for mankind. No religion, no other religious leader and no ritual could accomplish this crucial act for us to be connected to God, to have a relationship with Him and to receive the grace He offers.

> **2 Corinthians 5:21** *For He made Him who knew no sin to be sin for us, that we might become the righteousness of God in Him.*

In His act of sacrifice, Isaiah 53 highlights Jesus being viewed like the poor leper, as accursed of God, but, in fact, Jesus was doing this in our place so that, amongst other blessings, we could have access to His healing power.

> **Isaiah 53:4,5 AMPC**[8] 4 *Surely He has borne our griefs (sicknesses, weaknesses, and distresses) and carried our sorrows and pains [of punishment], yet we [ignorantly] considered Him stricken, smitten, and afflicted by God [as if with leprosy].* 5 *But He was wounded for our transgressions, He was*

bruised for our guilt and iniquities; the chastisement [needful to obtain] peace and well-being for us was upon Him, and with the stripes [that wounded] Him we are healed and made whole.

We need to engage with this truth for it to impact us. Receiving healing doesn't come only from praying or receiving prayer, but through the engagement with, the application of and the receiving of revelation of Jesus and His Word. The Holy Spirit moves on the revelation of Jesus and on His Word. There is a depth and power when we push in to really feel the weight and impact of what Jesus did; to get a revelation of it and to allow it to change us.

For example, with Jesus dying in our place for our sins - if one treats this lightly and doesn't give too much thought to the cost or stop to really appreciate it, or fails to recognise that this was the ONLY hope that we have, then, the impact on that person's life is little, and they continue to struggle with things that Jesus has actually already set them free from.

For the person who stops and appreciates the immense cost of their salvation; feels the weight of it; feels the conviction that it brings, then that person is actually less likely to struggle with sin, experiencing more breakthroughs and power to transform their lives.

It's the same with healing. When you stop and feel the weight and the cost, a free gift to us, but one that came at a huge cost to Jesus, then, there is an impact on us that crosses from spirit to soul to body. When we value the cost, it brings us to our knees in appreciation, brings worship and honour, even before we receive the healing - as did the leper in the story.

It also brings, I believe, a far greater and more lasting healing and a truth that can be drawn on at any time, if needed. We have to engage with what He did for us and not just be surface believers. We are to allow the divine transfer that took place spiritually to be released physically into every part of our being. When it impacts our own life, we can then help others to also engage with Him and see their lives transformed.

Going back to our story in Matthew 8, Jesus tells the now healed man to go show himself to the priest and to offer the gift that Moses commanded as a testimony to them and in fulfillment of the law. What a testimony that would have been! Leprosy at the time was incurable and while the priests would presumably have seen minor skin afflictions healed, or the lifting of the seven days of leprosy from Miriam, never would someone have presented themselves as being healed from the actual condition of leprosy. All the provision of the law for the healing of a leper would have been made for this man who thought that he had been rejected by God. At a later date, ten more lepers would have presented themselves to the priests as an extraordinary sign that Jesus brings healing to that which is deemed incurable. For with God nothing will be impossible (Luke 1:37).

In addition, the gift, the sacrifice, was so full of details that prophesied of Jesus and what He would do for us and these details needed attention; and it had a cost associated with it. So, the details of what He would do (and for us, has done) and the cost associated with it needs to be recognised, appreciated and applied to a person's life.

The detailed offering is described in Leviticus 14, but in brief, there would be a process over eight days where the man, washed and shaved, would present two birds- one sacrificed and the other, with cedar wood (signifies incorruptibility), scarlet (signifies the blood) and hyssop (contains water in the stem - signifies both cleansing and Jesus' death where blood and water came out as He was pierced) dipped in the blood of the first bird. The blood was applied to the man and the live bird set free.

This is a picture of Jesus' sacrifice and Atonement and by it, the removal of sin and sickness, with the live bird being set free as a picture of this. On the eighth day, there was the further sacrifice of two lambs and the blood of the sacrifice and the oil, that signified the Holy Spirit, had to be applied to his life. The whole process required great attention and great cost.

How does this apply to us today? Jesus has fulfilled all of the law for us and no financial offering is required. If anyone suggests that you need to give a financial gift to receive healing this is false doctrine and a corruption of the beautiful truth that God gives His grace freely to us, solely through faith in Jesus and what He has done.

I think that the message for us is that there needs to be a focused recognition that the healing comes from God, that it is a result of the Redemption that comes through Jesus - His shed blood, His incorruptibility and His cleansing - and the fact that there was a great cost to that healing. Giving due appreciation to the cost, being thankful and honouring (which means to give weight to) God, taking time to engage with God and the Scriptures, allowing what Jesus did to impact us, brings far greater and lasting healing and an internal reservoir of truth that can be drawn on whenever needed.

Thankfulness is a bit like fasting in that you are intentionally shutting off the voice of the flesh, not voicing your complaint but rather praise to God for who He is and what He has done, this bringing a deeper connection with the Spirit. Complaining, as its opposite, limits the expression of the power of God. Thankfulness keeps our eyes on Jesus no matter what we are going through and, as one of God's ways, brings His power.

Reading:

- Matthew 8:1-4
- Mark 1:40-44
- Luke 5:12-14
- Deuteronomy 28
- Galatians 3:13,14

Thought for the day: Healing is free to us but came at a great cost that needs to be acknowledged and appreciated.

Reflection: Write down any insights or revelations that you have had today as you reflect on Jesus; what He did for you; the price He paid to bring you forgiveness, healing and freedom. Let it sink into your soul and let it bring deep gratitude.

_____
_____
_____
_____
_____
_____
_____
_____
_____

Write down three Scriptures below that describe Jesus' suffering on your behalf and meditate on them.

Scripture 1:

Scripture 2:

Scripture 3:

8

HEALING IS THE CHILDREN'S BREAD

Matthew 15:28 *Then Jesus answered and said to her, "O woman, great is your faith! Let it be to you as you desire." And her daughter was healed from that very hour.*

Matthew 15:21-28 ²¹ *Then Jesus went out from there and departed to the region of Tyre and Sidon.* ²² *And behold, a woman of Canaan came from that region and cried out to Him, saying, "Have mercy on me, O Lord, Son of David! My daughter is severely demon-possessed."* ²³ *But He answered her not a word. And His disciples came and urged Him, saying, "Send her away, for she cries out after us."* ²⁴ *But He answered and said, "I was not sent except to the lost sheep of the house of Israel."* ²⁵ *Then she came and worshiped Him, saying, "Lord, help me!"* ²⁶ *But He answered and said, "It is not good to take the children's bread and throw it to the little dogs."*

²⁷ *And she said, "Yes, Lord, yet even the little dogs eat the crumbs which fall from their masters' table."* ²⁸ *Then Jesus answered and said to her, "O woman, great is your faith! Let it be to you as you desire." And her daughter was healed from that very hour.*

This passage is often quoted with a negative connotation - that Jesus was reluctant to heal this woman's daughter but, in fact, Jesus wanted her to have an encounter with Him and to draw out of her a faith that He called great. Jesus wants you to be healed and is in no way reluctant or in need of pressuring to bring this about. God cannot be coerced and will do exactly what is His will to do. What Jesus did for us at the Cross of Calvary, paying the price for all to be healed, demonstrates both His will and His willingness to heal. We don't want to be approaching God as if He is One who is reluctant and needs us to pressure or coerce Him. Not only does this show no honour to Him, but it also reveals unbelief and a distorted perception of His character and how to relate to Him.

Healing and miracles are what God does, but He also wants us to have an encounter with Him, rather than just wanting the miracle alone, and a relationship that will sustain us all of our days and into eternity. Then He wants us to have revelation of His Word and to understand what He is saying to us - not just a head knowledge - because His words have the power to continually sustain and empower us.

The woman in this story was a Canaanite, someone who Jesus' audience would be prejudiced against; someone outside the kingdom of God. The Jews at the time referred to Gentiles and dogs as unclean, and often insultingly referred to the Gentiles as dogs. So, she is in a hostile environment where she is prejudiced against and, being a woman in the culture of the time, not valued and so there is great cause for offense to come into her heart.

The woman comes to Jesus, pleading for her daughter's healing, acknowledging Jesus as Lord, and using the Messianic title of 'Son of David'. So, she knows about Jesus but doesn't yet know Him. It is not enough for us to just know about Jesus, but we need to have an encounter with Him and know Him in a personal relationship. It is an encounter with God that carries us through all the seasons of life and into eternity.

'But He answered her not a word'. Jesus doesn't give a response. Note that He doesn't say "no". This is important because often we can read over these things quickly, or make assumptions about someone's healing journey quickly, and conclude that God is saying "no" or that it's not His will. When God says "no" He makes it very clear - it's not just silence. This passage is not revealing that God was saying "no" - in fact, quite the opposite, because the woman's daughter is healed.

Jesus wants to draw the woman into an encounter with Him and to not just receive her miracle and go. She is also not to see the healing as being like 'magic' or a performance like that of one of the pagan magicians.

When God is silent, it is an invitation to draw nearer to Him. If He answered everything quickly, by nature we would stay in a shallow relationship with Him, taking the answers and moving on without needing to press in deeper. The answer is not "no" but "come closer". Jesus wants this woman to press in, go to a greater depth in her encounter with Him and allow Him to bring her to a place of revelation and greater understanding of Himself.

Note also that Jesus does not send her away when encouraged to do so. He values her and her daughter, unlike His disciples, and He wants to draw the woman to Himself and take time with her, to take her through a process.

Jesus then responds in verse 24 with a statement about the boundaries of His own call, that He was to focus on Israel over three years with the intent that, after the coming of the Holy Spirit in Acts 2, believers would carry it to the rest of the world. Often, the Lord will give you a response or a Scripture that is not a direct answer to your question and may even seem enigmatic, but this too, is an invitation to press in deeper to receive revelation and understanding of Him and what He wants to bring about in your life.

As an example, the Lord spoke to me as a young believer, in the midst of many trials and many questions, "My grace is sufficient for you". My immediate response was to think, "That doesn't answer any of my questions and I don't understand what You are saying to me". However, being drawn in to study the passage in 2 Corinthians 12;9,10 (and its wider context) I received such revelation and understanding that have now sustained me for more than 30 years and brought breakthroughs in so many areas - far more than the original ones that I was praying about. This Scripture now stirs up faith and an expectation that God will intervene with His miracle working power and demonstrate His strength in my weakness. This revelation that is sought for is life giving and becomes sustaining 'bread' from the Lord and brings far more than a quick answer would.

> **Proverbs 4:22 AMPC**[8] (speaking of God's words) *For they are life to those who find them, healing and health to all their flesh.*

The woman now comes and worships Jesus. Worship is reserved for God alone and she demonstrates that she has received revelation that He is not just a teacher or a prophet but God Himself. If He had immediately given her what she wanted, she would have missed the opportunity to know Him.

Then Jesus comes out with a challenging statement - *"It is not good to take the children's bread and throw it to the little dogs"*. Jesus is putting His finger on the area of offense and, using the language of those she's offended with, referencing the term 'dog' for a Gentile in His response. Wow! Even though He uses the term for a domestic dog it would still be a comment that could trigger existing offense or bring offense.

What triggers you on the inside is your point of offense. Is there something for you that can cause anger, or intense emotion, to ignite either internally or be released externally? It can be offense with a person or even with God if you feel that He hasn't responded as you hoped or expected. It can be with a church if you feel that they haven't met your expectations or even around a divisive opinion. It's okay to have different opinions around issues that fall outside the foundational tenets of Scripture. Romans 14 tells us that we are not to have disputes over doubtful things but rather be fully convinced in our own mind and at the same time respectful of the convictions of others. Some carry such conviction that they are enraged or judgmental at someone else having a different view - this is the point where it has progressed from conviction to offense.

God will test our hearts and put His finger on offense because He loves us and wants our hearts to be free of a bitterness or emotion that internally causes destruction. Offense of any kind can block our relationship with Him and block answer to prayer.

When we seek to receive mercy and grace from God it comes with the understanding that we are expected to release it to others. The Lord's prayer in Matthew 6:9-15 and the prayer of faith in Mark 11:22-26 both expand on the issue of needing to forgive others in response to the grace we seek from God. What we receive freely we must freely give.

So, there is a test here for the Canaanite woman - what will she do with the offense? Will she walk away at this point, angry at God, or will she respond to Him and still worship Him? Frustratingly, He doesn't address all those around her who are the source of offense. There can be a feeling of "What about them Lord?"; "Why aren't you dealing with them?". I feel like the answer would be similar to the one Jesus gives Peter, in another situation in John 21. After Jesus has prophesied to Peter of the manner of his later death, Peter points to John and asks "What about him?" Jesus' response, paraphrased, is basically 'what is that to you - you just follow Me'. Jesus will deal with things His way and, in this case with the woman, He will make His point to the crowd by showing her off, this Gentile woman who reveals more faith and revelation than Jesus' followers do.

Many believers leave when offended and many take offense at Jesus for not doing what they expected, missing their miracle in doing so. However, this woman is smart and comes right back at Him, even using the 'dog' reference and demonstrating the revelation on His word that she has received - *"Yes, Lord, yet even the little dogs eat the crumbs which fall from their masters' table."*

She acknowledges that healing is the right of the children; part of God's kingdom provision but sees that His healing provision is so great that, just the crumb she appeals for will be enough to heal her daughter.

Healing is indeed the provision of the children of God, made available through Jesus' bearing of our sickness and pains, as well as our sin, at the Cross of Calvary. In the same manner as the provision of bread or food for children in their own home, it's not something that the children have to beg for but nor is it something that they make a demand for, in an entitled manner. They believe and trust that it is there for them, as a provision of grace, and gratefully just receive it. In the account of this story in Mark 7:24-30, Jesus reveals that He wants the children (believers) to be filled with what He has provided for us.

Matthew 15:28 *Then Jesus answered and said to her, "O woman, great is your faith! Let it be to you as you desire." And her daughter was healed from that very hour.*

Two Gentiles, this woman and the Centurion, are commended for having great faith and the receiving of great revelation, beyond that of those around them who know the Word of God.

So be encouraged that God's response to you isn't "no" but "come closer". Press into His Word for revelation and allow Him to bring freedom to your heart. Trust and allow Jesus to lead you into the healing that He longs for you to receive.

Reading:

- Matthew 15:21-28
- John 6:28-35
- James 4:8-10

Thought for the day: The answer is not "no" but "come closer".

Reflection: Prayerfully consider if there is any area of your life that you feel the Lord may be challenging you on. Are you ready to step over the challenge or the offense of it? Are you ready to push in and come closer to God? Write down any thoughts you have around this.

9

AS YOUR SOUL PROSPERS

3 John 2 *Beloved, I pray that you may prosper in all things and be in health, just as your soul prospers.*

John 5:2-14 ² *Now there is in Jerusalem by the Sheep Gate a pool, which is called in Hebrew, Bethesda, having five porches.* ³ *In these lay a great multitude of sick people, blind, lame, paralyzed, waiting for the moving of the water.* ⁴ *For an angel went down at a certain time into the pool and stirred up the water; then whoever stepped in first, after the stirring of the water, was made well of whatever disease he had.* ⁵ *Now a certain man was there who had an infirmity thirty-eight years.* ⁶ *When Jesus saw him lying there, and knew that he already had been in that condition a long time, He said to him, "Do you want to be made well?"*

⁷ The sick man answered Him, "Sir, I have no man to put me into the pool when the water is stirred up; but while I am coming, another steps down before me."

⁸ Jesus said to him, "Rise, take up your bed and walk." ⁹ And immediately the man was made well, took up his bed, and walked.

And that day was the Sabbath. ¹⁰ The Jews therefore said to him who was cured, "It is the Sabbath; it is not lawful for you to carry your bed."

¹¹ He answered them, "He who made me well said to me, 'Take up your bed and walk.' "

¹² Then they asked him, "Who is the Man who said to you, 'Take up your bed and walk?'" ¹³ But the one who was healed did not know who it was, for Jesus had withdrawn, a multitude being in that place. ¹⁴ Afterward Jesus found him in the temple, and said to him, "See, you have been made well. Sin no more, lest a worse thing come upon you."

In the story in John 5:2-14, we find a 'great multitude' of people waiting for a miracle through a special sign from God. The pool is called Bethesda in the Hebrew, meaning 'Place of Outpouring' or 'House of Grace'. Like many believers today, they have come to a place which they identify as somewhere where God will move, believing that there they will find their miracle.

Perhaps, over time as they wait, there can creep into their believing that they can only be healed if there is a special sign from God, like the moving of the water in the story. Perhaps, as appears with the man in this story, they can feel that "It happens for them but not for me"; "I can believe it will happen for someone else but not for me"; or "If only there was someone to make this happen for me - take me to the special place with the special manifestations of God and His anointing - then I could be healed".

> **Hebrews 1:1,2** ¹*"God, who at various times and in various ways spoke in time past to the fathers by the prophets,* ²*has in these last days spoken to us by His Son'.*

Hebrews 1:3 goes on to describe Jesus as being *'the brightness of His glory and the express image of His person'.*

God, in former times, sovereignly did signs at various times for people through the intermediary ministry of the prophets - through a certain person in a certain place. Now, He speaks to us and works signs or miracles for us through Jesus, who is the exact representation of the Father (AMPC version[8]). It comes through relationship with Him, through His finished work, His Word and through the ministry of the Holy Spirit. Through Jesus, the work of God is not just for one, on one occasion, but for all on any occasion. Any ministry of healing must have Jesus as the focus and not the minister themselves, despite the fact, that Jesus moves through the prayers and laying on of hands by the one ministering.

Jesus comes to this man who had an infirmity thirty-eight years and asks this strange question "Do you want to made well?" This seems so obvious that we can wonder why Jesus would ask it. Perhaps, the man needed to refocus on the Lord and that what he sought was to come from Jesus Himself, and to not focus on the need for a special place or event. I believe that Jesus is looking for the man to respond to Him and not just wait for ministry to happen for him. Interestingly, the man doesn't answer the question but complains that there is no one to make the effort for him, in placing him in the water. His focus is on needing someone else to do something, and on his helplessness and not, as yet, in responding to Jesus.

It is interesting that Jesus doesn't lay hands on him or give him special attention as He had to others because this, presumably, would have fed the incorrect mindset that the man already had. Instead, Jesus just tells him to get up - he doesn't need a special manifestation but simply to respond to Jesus and His word. The man makes the adjustment; he responds to Jesus and receives his healing immediately.

In John 5:10, we can again see the contrast of legalistic religious teaching to the Word of God, as revealed through Jesus. Jesus has told the man to take up his bed and walk and the Jews are telling him that "it's not lawful to carry your bed" on the Sabbath. So, whose law would that be if it conflicts with what Jesus, God in the flesh, has said? If you hear religious teaching that is not substantiated by Scripture, put that teaching aside and respond to the Word of God. This is not saying that one can't do the practical things nor seek medical help but is, rather, referring to what you allow into your belief system regarding God, how to respond to Him and how to receive from Him.

It appears that, in this case, the man's infirmity was connected to sin as seen in Jesus' response in John 5:14. Jesus doesn't want to just give him physical healing but for him to turn and to be restored spirit, soul and body.

> **John 5:14** *Afterward Jesus found him in the temple, and said to him, "See, you have been made well. Sin no more, lest a worse thing come upon you."*

Sickness had its original entry into the Earth through sin and has been present ever since the Fall. If someone is sick this does not mean that it is due to an area of sin in their life, but rather the consequence of living in an imperfect world. In John 9:3 Jesus makes the point that not all suffering is due to the individual's sin. However, sometimes, as with the man in this story, it can be the case. His own conscience would have resonated with which sin Jesus was referring to.

If we do sin, then we need to repent, turn away from it and receive God's forgiveness. In that place, we live with access to the benefits of a sinless life through the receiving of Jesus' righteousness, including healing. However, if we choose to wilfully hold onto an area of sin then the impact of sin, including sickness can remain upon our life. Again, I want to clarify that if someone is living with a long-term illness, I am not saying it is due to sin - but this story just highlights that there can be occasion where it can be the case.

Sometimes it is not even wilful sin but an area in our life that is just 'not on the radar' or seems out of our control. It might be an area of unforgiveness with someone that seems too great to deal with, that hasn't yet been brought to the Lord. It might be an attitude that, having lived with it for so long, one is not aware of its presence being an issue. It may even be the impact from a hurt, trauma or abuse i.e., something that has been done to you not by you, that, while not being the result of your own sin, has created a pain response that becomes a blockage to receiving from God. If there is a challenge in receiving healing, it is good to ask the Lord to show you if there is an area that is causing a blockage. Sometimes the soul needs to be healed and restored before a physical healing occurs.

3 John 2 *Beloved, I pray that you may prosper in all things and be in health, just as your soul prospers.*

John 15:1-3 *"I am the true vine, and My Father is the vinedresser.* ² *Every branch in Me that does not bear fruit He takes away; and every branch that bears fruit He prunes, that* *it may bear more fruit.* ³ *You are already clean because of the word which I have spoken to you.*

When pruning, branches that are unhealthy or dead are removed, so that they won't impact the rest of the plant. Even healthy branches are pruned back, so that the concentration of life and nutrients will bring even a stronger and more beautiful future growth. There are 'branches' in our lives that are not of Jesus, that if left, will sabotage our life e.g., rejection, unforgiveness or emotional pain. They can create patterns in someone's life that can even look like the result of others' behaviour or circumstances but it's actually a branch that needs to be cut out. So, there will be branches in our lives that God wants to cut out and remove for our own good, and when He cuts something out, He completely destroys it, and it is no longer empowered to affect your life.

There is power in identifying and laying issues down at the Cross- a 'drawing a line in the sand' moment. There may be sins that need to be repented of, but also areas that are just not part of God's plan for you, that you want to leave behind e.g., burdens, anxieties, rejection etc. How to deal with this will be expanded on further in chapters 28-34 but, for now, look to Jesus and respond to Him. Consciously see yourself laying down what is unwanted, leaving it behind and receive the completeness of salvation that flows from Jesus - and healing, as well as forgiveness, will be imparted in that moment.

Reading:

- John 5:2-14
- 3 John 2
- John 15:1-8
- 1 John 1:9
- Proverbs 28:13

Thought for the day: It is God's will for you to prosper in all things and to be in health.

Reflection: Prayerfully consider if there is any area of your life that you feel the Lord may have His finger on; that needs to be laid down so that you can move on without it. Write down what you are leaving behind today.

_____
_____
_____
_____
_____
_____
_____
_____
_____
_____
_____
_____
_____
_____
_____
_____
_____
_____

10

IT'S ALL IN YOUR PERSPECTIVE

Numbers 21:9 *So Moses made a bronze serpent, and put it on a pole; and so it was, if a serpent had bitten anyone, when he looked at the bronze serpent, he lived.*

The third foundation that we need to have established in our heart, after those of God's character and God's will, as revealed in Jesus, is that of seeing and being positioned in God's perspective; having a supernatural, and not a natural, vision and response to the sickness or the problem.

Numbers 21:4-9 [4] *Then they journeyed from Mount Hor by the Way of the Red Sea, to go around the land of Edom; and the soul of the people became very discouraged on the way.* [5] *And the people spoke against God and against Moses: "Why have you brought us up out of Egypt to die in the wilderness? For there is no food and no water, and our soul loathes this worthless bread."* [6] *So the LORD sent fiery serpents among*

> the people, and they bit the people; and many of the people of Israel died.⁷ Therefore the people came to Moses, and said, "We have sinned, for we have spoken against the LORD and against you; pray to the LORD that He take away the serpents from us." So Moses prayed for the people.⁸ Then the LORD said to Moses, "Make a fiery serpent, and set it on a pole; and it shall be that everyone who is bitten, when he looks at it, shall live."⁹ So Moses made a bronze serpent, and put it on a pole; and so it was, if a serpent had bitten anyone, when he looked at the bronze serpent, he lived.

The people are exhausted and become discouraged on their journey through the wilderness. They anticipated a win at Edom, recorded in Numbers 20, but were defeated and now have to go on the journey for longer than they expected.

Sometimes we are expecting a quick breakthrough, and if it takes longer than expected, discouragement can come in.

The natural human reactions that come in here are complaining, discouragement and speaking negatively, even questioning God, but this clearly makes the situation much worse. So often we can justify and rationalise our reactions, complaining and negative speaking but, however much it may seem justifiable, it will never bring about the response of God. We need to respond to God's answer and not the problem.

The people ask Moses to pray to the Lord that He "take away the serpents from us". In other words, the prayer "God I want <u>You to</u> take away the problem; take away the sickness". God's response is to direct <u>them to</u> put a type of the Cross into the situation. God's perspective and answer has never changed - put the work of the Cross into your situation! Jesus says in John 3:14, that as Moses lifted up the serpent in the desert so too, He must be lifted up that all who look to Him would be similarly forgiven, healed and delivered from the serpents still around.

The Amplified Bible[8] interpretation for *'looked at'* (Numbers 21:9) is to *'look attentively, expectantly, and with a steady and absorbing gaze'*. If we look at something attentively, it means that it has all of our focus; we are looking at it carefully, noting every detail. So, our vision is to be filled with God's perspective - His character, Jesus' work at the Cross of Calvary, the promises and will of God for the situation - seeing yourself healed.

To look at it expectantly implies that we are expecting something to happen in response to that look i.e., the look of faith. You can't 'hype up' faith but rather, it is the automatic response when we <u>see</u> our God and what He has done.

To look with a steady and absorbing gaze means that we not only keep looking at it, as opposed to a mere glance, but we are absorbing something from it. Therefore, we are influenced and are changed by what we are looking at.

We all need to renew our minds and see the Word in our heart to the point where we are consumed with God's truth, and not the facts of the situation. Don't look to your circumstances but to what God has said, who Jesus is and what He has done for you and He can bring the healing or miracle to pass. The Israelites couldn't keep their vision on the brazen serpent and their symptoms of snake bite at the same time, if they wanted to be healed.

Faith is the perception or vision of God's perspective. We need to shift to His perspective, and off ours, to be positioned for the power of God.

Our perspective is so often fed by our feelings, problems, symptoms and input from what we might call 'our reality'. So often people say to me, "Kate I just have to face reality" - and it is a reality.

God, however, has a completely different perspective, an even greater reality. His reality is eternal, unchangeable; ours is temporal which, by definition, means it is subject to change. The eternal changes the temporal. God sees sickness, pain and weakness placed on Jesus, nailed to that Cross with resultant healing to us.

I wrote in my earlier book, 'A Picture of Health'[9], '*Faith is not blind but the perception of another and far greater reality. When Paul the apostle says that we walk by faith and not by sight (2 Corinthians 5:7) he is not saying that we walk blindly, not knowing or perceiving where we are going. Faith sees into God's reality and walks in the light of that.*'

His power is released from His perspective and not ours. So, we can be praying and believing the promises, but if we are still seeing things from our perspective and responding according to the problem, then we are not positioned for God's power.

It's a simple shift that changes everything - we choose to fix our vision on God's perspective remembering that it is the truth despite contrary feelings or symptoms.

> **Joshua 1:8** *This Book of the Law shall not depart from your mouth, but you shall meditate in it day and night, that you may observe to do according to all that is written in it. For then you will make your way prosperous, and then you will have good success.*

The Amplified version of the Bible[8] for this verse reads 'that you may observe and do'. We are to meditate on the Word until we can see it, and when we see it, we find that we automatically will do it. We are not just to read or study the Bible but to meditate on it. Meditating on the Word is not like Eastern meditation, where a person seeks to empty their mind, but it is where one fills the mind, heart and inner vision with the Word of God.

The word 'meditate' in Joshua 1:8 means to 'ponder while speaking to oneself or imagine'. In other words, it means to think about the passage, speak it out and visualise it. So, you take a Scripture and think about "What is this saying?"; "How do I apply this to my life?". Then speak out the Scriptures - Romans 10:17 tells us that 'faith comes by hearing, and hearing by the Word of God'. Then you start to visualise - "What does my life look like in light of this Scripture or promise?" This starts to build the picture in your inner vision or spirit, where the Holy Spirit speaks to you.

> **Habakkuk 2:1** *I will stand my watch and set myself on the rampart, and watch to see what He will say to me, and what I will answer when I am corrected.*

We have to see what God is saying to us. When the Holy Spirit inspires to us that written Word that we are attending to, we start to see what God is saying to us and not merely believe it. See Jesus on the Cross, His suffering; the affliction laid on Him; the blood He shed for us. That's our sickness that He suffered for, just as He suffered and paid for our sins - so that we could be set free.

It's not just a vision of what you want to do when healed, which though being good and something many people choose to focus on, still comes from the flesh and what you want from God. Rather, look to what He sees, Jesus, and then you find that the Holy Spirit starts to give you His vision for your healing - born of the Spirit and not of the flesh.

> **2 Corinthians 3:18** *But we all, with unveiled face, beholding as in a mirror the glory of the Lord, are being transformed into the same image from glory to glory, just as by the Spirit of the Lord.*

The mirror is the Bible, where we see and behold Jesus, the Word of God who was made flesh, who bore our sins and carried our sicknesses on that Cross and *'by whose stripes we are healed'*. As we look, we are increasingly transformed into the image we behold. What we look at and what we hold in our vision matters.

The Israelites beheld a type of Jesus' work at the Cross of Calvary in the form of the brazen serpent. This is not to say that Jesus Himself was portrayed as a serpent, but the brazen serpent was a type of what He would nail to that Cross - sin, sickness, Satan and his works. They had to see the 'serpent' disempowered over them.

As they were attentive to the image of sin and sickness being put to death, they were influenced by what they saw and expectant to receive - with transforming power being released to bring forgiveness, healing, life and deliverance from all the serpents still around them.

Now, if they received healing and deliverance through faith in a type of Christ's work at the Cross, how much more shall we receive healing and deliverance through faith in Jesus Himself as we behold Him and what He has done for us.

Reading:

- Numbers 21:4-9
- 2 Corinthians 3:18
- 2 Corinthians 5:7
- Joshua 1:8
- Psalm 1:2,3
- Psalm 16:8

Thought for the day: Faith is the perception or vision of God's perspective. We need to shift to His perspective, and off ours, in order to be positioned for the power of God.

Reflection: Write down any insights or revelations that you have had as you reflect on God's perspective versus your own perception of the situation.

_____
_____
_____
_____
_____
_____
_____
_____
_____
_____

Write down three Scriptures below that reveal God's perspective for healing.

Scripture 1:

Scripture 2:

Scripture 3:

11

GOD'S PERSPECTIVE BRINGS HIS POWER

John 11:40 *Jesus said to her, "Did I not say to you that if you would believe you would see the glory of God?"*

John 11 recounts the raising of Lazarus from the dead. This story displays so many contrasts between the natural perspective of people and God's radically different perspective, and it is always His perspective which brings His power.

John 11 starts with Mary and Martha calling for Jesus to come to their sick brother Lazarus. They loved God, they were friends of Jesus and God loved them (verses 3- 5) and so, just because Lazarus got sick doesn't mean that God didn't love him or that he didn't love God or that Lazarus had done anything wrong.

In verse 4, Jesus declares right away God's perspective of the situation, given to them to focus on, *"This sickness is not unto death, but for the glory of God, that the Son of God may be glorified through it."* For us, we have the

Bible to reveal His perspective, given to us to set our vision on, and our response of faith is to shift in how we see things, to align with it. That He says the situation is for the glory of God does not mean that God brought or allowed the sickness so that He could be glorified through it. Situations happen to us in life and while God doesn't bring the bad things (James 1:17), He desires to bring His answers, which in turn, brings glory to Him.

Now Lazarus did die before being raised up. There was a time when it didn't look like this prophetic word was coming to pass, if you are only looking at the circumstances and not at what Jesus said. If we only look at things from our perspective, we can miss being positioned for the miracle that comes from being in God's perspective.

As the chapter goes on, we see the two perspectives contrasted - the disciples saw persecution and even death (verses 7 and 16) awaiting them; Jesus saw a resurrection and life. Mary and Martha saw death; Jesus saw the raising of the dead.

> **John 11:9,10** *Jesus answered, "Are there not twelve hours in the day? If anyone walks in the day, he does not stumble, because he sees the light of this world. *¹⁰* But if one walks in the night, he stumbles, because the light is not in him."*

Again, we have the two perspectives contrasted. To walk in the light is to walk in the revelation of God's perspective where we won't stumble. This doesn't say that we won't have any challenges but if we walk, as John writes here, seeing 'the light of this world', Jesus, then we won't stumble in our faith, won't stumble in our attitude toward God along the way, and we will find ourselves positioned for His power that brings His answers.

To walk in the night is to walk in one's own perspective and fears, which causes one to stumble - in faith and in attitude towards God, as disappointment and cynicism can set in when prayers seem to go unanswered. The language of walking 'in the night' is asking God the questions of "Why is this happening?", "When are You going to do something?" and needing to know how He will do it before believing.

We have to shift from the 'why of the problem' to the 'Who of the answer' and what He has already done. We will look at Job later on, but before God turned Job's situation around, He went to great lengths to reveal Himself, the 'Who of the answer' to Job. He never did answer the why questions, the how and the when - all He did was give Job a greater revelation of Himself until Job declared "I know that my Redeemer lives" (Job 19:25). The shift from the 'why' to the 'Who' preceded his restoration.

Jesus approaches the situation declaring God's answer, avoiding speaking the problem (John 11: 11 speaking of Lazarus as being asleep) and only stating the problem (verse 14) when the disciples fail to understand what He is saying.

> **John 11:11-14** [11] *These things He said, and after that He said to them, "Our friend Lazarus sleeps, but I go that I may wake him up."* [12] *Then His disciples said, "Lord, if he sleeps he will get well."* [13] *However, Jesus spoke of his death, but they thought that He was speaking about taking rest in sleep.* [14] *Then Jesus said to them plainly, "Lazarus is dead".*
>
> **John 11:17** *So when Jesus came, He found that he had already been in the tomb four days.*

The Jews had a theory that a person's spirit remained over their body for three days and that they could come back into their body during that time. So, if Jesus raised Lazarus within that time, it would be seen as a healing. They already knew Jesus as Healer, but He wants to reveal Himself in a greater way, now as the Resurrection and the Life. So, it is intentional that Jesus waits until the fourth day to raise Lazarus from the dead.

Now look at people's responses to Jesus when He comes:

> **John 11:21** *Now Martha said to Jesus, "Lord, if You had been here, my brother would not have died".*

> **John 11:32** *Then, when Mary came where Jesus was, and saw Him, she fell down at His feet, saying to Him, "Lord, if You had been here, my brother would not have died."*

> **John 11:37 The Message**[4] *Others among them said, "Well, if he loved him so much, why didn't he do something to keep him from dying? After all, he opened the eyes of a blind man."*

Martha, Mary and so many Christians have said, "God if You had come, this wouldn't have happened; where were You?", "Why didn't You respond when I prayed?" If we are set in our perspective and the 'why' of the problem we can often end up accusing God for what we perceive He has failed to do, or for not caring. From His perspective, He has done everything in Jesus and "It is finished" for all that we will ever need, including miracle healing. We need to shift to the 'Who' of the answer and see Jesus and what He has done for us, in order for the power of God to be revealed.

> **John 11:23,24** *Jesus said to her, "Your brother will rise again." Martha said to Him, "I know that he will rise again in the resurrection at the last day."*

Martha takes the word that Jesus has spoken and interprets it within her current and limited framework of theology - while the future resurrection is correct theology, she is missing what Jesus is trying to say to her. She is taking the Word to interpret it within her perspective when Jesus wants her, and us, to take the challenge/ sickness/ circumstance and bring them into His perspective and Word and interpret them in that light.

> **John 11:25-27** *Jesus said to her, "I am the resurrection and the life. He who believes in Me, though he may die, he shall live.* [26] *And whoever lives and believes in Me shall never die. Do you believe this?"* [27] *She said to Him, "Yes, Lord, I believe that You are the Christ, the Son of God, who is to come into the world."*

Jesus now shifts Martha from a problem focus and "Why weren't you here?" to who He is - the Christ, the Son of God. It is always a focus on Jesus, who He is and what He has done which brings the power of God and not a focus on what we want from God. He is the Healer, the Resurrection, the Life, the One who raises things that have gone dead, back to life and the One with whom nothing is impossible. Seeing Jesus isn't merely taking our eyes off the problem and looking to Him to fix it, but rather letting who He is and what He has done have our attention, fill our thoughts, fill our hearts and fill our vision.

> **1 John 5:4,5** *For whatever is born of God overcomes the world. And this is the victory that has overcome the world— our faith. Who is he who overcomes the world, but he who believes that Jesus is the Son of God?*

This is the victory, when we believe and see Jesus, and that shift of focus automatically brings any ensuing step of faith and the power of God. We don't have to figure out how God will do it, when He will do it but just need to position ourselves in His power - that is in the 'Who' of the answer, Jesus!

> **John 11:33** *Therefore, when Jesus saw her weeping, and the Jews who came with her weeping, He groaned in the spirit and was troubled.*
>
> **John 11:35** *Jesus wept.*

Jesus didn't weep over Lazarus because He knows that He is about to raise him from the dead. He is possibly weeping at the impact of sin on the earth and the suffering that people were never meant to experience; and, perhaps, because they still don't get it and can't see Him for who He is, nor see God's perspective. Or was this one of many moments that, in grieving at the impact of the Fall, He would be strengthened to take on the suffering that would destroy sin and death itself?

> **John 11:39** *Jesus said, "Take away the stone." Martha, the sister of him who was dead, said to Him, "Lord, by this time there is a stench, for he has been dead four days."*

Lazarus isn't just dead- by now, he is decaying and there is a stench. We can complain to God saying, "Don't You know how dead and rotten this situation is?" A better response is to take away any stone or blockage, choose to see what He sees and be positioned for a miracle.

> **John 11:40** *Jesus said to her, "Did I not say to you that if you would believe you would see the glory of God?"*

Obviously, Jesus had previously said this to them because He says, "Did I not say". What has God already said to you? Did He not say He is the Healer? Did He not say that He took our sicknesses and pains on the Cross? If we will believe and see what He has done, we will see His glory and power revealed.

John 11:41,42 *Then they took away the stone from the place where the dead man was lying. And Jesus lifted up His eyes and said, "Father, I thank You that You have heard Me. And I know that You always hear Me, but because of the people who are standing by I said this, that they may believe that You sent Me."*

Jesus says He is praying, knowing that the Father had already heard Him. Be assured that God has heard your prayers and He does care! He has also already provided the answer - Jesus Himself and what He did on the Cross. In healing, we are praying a prayer in which we have an assurance of an answer already provided - Jesus and His finished work.

John 11:43 *Now when He had said these things, He cried with a loud voice, "Lazarus, come forth!"*

Only a very simple prayer is required when you know that God has already heard and has already answered before you ask- it's all in Jesus.

Reading:

- John 11:1-44

Thought for the day: God's perspective is very different to our natural perspective - His power operates from His perspective and not from ours.

Reflection:

1. What do you see over your health and circumstances.

   _____
   _____
   _____
   _____
   _____
   _____
   _____

2. What has God said about your health? Particularly from the Bible, but maybe also through a personal prophecy (given through a reputable source i.e., a person who has a recognised prophetic gift and is living a lifestyle consistent with Scripture) or the 'still small voice 'of the Holy Spirit in your own devotional time.

   _____
   _____
   _____
   _____
   _____
   _____
   _____
   _____

12

A SPIRIT OF WISDOM AND REVELATION

Ephesians 1:17 *'that the God of our Lord Jesus Christ, the Father of glory, may give to you the spirit of wisdom and revelation in the knowledge of Him..'*

Often, we want God to come into our situation and fix the problem and, while He is not limited to a method and He can do something sovereignly, the Bible often reveals that He wants us to shift into His perspective to experience His power, with that bringing the healing, miracle or desired change. Psalm 103:7 says, *'He made known His ways to Moses, His acts to the children of Israel'*. Israel, like many, wanted the acts of God without His ways, but when we take on His ways, His acts follow.

Ephesians 1:17-21 [17]*that the God of our Lord Jesus Christ, the Father of glory, may give to you the spirit of wisdom and revelation in the knowledge of Him,* [18]*the eyes of your* *understanding being enlightened; that you may know what is the hope of His calling, what are the riches of the glory of His inheritance in the saints,* [19] *and what is the exceeding greatness of His power toward us who believe, according to the working of His mighty power* [20] *which He worked in Christ when He raised Him from the dead and seated Him at His right hand in the heavenly places,* [21] *far above all principality and power and might and dominion, and every name that is named, not only in this age but also in that which is to come.*

Paul prays that we may have the spirit of wisdom and revelation in the knowledge of God Himself - that we will see Him. Paul then prays for our spiritual eyes, our inner vision, to be opened to see three things.

Firstly, that we will see salvation, which is the hope to which He has called us. When we come to Christ and receive His free gift of salvation, there is a moment when we 'see' Him and the gospel. Before, we didn't see, but the gospel brings a revelation and understanding, that is not of the intellect, but an illumination of a spiritual truth brought by the Holy Spirit. This illumination brings faith, and the response of faith brings the power of God. This power is in such great measure that, in a moment in time, you are forgiven of all your sins, the former separation between you and God is removed, the Holy Spirit brings the life of God into your spirit and connects you to your Heavenly Father - and you are given the free gift of eternal life with Him. So much power, in fact, the greatest miracle that you will ever receive, all in an instant of time, as the result of the illumination of your spirit to the truth of God!

The second thing that Paul prays we will see is our inheritance, as in all that God has already given to us in Christ.

A SPIRIT OF WISDOM AND REVELATION

> **2 Peter 1:2-4** ²*Grace and peace be multiplied to you <u>in the knowledge of God and of Jesus</u> our Lord, ³as <u>His divine power has given to us all things</u> that pertain to life and godliness, <u>through the knowledge of Him</u> who called us by glory and virtue, ⁴by which have been given to us exceedingly great and precious promises, that <u>through</u> <u>these</u> you may become partakers of the divine nature, having escaped the corruption that is in the world through lust.*

His divine power has already given to us all we need, including our healing. He has accomplished it all for us and then His provision is sealed in His Word, which contains the power of God to bring itself to pass. Once faith is applied to the seed of the Word, the power of God is released by the Holy Spirit to bring it to pass.

The power comes through revelation knowledge of Him. When we see who He is to us and what He has done for us, the Scriptures are opened to us and the promise, although already given, is now released to us through that revelation. Then, the power of God, His divine nature is released through those same promises, bringing them into our experience.

A key is to study the promises of God not just trying to get something from Him but to see Him in them. The power is released in the knowledge of Him and not merely in knowing the promises He has given. For example, for healing there is far more power released in getting a revelation of God as your Healer and seeing what Jesus has done, than in just trying to get healed through reading and speaking the promises.

Once you see God and what He has done for you, the power is released to you, rather than striving to get something from Him. The world's way is to strive and grab at the things we desire ('lust' in the context of 2 Peter 1:4) which, by its nature, brings corruption. God's way is for us to simply receive what Jesus has already done for us. The bridge between God giving it and us receiving it is the revelation knowledge of Him.

> **1 John 3:2** *Beloved, now we are children of God; and it has not yet been revealed what we shall be, but we know that when He is revealed, we shall be like Him, for we shall see Him as He is.*

While this relates to a future transformation, it also has a temporal application. The more we see Jesus, the more the power of the Holy Spirit transforms us into the same image (2 Corinthians 3:18). The Holy Spirit moves on the revelation of Jesus.

> **1 Corinthians 13:12** *For now we see in a mirror, dimly, but then face to face. Now I know in part, but then I shall know just as I also am known.*

We currently see a dim reflection, but the more we see of Jesus, the more His power is revealed in our lives. Many interpret this passage as "Well, we can't see the whole picture. God must have some other plans for this person that includes their suffering". This gives an impression of God as harsh, a respecter of persons (which He is not) or not being good. From this, we can see that such inferences against His character are from the pit of hell and remind us of the temptation that led to the Fall, where Satan's deception was that God was not good and was withholding.

The salvation and healing that Jesus provided was provided equally and graciously to all (Romans 4:16 the promise is sure to all the seed having being given by grace). While we do not understand why some suffer more than others, such sufferings are the result of the impact of the Fall on the Earth and are not from God. The redemption in Christ offers hope, mercy and power to us all to experience God's goodness in its various manifestations, including healing.

The third thing Paul prays for in the Ephesians 1 passage (verses 19 - 21) is that we will see the exceeding greatness of God's power to bring all of this to pass when we believe, that is, when we see it. The measure of this available power is the same power that it took to raise Jesus from the dead when He was bearing all of our sins and all of our sicknesses and pains. That is more than enough power to completely heal you!

We don't need to keep asking for what He has already done, which includes healing, but we need to get a greater vision of it. The Holy Spirit brings this revelation to us, that we could not have 'seen' otherwise.

> **1 Corinthians 2:9,10** *⁹ But as it is written: "Eye has not seen, nor ear heard, Nor have entered into the heart of man the things which God has prepared for those who love Him." ¹⁰ But God has revealed them to us through His Spirit. For the Spirit searches all things, yes, the deep things of God.*

When we see God as the Healer and the finished work of the Cross, then healing is released. The more we see Jesus and what He has done for us, the more His healing power is released. I'll say it again - the Holy Spirit moves on the revelation of Jesus!

> **Proverbs 4:20-23** *²⁰My son give attention to my words; incline your ear to my sayings. ²¹Do not let them depart from your eyes; keep them in the midst of your heart; ²²For they are life to those who find them, and health to all their flesh. ²³Keep your heart with all diligence, for out of it spring the issues of life.*

Proverbs 4:20-23 is like a pattern for receiving healing. We are to give attention to God's words, allowing them to have priority over other words that will come to us in the situation. We are to incline our ear to what He says, with faith coming by hearing and hearing by the word of God (Romans 10:17). What is God saying to you in His Word?

We are then, not to let God's words depart from our eyes. Now I love the Word of God but even so, I can't be in front of it physically all the time. I believe that this is talking about not letting the Word of God depart from our inner vision. We are to be seeing God's perspective all the time. If I am seeing the sickness or the problem above His Word, then the Word has departed from my vision. I know that the Word of God is in my vision when it's what I see above all else and is my first response when any challenge comes.

The best way to keep the Word of God before your eyes or inner vision is to meditate on it (Joshua 1:8). I find that if I meditate on a Scripture for even ten minutes in my devotional time, which is generally for me first thing in the morning, then I continue to ponder on it throughout the day, and thus, it remains before my eyes.

This transfers the Word from your mind to your heart. Jesus' words carry His life and Spirit (John 6:33). The healing anointing is the life of God overcoming the law of sin and death (Romans 8:2). With the Word in our hearts and set as our vision, it brings the Holy Spirit and God's healing power into our flesh. The word 'health' in Proverbs 4:23 means 'medicine' - the Word acts as medicine to all your flesh. Just like any other medicine, you need to take it regularly until healed.

Reading:

- Ephesians 1:15-23
- Proverbs 4:20-27
- 2 Peter 1:2-4
- Psalm 119:15,18 and 130

Thought for the day: God's Word is medicine to all your flesh.

Reflection: Write down any insights or revelations that you have had as you reflect on what God's Word reveals to you about your health or situation, despite anything you are experiencing to the contrary.

13

SEEING THE IMPOSSIBLE BECOME POSSIBLE

Romans 4:17... *God who gives life to the dead and calls those things which do not exist as though they did.*

God gives life to those things that seem impossible, incurable, generational and any report that brings its own kind of death with disappointment and discouragement.

God calls those things which do not exist (e.g., promises that have not yet come to pass in the physical realm) as though they did (past tense). Once He has declared it, it is considered done, and faith aligns with that perspective.

> **Romans 4:16-21** [16]*Therefore it is <u>of faith that it might be according to grace,</u> so that the <u>promise might be sure to all the seed</u>, not only to those who are of the law, but also to those who are of the faith of Abraham, who is the father of us all,* [17]*(as it is written, "I have made you a father of many nations") in*

> the presence of Him whom he believed - God who gives life to the dead and calls those things which do not exist as though they did; ¹⁸ Who, contrary to hope, in hope believed, so that he became the father of many nations, according to what was spoken, "So shall your descendants be". ¹⁹ And not being weak in faith, he did not consider his own body, already dead (since he was about a hundred years old) and the deadness of Sarah's womb. ²⁰ He did not waver at the promise of God through unbelief, but was strengthened in faith, giving glory to God, ²¹ and being fully convinced that what He had promised he was also able to perform.

Abraham progressed from one who waited for the promise for twenty-four years, not seeing anything, to someone who received the promise within three months from the time a shift took place (Genesis 15-18).

In Genesis 15:1-6, God comes to Abram (as Abraham was then known), saying, "Do not be afraid, Abram. I am your shield, your exceedingly great reward" (Genesis 15:1). Abram's response (paraphrased here) is basically, "What good is that to me God, since I have no child to be my heir? What is the use of blessing me so much if I have no one to pass it on to?"

God immediately promises him that one from his own body will be his heir and straight after that, takes Abram outside and says, "Look now toward heaven, and count the stars if you are able to number them" and He said, "So shall your descendants be" (Genesis 15:5). God was telling him what to see.

The next thing that God does is to make a blood covenant with Abram as Abram asks, "How shall I know that You will keep Your word to me?" Now, we don't understand a lot about blood covenants in our western culture but in ancient culture, they were understood to be an unbreakable pact.

When two parties entered into a covenant, they were saying that they and all that they owned were at the disposal of their covenant partner should they ever need it. Attached to the covenant would be promises made, that could not be broken, such was the sanctity of the covenant. The covenant was then sealed with blood and the partaking of a covenant meal. So, when God immediately initiates a blood covenant with Abram along with the promise, Abram would understand just how serious God was about keeping His Word. God was attaching His life to His promise to guarantee it.

So, Abram has a promise, God has told him what to see regarding the promise and he has a blood covenant with God. Then twenty-four long years go by. In that time the couple has tried to take things into their own hands and make God's promise happen according to their interpretation of events, rather than considering God to be faithful and powerful enough to bring the impossible to pass. For Sarai has been barren all her life and the promise was first given when she was sixty-five years old! By the time it is fulfilled she will be ninety years of age.

Isn't it the same with us at times? We have a promise from God and a covenant sealed in the blood of His precious Son, Jesus, that guarantees the promise to us, and yet still not seeing the promise come to pass, we can start to reason and find ourselves putting a different interpretation on what God originally said. I believe the key to breakthrough is seeing what God has told us to see regarding that promise.

God again comes to Abram and Sarai in Genesis 17, twenty-four years after He had given the promise that Abram would have a child. Abram is now ninety-nine and Sarai eighty-nine and as the promise is reaffirmed, both Abram and Sarai respond by laughing (Genesis 17:17 and Genesis 18:12-15). They <u>can't see it</u> happening!

God now comes to bring a shift in their perspective that brings His power. God breathed Himself (and imparting His Name, with 'JHWH' or

SEEING THE IMPOSSIBLE BECOME POSSIBLE

'Jehovah' being spoken as a breath - 'ah') into Sarai and Abram, changing their names to Sarah and Abraham (Genesis 17:5,15) and they embraced the new identity that God gave them. Abraham means 'father of a multitude' which was in line with the promise God gave him. So, Abraham had to go and tell everyone that his name was now 'the father of a multitude', even before he had a child, and that is what others had to call him from now on. He would have received mocking, criticism, "Why would you believe that? You are not facing reality". However, at a word from God, he embraced who God was declaring him to be.

The NIV[2] says of Romans 4:18, that *'against all hope, in hope he believed'*. In what seemed a hopeless situation Abraham chose to believe in the hope that God would be faithful to His promise. Nothing is impossible for God (Luke 1:37) and nothing is impossible to he or she who believes (Mark 9:23).

God had made a promise, but He still required Abraham to believe it, see it and speak in line with the vision, in order for it to come to pass. He had to call those things that did not exist (still in the future) as though they already did (past tense) in line with the way God Himself speaks.

Abraham believed according to what God had already said. This is important. We are not just hyping something up or trying to manipulate God (as if we could), to give us what we want. We speak what is already His revealed will to us, including healing. We believe according to what <u>He has already said.</u>

Next, Abraham didn't focus on the problem. He knew it was impossible. Abraham did not consider his own body (parallel of symptoms or weaknesses), nor the deadness of Sarah's womb (parallel of impossible circumstances around us). He did not deny the problem, but he did choose to primarily focus on the answer instead.

Many Christians confuse believing God's Word and declaring it in the face of opposing circumstances to be expressed as denial of the sickness or problem, going around saying "I'm not sick". Faith is not denial but choosing to believe that God's promise is enough to override the problem that you do acknowledge exists. As Abraham did, faith faces the worst facts head on; then sees God, His character and His promises in the midst of those facts and from there, declares the promise in faith.

So, we know that there is a sickness to be dealt with; we don't deny it but choose to focus on and see the promise of God's Word instead, understanding that what we see of Him releases His power for us to receive.

For Abraham and Sarah, the wait was twenty-four years with a promise and the covenant with no results, but only three months from seeing God's perspective of the situation and aligning their faith, perspective and actions with that. I know the timing of God comes into things as well, but I do believe that this situation highlights the importance of seeing God's perspective and aligning ourselves, in all our being and ways, with that.

Just because things don't change immediately doesn't mean that it won't happen. If you received everything from God, as soon as you asked for it, you wouldn't need faith. Faith is believing for what you cannot see with the natural eyes, and it is 'through faith and patience' that we inherit the promises of God (Hebrews 6:12). The fact that we also need patience indicates that a waiting period may be involved.

God, Jehovah Rapha, the God who heals us has declared us to be healed because of what Jesus did for us on the Cross. While this is possibly not what you are experiencing now, allow that truth to change how you see yourself. Faith calls the promise that is not yet visible as if it's done - 'by whose wounds you were healed' (1 Peter 2:24).

Reading:

- Romans 4:16-21
- Isaiah 55: 8-11
- Genesis 15:1-6
- Genesis 18:1-15
- Genesis 21:1-7

Thought for the day: 'God who gives life to the dead and calls those things which do not exist as though they did'.

Reflection: What has God already told you to see? Are you seeing it, aligning yourself and speaking in line with that - or the circumstance?

_____
_____
_____
_____
_____
_____
_____
_____
_____
_____
_____
_____

Write down three Scriptures regarding what God wants you to believe, see and speak over your health.

Scripture 1:

Scripture 2:

Scripture 3:

14

BELIEVE THAT YOU RECEIVE (part 1)

John 4:50 *Jesus said to him, "Go your way; your son lives." So the man believed the word that Jesus spoke to him, and he went his way.*

John 4:46-53 [46] *So Jesus came again to Cana of Galilee where He had made the water wine. And there was a certain nobleman whose son was sick at Capernaum.* [47] *When he heard that Jesus had come out of Judea into Galilee, he went to Him and implored Him to come down and heal his son, for he was at the point of death.* [48] *Then Jesus said to him, "Unless you people see signs and wonders, you will by no means believe."*

[49] *The nobleman said to Him, "Sir, come down before my child dies!"* [50] *Jesus said to him, "Go your way; your son lives." So the man believed the word that Jesus spoke to him, and he*

BELIEVE THAT YOU RECEIVE (PART 1)

went his way. ^{51} And as he was now going down, his servants met him and told him, saying, "Your son lives!" ^{52} Then he inquired of them the hour when he got better. And they said to him, "Yesterday at the seventh hour the fever left him." ^{53} So the father knew that it was at the same hour in which Jesus said to him, "Your son lives." And he himself believed, and his whole household.

Jesus doesn't withhold healing from those who don't present to Him with perfect faith but frequently, He does first reveal what He wants to correct or what He wants a person to respond to. As the person responds to His direction, i.e., a step of faith, the power of God is released.

The story in John 4:46-53 starts with the nobleman begging for healing. He is desperate and wants Jesus to come to his situation at his direction. Despite the man's desperation, Jesus makes a statement that may not immediately seem clear unless the man ponders it. Jesus is directing him to faith. The required shift in perspective and response is not a lack of sympathy or mercy, but rather, real mercy because faith aligns us to God and His provision of healing.

> **John 4:48** *Then Jesus said to him, "Unless you people see signs and wonders, you will by no means believe."*

Jesus is addressing the natural tendency to believe when we see evidence of a thing, and the human tendency to want God to come and do things our way.

However, God's way is that we believe before we see, as a response of trust in Him, and that we do things His way.

The man pleads with Jesus to come but Jesus is undeterred and again presents the required shift to have faith in Him and His Word - "Go your way; your son lives." The nobleman's response reflects a shift from "I'm asking You to come and do a miracle" to "I will trust what You have said to me". He believed and went his way believing.

The boy's healing started as soon as the nobleman believed, even though the man wouldn't have been able to physically see that, as he was still on a long journey back to his house - an estimated thirty-eight kilometres from Cana to Capernaum. When he heard about his son's recovery, then he believed even more, along with his household. In other words, there was a progression of faith in the process, and it wasn't about having perfect faith at the beginning before Jesus would respond. He heard the word that Jesus spoke, he took Him at His word, he responded to it and then later he really believed in Jesus and His Word.

In Matthew 9:27-31 Jesus asks two blind men before they receive their healing, "Do you believe that I am able to do this?" Their response in the affirmative precedes them receiving their healing and Jesus states "According to your faith let it be to you".

In Mark 11:12-14, Jesus speaks a word to a fig tree that no one shall eat from it again and then, twenty-four hours later, they again pass the tree and Peter sees that it has withered away. The disciples didn't believe at the exact moment that Jesus spoke to the fig tree but only when they saw the results the next day. Jesus uses this moment to teach them about how faith works.

> **Mark 11:22-26** [22] *So Jesus answered and said to them, "Have faith in God.* [23] *For assuredly, I say to you, whoever says to this mountain, 'Be removed and be cast into the sea,' and does not doubt in his heart, but believes that those things he says will be done, he will have whatever he says.* [24] *Therefore I say to you, whatever things you ask when you pray, believe that you receive them, and you will have them.* [25] *"And whenever you*

BELIEVE THAT YOU RECEIVE (PART 1)

> *stand praying, if you have anything against anyone, forgive him, that your Father in heaven may also forgive you your trespasses.* ²⁶ *But if you do not forgive, neither will your Father in heaven forgive your trespasses."*

There is so much to discuss in this passage, but the following will focus on three alignments of faith that bring us closer to God and the manifestation of His authority and power.

The first alignment is to have faith in God Himself and, by association, His Word. This is expressed in believing what He says and going your way believing - before you see any evidence of it physically.

> **Mark 11:24** *Therefore I say to you, whatever things you ask when you pray, believe that you receive them, and you will have them.*

> **John 4:50** *Jesus said to him, "Go your way; your son lives." So, the man <u>believed the word that Jesus spoke to him</u>, and he went his way.*

So, we believe first in the present, and then, we will have in the future (be it near or distant). In verse 22, Jesus says "Have faith in God". He didn't say have faith in a desired outcome or have confidence in how much faith you have. The former looks like "I want God to do this (and at, or by, this time) and therefore I choose to believe it and now, I want God to come into alignment with that and for Him to do it just how I have asked". That is presumption rather than faith and is treating God like the genie in the bottle rather than Lord. Often believers make the request, "I want you to believe with me that this is going to happen". It may be around healing, that is clearly God's will, but its presentation is such that it requires no alignment with God on their part, but rather, that He would respond to (and thus align with) them, their ways, desires and timing.

Putting faith in God for a specific outcome or timing comes with great risk because God has never said that He would do our will in our timing. Then, when a thing doesn't happen, people become disappointed or step back in their faith - the very faith they needed to place in Him to see a healing or miracle take place. So, this kind of presumptive prayer or misguided expectation becomes a great trap and hindrance to seeing a healing take place. People set themselves up for disappointment when they are believing for things to be their way, in their timing and for their will to come to pass.

> **Isaiah 55:8,9** [8] *"For My thoughts are not your thoughts, nor are your ways My ways," says the Lord.* [9] *"For as the heavens are higher than the earth, so are My ways higher than your ways, and My thoughts than your thoughts."*

So how does this work? There can be a fine line between faith and presumption and it's important that we respond to God appropriately. Presumption is centred around my will, what I want and how I want God to move. Faith is centred around Jesus, His will, His Word and alignment with that.

You could pray, for example, "God I am so grateful that You are the Lord Who heals me and I put my trust in You. I thank you Jesus for dying in my place and that You took my sicknesses and pains and that by Your stripes I have been healed. I take you at Your word: I believe it; I receive it; and I ask the Holy Spirit to fill me with the healing grace that You have provided, in Jesus' name. Amen."

> **Luke 17:5-10** [5] *And the apostles said to the Lord, "Increase our faith."* [6] *So the Lord said, "If you have faith as a mustard*

> seed, you can say to this mulberry tree, 'Be pulled up by the roots and be planted in the sea,' and it would obey you. ⁷ And which of you, having a servant plowing or tending sheep, will say to him when he has come in from the field, 'Come at once and sit down to eat'? ⁸ But will he not rather say to him, 'Prepare something for my supper, and gird yourself and serve me till I have eaten and drunk, and afterward you will eat and drink'? ⁹ Does he thank that servant because he did the things that were commanded him? I think not. ¹⁰ So likewise you, when you have done all those things which you are commanded, say, 'We are unprofitable servants. We have done what was our duty to do.' "

Interestingly, while Jesus commends great faith, He also highlights that it's not the magnitude of our faith that determines whether the miraculous is experienced. His miraculous power is available to all levels of faith - if that 'mustard seed' of faith is placed in Him and worked out in obedience to Him. Faith in God, alignment with Him, obedience to Him and submission under His Lordship, position us to partner with Him - to see His will and His great power released.

In Luke 17:7-10 Jesus pulls us out of having pride in our faith, and any arrogance that we could walk into any situation and have the power to command what we want done, operating independently of Him. Faith operates from the place of an obedient servant obeying the Master's command. All the power is God's, all the authority, all the glory and we need to discern what He is doing, align with Him and then, from that place we do need to minister that authority and power delegated to us, to see His will be done.

Then, when extraordinary things happen, don't expect any glory or think it was because of a person's or your own great faith that they occurred - we are just servants doing what is our duty to do and to God be all the glory who does all the wonderful healings and miracles.

The second alignment we require from Mark 11:23 is that of the heart and the mouth.

> **Mark 11:23** *For assuredly, I say to you, whoever says to this mountain, 'Be removed and be cast into the sea,' and does not doubt in his heart, but believes that those things he says will be done, he will have whatever he says.*

"Does not doubt in his heart" literally means 'does not differ in his heart to what he says with his mouth'. What we say, what we believe and what we see must align. We can't believe one thing and then be speaking words that contradict it - or vice versa.

God's word has power. We speak it to build faith (Romans 10:17), release our faith and it has creative power to change things. Jesus just saying "your son lives" is enough for a young boy to be healed thirty-eight kilometres away, once that word was believed.

It's not just mechanically speaking it out as a religious exercise but rather, a submission and alignment with God's way. Speaking God's word, thankfulness and giving glory to God are His ways and align us with Him and release His power.

Complaining, problem-talking words do the opposite and create unbelief and a blockage to the power of God. So, you may have believed and gone your way, but unbelief can still come in through words expressing doubts, feelings, disappointments etc and crowd out the faith that is there.

BELIEVE THAT YOU RECEIVE (PART 1)

Thankfulness and speaking God's word instead of the issue are like fasting, shutting down the voice of the flesh and in so doing, connecting us deeper with the Spirit.

> **Philemon 6** *that the sharing of your faith may become effective by the acknowledgment of every good thing which is in you in Christ Jesus.*

The word 'sharing' in this verse, in the Greek is 'koinonia', that being the fellowship or a unity brought about by the Holy Spirit, which, in Scripture, results in the works of God being revealed. Connecting faith to the acknowledgement and declaration of what we have in Christ is a Holy Spirit empowered fellowship that makes it effective.

We need to connect our measure of faith to something that it is designed to have Holy Spirit empowered fellowship with - to what God has declared in His Word and revealed through Jesus. Again, noting, that there is no Holy Spirit empowered fellowship with complaining, religious teachings that contradict the word of God, reasons why it may not happen or focusing on the problem.

The third alignment is that of our heart to God's heart of mercy, forgiveness, love and His character, expressed through forgiveness. The important "and" in Mark 11:25 impacts our faith.

> **Mark 11:25, 26** *"And whenever you stand praying, if you have anything against anyone, forgive him, that your Father in heaven may also forgive you your trespasses. [26] But if you do not forgive, neither will your Father in heaven forgive your trespasses."*

At the end of the Lord's prayer also, the importance and power of forgiveness is emphasised. It may seem unrelated in our thinking but Jesus links it with answered prayer. Forgiveness is God's way and if we don't align with Him, it blocks us from receiving the power of God.

God is merciful and forgives us - but it's not as a casual 'light' thing but it came at a great cost to Himself. In response to this mercy, we are commanded to also release forgiveness to others.

So, like the nobleman (John 4:46-53) we are to listen to what Jesus is saying to us; align to His Word, His nature and His ways; believe before we receive and go our way believing.

Reading:

- Mark 11:12-26
- John 4:46-53
- Matthew 9:27-31
- Romans 10:6-11

Thought for the day: 'So the man <u>believed the word that Jesus spoke to him</u>, and he went his way.'

Reflection: Write down any insights or revelations that you have had as you reflect on "Is there something God has been saying to me in His Word and through an impression in my spirit that is showing me an area I need to align with?"

15

BELIEVE BEFORE YOU RECEIVE (part 2)

Mark 11:24 *Therefore I say to you, whatever things you ask when you pray, believe that you receive them, and you will have them.*

Revisiting Jesus' teaching on faith in Mark 11:12-14 and 20-24, we find that it highlights both the power of God's Word and the power that comes from having faith in God, that leads us to believe and speak His Word.

In Mark 11:12-14, Jesus speaks a word to a fig tree that no one shall eat from it again but when they pass it again at the end of the day, no one comments on any change in it. The Word of God had been spoken to it, but they didn't see any physical change yet. Then twenty-four hours later, they again pass the tree, and Peter sees that it has withered away.

Normally a tree dies from the extremities down and while the root is viable, it can still have life, if the dead parts are pruned. However, Jesus' Word goes to the root and it dies from the root up.

Jesus' Word and redemptive work have also gone to the root of sin and sickness, even though they may still be visible to the eye. 1 Peter 2:24 describes how we can be dead to sin because of Jesus bearing it on our behalf but this doesn't mean that it no longer exists. Rather, Jesus has broken its power off our lives, and in looking to Him in faith, we can receive forgiveness and the Spirit of holiness, who transforms us to leave the pursuit of sin and live for righteousness. In the same way, in Jesus bearing our sicknesses and pains at the same time, we can see ourselves as being 'dead to sickness' – this, not meaning that it doesn't exist, but that Jesus' redemptive work has broken its power off our lives and, in looking to Jesus in faith, we can receive His healing and the power of the Holy Spirit to transform our earthly bodies.

> **1 Peter 2:24** *who Himself bore our sins in His own body on the tree, that we, having died to sins, might live for righteousness—by whose stripes you were healed.*

> **Romans 8:11** *But if the Spirit of Him who raised Jesus from the dead dwells in you, He who raised Christ from the dead will also give life to your mortal bodies through His Spirit who dwells in you.*

Jesus cursed sickness at the root and declared "It is finished" along with all that He accomplished for us. As you identify with, and see, what He has done for you, that spiritual reality starts to be demonstrated physically in your body and the symptoms wither. See that sickness pulled out by the root from your body!

Mark 11:22-24 [22] *So Jesus answered and said to them, "Have faith in God.* [23] *For assuredly, I say to you, whoever says to this mountain, 'Be removed and be cast into the sea,' and does not doubt in his heart, but believes that those things he says will be done, he will have whatever he says.* [24] *Therefore I say to you, whatever things you ask when you pray, believe that you receive them, and you will have them.*

Jesus said to have faith in God. The confidence to believe comes from confidence in God Himself, that His Word carries His power and that the Holy Spirit moves on the Word of God. It's not a 'hype' or a confidence in who we are or in our own level of faith - it's faith in God.

Then, Jesus, standing at the Mt of Olives, says in verse 23 to speak to your mountain (not speak about it!). You may not have a word to move a specific mountain, but you do have a word that says 'I am the Lord who heals you', 'He Himself took our infirmities and bore our sicknesses', and 'by whose stripes you were healed'.

Believe His word, see it in your inner vision and from that heart of faith, align your mouth and speak. Declare Jesus' victory to your problem.

There are two ways we can experience healing - the immediate manifestation, which we love and then there's the healing where you believe that you receive it first, seeing that sickness destroyed at the root; declare it boldly and then over time you will see the symptoms wither away.

There are two stories in the Old Testament that while not speaking of healing, illustrate how God does a miracle. Often the first time, or in the initial stages of our faith, He does it 'before your eyes' and then, thereafter, He expects a faith that takes Him at His Word and believes before it receives.

BELIEVE BEFORE YOU RECEIVE (PART 2)

The first story is that of the 'immediate' or 'before your eyes' physical manifestation.

> **Exodus 14:21,22** *Then Moses stretched out his hand over the sea: and The Lord caused the sea to go back by a strong east wind <u>all that night</u>, and made the sea into dry land, and the waters were divided. So the children went into the midst of the sea on the dry ground, and the waters were a wall to them on their right hand and on their left.*

They believed because they saw it happen in front of them, even though it took all night to finish. The seeing of a miracle, and many others, however, didn't change them or bring great faith in God, preventing the Israelites living in the fullness of His promises. The crossing of the Red Sea was into the wilderness, not into the Promised Land.

The way of faith is believing that you have received the answer, before you see it with your physical eyes. This 'standing in faith', believing what God has said despite contrary circumstances causes you to be someone who steps into the Promised Land of God's provision. Most sustained healings are the result of the person having put the Word of God in, believed it and having stood in faith until it manifested.

The second illustration is that of the crossing of the Jordan into the Promised land - a 'believing before they received'.

> **Joshua 3:8** *⁸You shall command the priests who bear the ark of the covenant, saying, 'When you have come to the edge of the water of the Jordan, you shall stand in the Jordan.'"*

> **Joshua 3:13-17** *¹³ And it shall come to pass, as soon as the soles of the feet of the priests who bear the ark of the Lord, the Lord of all the earth, shall rest in the waters of the Jordan, that*

> the waters of the Jordan shall be cut off, the waters that come down from upstream, and they shall stand as a heap." ¹⁴So it was, when the people set out from their camp to cross over the Jordan, with the priests bearing the ark of the covenant before the people, ¹⁵and as those who bore the ark came to the Jordan, and the feet of the priests who bore the ark dipped in the edge of the water (for the Jordan overflows all its banks during the whole time of harvest), ¹⁶that the waters which came down from upstream stood still, and rose in a heap very far away at Adam, the city that is beside Zaretan. So the waters that went down into the Sea of the Arabah, the Salt Sea, failed, and were cut off; and the people crossed over opposite Jericho. ¹⁷Then the priests who bore the ark of the covenant of the Lord stood firm on dry ground in the midst of the Jordan; and all Israel crossed over on dry ground, until all the people had crossed completely over the Jordan.

Joshua 3:9-13 reveals the plan that God has given to Joshua to get the people over the Jordan river which was in flood at the time (verse 15). The priests are to take the Ark of the Covenant, the manifest presence of God, which contained the Word of God; put their feet into the river and *'as soon as the soles of the feet of the priests who bear the ark of The Lord, The Lord of all the earth, shall rest in the waters of the Jordan, that the waters of the Jordan shall be cut off, the waters that come from upstream, and they shall stand as a heap'* (verse 13).

They had to bring the presence of God and His Word to the problem, to face it and not deny it. The gift of the Spirit, called the working of miracles, is just that - 'a working', because there are things that we do that allow the miracle to be worked out. God could and occasionally does do it sovereignly but has designed the general method to be faith in His Word and cooperating with the Holy Spirit.

As soon as they put their feet in the water, the 'waters which came down from upstream stood still, and rose in a heap' - just as God said BUT it's at Adam, nineteen miles up the river! Not right in front of their eyes.

The New Living Translation[5] says - '*the water above that point began backing up a great distance away at a town called Adam, which is near Zarethan. and the water below that point flowed on to the Dead Sea until the riverbed was dry. Then all the people crossed over near the town of Jericho.*'

The water is cut off nineteen miles upriver at Adam - God's redemption has even worked backwards to Adam. This means that where the priests were standing in the river, the water is still going to be flowing until those nineteen miles worth of water have flowed past, down to the Dead Sea. Now it's harvest season for the Israelites (verse 15), the time when the Jordan was in flood. In those days, before irrigation drew on its waters, the water would flow over the banks and so nineteen miles worth of it will take a bit of time to pass them by. Therefore, those priests would have been standing in the water for maybe hours, maybe days, seeing no outward change in their circumstances but standing on the Word of God. Even though they can't see an immediate change, God has done what He said He would do at the time He said He would do it - it's just happened before them, and they have to wait for it to be revealed in front of them.

He had split the waters at the Jordan just as much as He had done at the Red Sea- in fact at the Jordan it was even more immediate - it's just that it wasn't done in front of them. God has healed you just as much when you can't see an immediate change as when you get the immediate miracle. He has just done it beforehand at the Cross, in a moment in time, that will catch up with your circumstances as long as you stay in position with the presence of God and believing the Word that He spoke. UNTIL!

God has given us His irrefutable Word, guaranteed to us by the blood of Jesus, in whom all the promises of God are 'yes and amen'. He has said that He is the Lord who heals us, that He has removed sickness from us, that Jesus bore (in order to carry away) our sicknesses at the Cross and that by His stripes we have been healed.

At His Word we stand on the edge of the impossibility, with the presence of God and believing the Word of God and we stand until the act that God did in Christ nearly two thousand years ago catches up with us.

Reading:

- Galatians 3:1-9
- Hebrews 11:1-6
- Hebrews 12:1,2

Thought for the day:

> **Mark 11:24** *Therefore I say to you, whatever things you ask when you pray, believe that you receive them, and you will have them.*

Reflection: Write down what you are deciding to believe God for - as He has said in Scripture and not of your own will. Write down Scriptures to support it; meditate on them and make a decision to believe and 'stand' for your healing despite any contrary circumstances. Pray over them and ask the Lord to perfect your faith in Him and His Word.

16

I BELIEVE; HELP MY UNBELIEF

> **Mark 9:23,24** *Jesus said to him, "If you can believe, all things are possible to him who believes." [24] Immediately the father of the child cried out and said with tears, "Lord, I believe; help my unbelief!"*

In Mark 9, the disciples, the best ministers of the day apart from Jesus, who themselves had seen many healings (Mark 6:13) have prayed for a boy with epilepsy, and he wasn't healed. From this, many would conclude that it wasn't God's will to heal him or a variety of other reasons that people come up with as to why someone wasn't healed. Then, Jesus comes down from the Mount of Transfiguration and heals the boy. Was it God's will to heal the boy? Absolutely! Was he healed when all the best ministers prayed? Not on that occasion. Jesus points to the reason as being unbelief in both the father of the boy (recipient) and the disciples (ministers).

> **Mark 9:21-24** [21] *So He asked his father, "How long has this been happening to him?" And he said, "From childhood. [22] And*

> *often he has thrown him both into the fire and into the water to destroy him. But if You can do anything, have compassion on us and help us."* ²³ <u>*Jesus said to him, "If you can believe, all things are possible to him who believes."*</u> ²⁴ *Immediately the father of the child cried out and said with tears, "Lord, I believe; help my unbelief!"*

Jesus then casts out a demon and the boy is healed. So, Jesus doesn't withhold healing from those who don't present to Him with perfect faith but, at the same time, He reveals what He wants to correct or what He wants a person to respond to. As the person responds to that, the power of God is revealed. It's like repentance - thinking and going one way and then turning in response to the Lord and the power of God comes immediately. But you then need to keep going that way to experience Him and all that He has for you.

Jesus addresses the man's unbelief "If You can" with "If you can believe, all things are possible to him who believes." So, He has revealed what He is looking for - for the father to believe Him. Again, it's not like we have to have perfect faith before we receive from Him but to rather, just take a step of faith and be consistently moving towards Him.

The moment the father 'switched on' faith God moved - even though, as he himself acknowledged, he didn't have strong faith. Healing doesn't just drop on us - we activate faith and engage with God. Faith is the key to receiving from God - everything is given freely by grace and received through faith. For the father in the story, he recognises in himself the presence of unbelief even in the midst of turning to Jesus and choosing to believe Him. Faith in Jesus and unbelief can be present at the same time.

Then the disciples ask Jesus why they couldn't heal the boy:

THE LORD WHO HEALS YOU

Matthew 17:20 *So Jesus said to them, "Because of your unbelief; for assuredly, I say to you, if you have faith as a mustard seed, you will say to this mountain, 'Move from here to there,' and it will move; and nothing will be impossible for you.*

That's a hard one to hear! They hadn't stopped loving Him; they hadn't stopped believing in Him or even believing that He was the Healer but perhaps, in the moment, as we can all do, their eyes had shifted onto the size of the problem, the circumstance, rather than on what Jesus had said to them earlier. In Matthew 10:1, Jesus had given them authority to cast out all demons and heal all diseases. Losing sight of the Word of God, had shut down the power of God in the situation.

Unbelief is believing something contrary to what God has said, or seeing the size of the problem above what Jesus has already said, or praying one thing and then countering it with "I wonder why God isn't doing something?" It might be focusing on and/or talking about the symptoms so much that doubt creeps in and eventually creates a stronghold of unbelief i.e., something that has a strong hold on your thinking, making it hard to stand in faith.

Most believers can be sensitive about this issue of needing faith. "I have faith!" and yes, they do, but again, unbelief and faith in God can be present at the same time. Often, we don't even know unbelief is there until we take a closer look.

It doesn't matter how long you've been a believer or how long you've been practising the principles of faith - we all need to guard ourselves in this area. If we don't keep pursuing the things of God, we not only stagnate but go backwards. We need to be consistently seeking God, getting revelation on His Word and staying full of faith.

Jesus then brings in the practice of prayer with fasting. In Matthew 9:14,15 Jesus reveals that fasting is required to bring us closer to God. Fasting is not about missing out on food, or anything else, as much as suppressing the voice and demands of the 'flesh' so that we sense and draw nearer to God in the spirit. In that place, we encounter His presence in a greater way and we receive a deeper revelation of Him and His Word.

In Matthew 17:21 Jesus advises the disciples, "However, this kind does not go out except by prayer and fasting". Many people believe that He was talking about the demon, but others would say that this would contradict what He had said earlier - that He gave them power to heal all sicknesses and <u>cast out all demons</u> - and that it rather refers to their unbelief.

Either way, He advises them to draw aside, fast and pray and receive fresh revelation of what they had been given and a greater measure of God's power to minister it.

> **Hebrews 11:6** *But without faith it is impossible to please Him, for he who comes to God must believe that He is, and that He is a rewarder of those who diligently seek Him.*

In diligently seeking Him, and praying with fasting, we are not earning the blessing because that would be contrary to what Scripture reveals. As we seek God, we find more and more of what He has already made provision of, for us all - and sometimes we really have to dig deeper and draw closer. Some of the blessings of God appear on the surface and others we have to dig deeply for. When we see more of what He has for us in the Word, it brings revelation, and revelation precedes the power of God being revealed.

Reading:

- Mark 9:14-29
- Isaiah 58:8
- Matthew 17:14-21
- Luke 9:37-42

Thought for the day: All things are possible to him (or her) who believes.

Reflection: Write down any insights or revelations that you have had as you reflect on whether there are areas of unbelief that God is revealing to you. Would you be prepared to make time to fast and pray to get a deeper revelation of God and His Word in that area?

17

THE HINDRANCE OF UNBELIEF

Hebrews 4:2 *For indeed the gospel was preached to us as well as to them; but the word which they heard did not profit them, not being mixed with faith in those who heard it.*

Mark 8:22-26 *²² Then He came to Bethsaida; and they brought a blind man to Him, and begged Him to touch him. ²³ So He took the blind man by the hand and led him out of the town. And when He had spit on his eyes and put His hands on him, He asked him if he saw anything. ²⁴ And he looked up and said, "I see men like trees, walking." ²⁵ Then He put His hands on his eyes again and made him look up. And he was restored and saw everyone clearly. ²⁶ Then He sent him away to his house, saying, "Neither go into the town, nor tell anyone in the town."*

Luke 10:13 *"Woe to you, Chorazin! Woe to you, Bethsaida! For if the mighty works which were done in you had been done* *in Tyre and Sidon, they would have repented long ago, sitting in sackcloth and ashes."*

Jesus has come to Bethsaida where, Luke 10:13 reveals, there is great unbelief, revealed through a lack of repentance in response to the mighty works done there. However, in the midst, there are some who reach out to Him for the healing of a certain blind man. The first thing Jesus does here is to take the blind man out of the town, physically removing him out of the place of unbelief, before He prays for him. So, if Jesus had to do this, how much more do we need to take steps to deal with the issue or environment of unbelief.

This might be something you need to consider. What do you need to do to remove yourself from any identified unbelief and into faith? To assist you in believing God for your healing, are there people or places you need to remove yourself from, even if for a time, until your faith can stand amid contrary statements and arguments? This is possibly what the blind man from Bethsaida needed. It is very difficult to believe for healing, or minister it, in an environment that is challenging what God can do, and what He has done.

It's not always a good idea to be telling everyone of what you are believing God for, but rather, just share it with those who will support you and lead you closer to Jesus, as the blind man's friends did. Just recognise, for those who like to post on social media and request everyone's prayers, that this may open you up to comments of unbelief that are not helpful. It also opens you up to all the health advice given by those not spiritually mature nor medically trained, with everything from vitamins to the latest diet or even an alternative practitioner who embraces another form of spirituality that is contrary to God. None of this helps you draw closer to God, build your faith in Him or receive healing from Him.

THE HINDRANCE OF UNBELIEF

There are certain blockages to the receiving of healing and unbelief is certainly one of them. In a discussion of Israel's failure to enter God's Rest, the author of Hebrews writes in **Hebrews 4:2** *'For indeed the gospel was preached to us as well as to them; but the word which they heard did not profit them, not being mixed with faith in those who heard it.'*

> **Hebrews 3:12** *Beware, brethren, lest there be in any of you an evil heart of unbelief in departing from the living God...*

Unbelief or hardening our hearts, in any way, to what God has said, causes us to depart or pull away from Him. It's not saying that you lose your salvation, but we can unconsciously (or consciously) take steps backwards when listening to or accepting arguments against what God has already said, or against His power. It's not like the Israelites stopped believing in God Himself, as much as they didn't believe what He said enough for them to act on it. The writer of Hebrews sums up the failure of the initial generation of Israel to enter the Promised Land (with the exception of Joshua and Caleb) in **Hebrews 3:19** *'So we see that they could not enter in because of unbelief.'*

Conversely, 1 Thessalonians 2:13 tells us that the Word of God works effectively in those who choose to believe.

> **1 Thessalonians 2:13** *For this reason we also thank God without ceasing, because when you received the word of God which you heard from us, you welcomed it not as the word of men, but as it is in truth, the word of God, which also effectively works in you who believe.*

In the passage of Hebrews 3 we also find one of the things that can help us on the journey, and that is encouragement found in faith-filled community. Hebrews 3:13 *'but exhort one another daily, while it is called 'Today' lest any of you be hardened through the deceitfulness of sin.'*

The blind man from Bethsaida perhaps didn't have a faith-filled community but he did have faith-filled friends who brought him closer to Jesus. Are there places, like a good Bible-based church for example, that you need to be positioning yourself in, and fellowshipping with those who will encourage your faith in God?

The healing of this man is the only two-stage healing that Jesus does, and a bit more dramatic with the spitting, possibly this was due to the unbelief on the man's part and that he needed something tangible to attach his faith to. There is no limitation on Jesus' part and His ministry of healing was directed by the faith of the person receiving healing. For the Centurion, who was in faith, He only had to speak a word but, for the blind man in Bethsaida, He needs to do something more.

Having said that, however, the Word is always revealing hidden truths to us and Jesus does everything on purpose. So, why the saliva in the eye rather than something else? In Revelation 3:18, Jesus counsels the lukewarm church to anoint their eyes with eye salve so that they could see. Spiritually speaking there was the need for the Holy Spirit to illuminate the eyes of their hardened and closed hearts. In Mark 8:23, He makes His own eye salve, that carried His DNA and life in it, to place on the man's eyes, not just to see physically but also spiritually. Interestingly, in the passage after the story of the blind man's healing in Mark 8, Jesus questions His disciples on who people see Him to be.

The first stage of the healing prayer shifts the blind man a little, to hope or even a seed of faith, and the second brings full healing. Jesus is so gracious that He will work with someone who is struggling to believe - just be real with Him and then, be prepared to take action to pursue Him and the healing He has for you.

This is the only time that Jesus asked someone if there was a result from His prayer, in this case, if the man saw anything. This is a good question to ask yourself, "What do I see regarding my health and healing?" Do you see the sickness or trouble? Or do you see what God has said and the finished work of the Cross? This is important because faith has vision.

This is not to discourage you if you are seeing something different to what God says, but it is important that we ask ourselves what we see and gauge where we are at. If you see the problem or the sickness more than the Word of God, then the problem has taken pre-eminence in your spiritual vision and is hindering you receiving from God. The answer is to meditate on the Word of God (Joshua 1:8), pray and fast until you see what God sees more than any argument or high thing (prideful thought) that would try and exalt itself against the knowledge of God.

> **2 Corinthians 10:4,5** *⁴ For the weapons of our warfare are not carnal but mighty in God for pulling down strongholds, ⁵ casting down arguments and every high thing that exalts itself against the knowledge of God, bringing every thought into captivity to the obedience of Christ,*

When you cast down unbelief, doubts, discouragement and deception and then, start to meditate on and see the Word, you feel the substance of faith come into your spirit. Yes, faith has substance - it is not some vague hope - and this substance is the evidence and assurance that God's Word is conceived and working in your life, even before you can see any change.

> **Hebrews 11:1** *Now faith is the substance of things hoped for, the evidence of things not seen.*

In Mark 8:25, as Jesus prays for the man a second time, He makes him 'look up'. We need to raise our vision from the sickness or problem that we are seeing with our natural eyes, to the healing provided for us in Christ, and the associated power of God to bring it to pass, with our spiritual eyes (inner vision).

Genesis 30:25-43, records a wonderful story regarding the power of a vision. Jacob wanted to leave his father-in-law Laban, but Laban knew that God was blessing him through Jacob. He asks Jacob to name his wages, the latter choosing all the sheep and goats that are spotted and speckled, and the brown lambs. The other even- coloured livestock would remain Laban's possession.

However, Laban tricks Jacob and removes all these uneven coloured sheep from the flock, giving them to his sons. This leaves only Laban's even-coloured sheep in the flock and they are going to reproduce after their own kind, according to the Law of Creation and the established laws of genetics, leaving Jacob with no wages.

God gives Jacob a dream, showing him to take sticks of poplar, almond and chestnut, tear into the bark, making the branches appear spotty and striped. He was then to place the branches before the watering troughs, where the animals mated and conceived, when they came to drink.

> **Genesis 30:39** *So the flocks conceived before the rods, and the flocks brought forth streaked, speckled, and spotted.*

What is this? The even coloured sheep are producing streaked, speckled and spotted progeny, contrary to the natural laws. Jacob recounts the key to this miracle in Genesis 31:11,12.

> **Genesis 31:11,12** *Then the Angel of God spoke to me in a dream, saying, 'Jacob.' And I said, 'Here I am.' And He said, <u>'Lift your eyes now and see</u>, all the rams which leap on the*

> *flocks are streaked, speckled, and gray-spotted; for I have seen all that Laban is doing to you.*

So, God told Jacob to see the rams as streaked, speckled and spotted, when according to the natural eye, they weren't! Jacob had to see what God was saying to him, above what his natural eyes or senses were saying to him, before the Word of God would be activated and work the supernatural.

We need to continually be looking up from our circumstances to God and what He has promised, if we want to see the works of God revealed. The man from Bethsaida looks up and receives the restoration of his vision.

> **Mark 8:26** *Then He sent him away to his house, saying, "Neither go into the town, nor tell anyone in the town."*

Finally, Jesus commands him to not return to the place of unbelief nor even tell what had happened, to those in unbelief. This is not the same as not sharing your testimony with someone about God's goodness and what He has done in your life, which is so important that we do, but rather not to tell it to those who will scorn or mock you for your faith in God. We just need some discernment in where, when and with whom to share it.

> **Matthew 7:6** *"Do not give what is holy to the dogs; nor cast your pearls before swine, lest they trample them under their feet, and turn and tear you in pieces".*

A phenomenon which is often seen, is when people can seem to 'lose their healing'. Now, they didn't lose it and it was real at the time. It is not just 'hype' because 'hype' cannot remove a sickness from your body. If a person, however, returns to old thoughts of unbelief, is too casual about the wonderful healing they have just received from the Lord, or the enemy comes to challenge that which has been received, and the person goes into fear and doubt at symptoms that may have appeared, then the original issue can be an issue again.

Jesus advises the man, and, I would suggest, us too, to not go back to that place of unbelief. So, this means that we need to intentionally take steps to achieve this. If we neglect the Word and prayer, then our faith levels will diminish and old issues can take hold.

Hebrews 2:1 *Therefore we must give the more earnest heed to the things we have heard, lest we drift away.*

We need to continually be filled with the Word, be in prayer and God's presence and pursuing what the Lord has for us. If we don't press forward, we go back.

Reading:

- Mark 8:22-26
- Hebrews 3:7- Hebrews 4:13
- Genesis 30:25 - Genesis 31:12

Thought for the day: The Word of God effectively works in you who believe.

Reflection: Write down any insights or revelations that you have had and reflect on what you are listening to and the environment you are in. Are there changes that you need to make to position yourself in an atmosphere of faith?

18

ARISE IN FAITH

Malachi 4:2 *But to you who fear My name the Sun of Righteousness shall arise with healing in His wings;...*

Malachi, prophesying of Jesus, declares that when He arises, healing will be a result. The word healing here is 'marpe' in the Hebrew, meaning 'health, healing, or literally a medicine or a cure'[3].

So, the first 'arise' was by Jesus - He went to the Cross taking our sicknesses, griefs, distresses and pains upon Himself, as well as our sins; was raised from the dead by the power of God having secured the provision of healing for us and by His stripes we were healed.

Then, there is an arising of a person seeking healing, which is the response of faith.

Acts 9:33-35 [33] *There he found a certain man named Aeneas, who had been bedridden eight years and was paralyzed.* [34] *And Peter said to him, "Aeneas, Jesus the Christ heals you.*

Arise and make your bed." Then he arose immediately. ³⁵ *So all who dwelt at Lydda and Sharon saw him and turned to the Lord.*

Aeneas had to make the decision to get up in response to Peter's healing prayer, resulting in him receiving a miracle. He didn't just lie there saying "Thanks for the prayer, I receive it; that was nice". He had to get up and do something, in this case, 'make his bed'. So, you don't have to do the impossible but what can you do in response to Jesus or healing prayer?

> **Mark 10:46-47** ⁴⁶ *Now they came to Jericho. As He went out of Jericho with His disciples and a great multitude, blind Bartimaeus, the son of Timaeus, sat by the road begging.* ⁴⁷ *And when he heard that it was Jesus of Nazareth, he began to cry out and say, "Jesus, Son of David, have mercy on me!"*

Matthew's account of this story has two blind men (Matt 20:29-34) but Mark and Luke (Luke 18:35-43) choose to focus on just one of them. Bartimaeus saw Jesus as the 'Son of David', the anticipated Messiah. There is great power released when we receive revelation of who Jesus is and Bartimaeus saw Jesus better than most people who had their eyesight. His faith came from hearing about Jesus and what He did. We get this faith from the Word of God (Romans 10:17).

> **Mark 10:48-49** ⁴⁸ *Then many warned him to be quiet; but he cried out all the more, "Son of David, have mercy on me!"* ⁴⁹ *So Jesus stood still and commanded him to be called. Then they called the blind man, saying to him, "Be of good cheer. Rise, He is calling you."*

As Bartimaeus cried out, those around him shouted him down, but when the pressure came for him to shrink back, he cried out all the more - and when Bartimaeus called out in faith, God stopped. It wasn't a passive thing, but Bartimaeus actively sought God.

> **Matthew 11:12** *And from the days of John the Baptist until now the kingdom of heaven suffers violence, and the violent take it by force.*

There is always a pushback against the things of God, spiritual or otherwise, and there needs to be some active taking of steps against it - against doubt and unbelief, thoughts of "What will people think?"; "What if it doesn't work?"; what people are speaking over you or how you see your condition versus how you see Jesus.

In spiritual warfare, believers focus so much on binding the devil (and you do need to do this) but not enough on taking steps of obedience that connect them to the power of God, irrespective of anything the devil is trying to do. Faith is revealed in actions of obedience.

No amount of opposition or pushback from the enemy can stop the power of God - if you decide to push in, believe and take steps of obedience. For example, the devil couldn't stop you receiving salvation, the greatest miracle of all, once you made a decision to believe and receive Jesus as your Lord and Saviour - and then took steps of obedience to align with and work out that belief. A lot depends on whether we will arise or not; to put our trust in Jesus; follow Him and intentionally obey.

> **Mark 10:50** *And throwing aside his garment, he rose and came to Jesus.*

Bartimaeus didn't just sit waiting for God to move - he doesn't say "Why doesn't God come to me?; Why doesn't He care?; He should know that I'm suffering and can't go to Him" or "I know God could do it if He wanted to" as is commonly heard. Jesus could have gone to him, but He required Bartimaeus to make the step. Bartimaeus didn't use his affliction, which was great, as an excuse to not step forward in faith.

Bartimaeus made an amazing step of faith as he threw away his garment before he asked for his healing. That garment defined him as a beggar; it allowed him to beg, earn a living and was an assured support, but he was already declaring that he was going to leave that behind and receive his healing in that moment.

Aeneas in the earlier story made a small step to get up and make his bed and received his healing. We see Bartimaeus taking a huge step, breaking away from his known support of income. Either way, do a step that you can do, without doing anything drastic. Please don't stop taking required medication or throw away your glasses before you get the report of being healed from a medical professional. Don't feel like that extreme step is required for faith to be active. Use wisdom with your faith, but the outworking of faith is a response to Jesus that has some kind of action.

> **Mark 10:51-52** [51] *So Jesus answered and said to him, "What do you want Me to do for you?" The blind man said to Him, "Rabboni, that I may receive my sight."* [52] *Then Jesus said to him, "Go your way; your faith has made you well." And immediately he received his sight and followed Jesus on the road.*

> **James 2:17** *Thus also faith by itself, if it does not have works is dead.*

> **James 2:17 AMPC**[8] *So also faith if it does not have works (deeds and actions of obedience to back it up) by itself is destitute of power (inoperative, dead).*

So, as we 'arise' and take a step of faith we find the power of God is released. Note, it's a step and not a whole journey - ask God "How can I respond to You and what You have said in Your Word?".

Now let's look at an Old Testament healing:

> **2 Kings 5:1-3** ¹*Now Naaman, commander of the army of the king of Syria, was a <u>great and honorable man</u> in the eyes of his master, because by him the Lord had given victory to Syria. He was also a mighty man of valor, but a leper.* ² *And the Syrians had gone out on raids, and had brought back captive a young girl from the land of Israel. She waited on Naaman's wife.* ³ *Then she said to her mistress, "If only my master were with the prophet who is in Samaria! For he would heal him of his leprosy."*

> **2 Kings 5:9-14** ⁹ *Then Naaman went with his horses and chariot, and he stood at the door of Elisha's house.* ¹⁰ *And Elisha sent a messenger to him, saying, "Go and wash in the Jordan seven times, and your flesh shall be restored to you, and you shall be clean."* ¹¹ *But Naaman became furious, and went away and said, "Indeed, I said to myself, <u>'He will surely come out to me, and stand and call on the name of the Lord his God, and wave his hand over the place, and heal the leprosy.'</u>* ¹² *Are not the Abanah and the Pharpar, the rivers of Damascus, better than all the waters of Israel? Could I not wash in them and be clean?" So he turned and went away in a rage.* ¹³ *And*

his servants came near and spoke to him, and said, "My father, if the prophet had told you to do something great, would you not have done it? How much more then, when he says to you, 'Wash, and be clean'?" [14] *So he went down and dipped seven times in the Jordan, according to the saying of the man of God; and his flesh was restored like the flesh of a little child, and he was clean.*

Naaman expected healing to come one way - that the minister, in this case the prophet, would do it all, pray for him and he would then be healed. However, the healing was to come as response to a word from the prophet and a step of faith that, in this case and many others, required him to lay down part of his fleshly nature - being, for him, pride.

Naaman didn't want to look silly in front of his men and felt no honour from the man of God who didn't even bother to come and speak to him personally. His responses of pride and offense could have hindered him receiving his healing. He needed to step over the reaction of the flesh and respond to the Word of God, given by the prophet, in order for healing to come. The healing part was easy, but the response was challenging to his pride. His sickness isn't recorded as being due to sin, but his healing was to come by submitting an area of his life to God, God using the situation to do a greater and deeper work in him.

Most of Jesus' healings had a step of faith involved, either initiated by the person or by Him, and many required the person to respond in a way that they had to relinquish something - be it of the flesh, fear, caring about what people think or a religious teaching that didn't align with Him, in order to pick up a greater measure of the grace of God.

The response is important as it engages our heart - there is a doing that accompanies the hearing of the Word.

> **Exodus 15:26** *and said, "If you diligently heed the voice of the Lord your God <u>and do</u> what is right in His sight, give ear to His commandments <u>and keep</u> all His statutes, I will put none of the diseases on you which I have brought on the Egyptians. For I am the Lord who heals you."*
>
> **James 1:22** *But be doers of the word, and not hearers only, deceiving yourselves.*

Healing is rarely passive, but Jesus never asked someone to respond in a way they couldn't do, for example, "Stretch out your hand." (Matt 12:13; Mark 3:5; Luke 6:10), nor in a way that risked putting them at harm. If healing is not immediate don't give up, but rather, seek God for a possible faith step. It usually involves submission of an area of our lives to Him, but not an unwise action.

There is sometimes the need for the believer or minister to 'arise' on behalf of someone who actually can't do it for themselves. An example is where Peter was called to Joppa to minister to Tabitha (translated Dorcas) who had died.

> **Acts 9:40-41** [40] *But Peter put them all out, and knelt down and prayed. And turning to the body he said, "Tabitha, arise." And she opened her eyes, and when she saw Peter she sat up.* [41] *Then he gave her his hand and lifted her up; and when he had called the saints and widows, he presented her alive.*

Now Tabitha (Dorcas) couldn't arise on her own in faith, so she needed someone else to 'stand in faith' for her. So, there will be times when God calls you to step out, in a response of faith to what He has done, for someone else's healing.

One way or another someone must 'arise', and step out in faith, in response to what Jesus has done. Peter started by praying and getting a sense from God on how to move forward and that is an important first step. We have access to the greatest power known but, in our response, it is best to seek God first and then, get up, take steps and access all that He has promised for us.

Reading:

- Acts 9:32-42
- Mark 10:46-52
- 2 Kings 5:1-14

Thought for the day: James 2:17 AMPC[8] *So also faith if it does not have works (deeds and actions of obedience to back it up) by itself is destitute of power (inoperative, dead).*

Reflection: Write down any insights or revelations that you have had as you reflect on the response of faith. Pray and ask the Lord what a step of faith might look like for you - remember it's just a step and not a huge leap that brings the power of God.

19
DO NOT BE AFRAID, ONLY BELIEVE

Mark 5:36 *As soon as Jesus heard the word that was spoken, He said to the ruler of the synagogue, "Do not be afraid; only believe."*

Mark 5:22-24 [22] *And behold, one of the rulers of the synagogue came, Jairus by name. And when he saw Him, he fell at His feet* [23] *and begged Him earnestly, saying, "My little daughter lies at the point of death. Come and lay Your hands on her, that she may be healed, and she will live."* [24] *So Jesus went with him, and a great multitude followed Him and thronged Him.*

Jairus, a leader of the synagogue has come to Jesus to plead with Him to come and heal his daughter. He has come to Jesus at a great personal cost, for as a ruler of the synagogue he would be condemned for doing so. He doesn't just come to Jesus, but he comes with honour, respect, and humility, bowing at Jesus' feet. Jairus makes a declaration of faith and trust. So, he is in faith and has done all the right things in approaching God for answered prayer.

The next thing that happens, is that the crowd starts to throng Jesus, which would have slowed everything down. So now there is delay to the prayer being answered; there is a hindrance occurring. Perhaps anxiety and frustration are coming to Jairus, and even though he was in faith before, delay can bring the temptation to doubt.

Then, Jesus makes time to heal a woman in the crowd who has demonstrated great faith. So, Jesus is now apparently side-tracked, and He is healing someone else.

How frustrating when you come to Him, you've done all the right things, there's been a delay, but you have stood, knowing that through faith and patience you inherit the promises, and now God goes and miraculously heals someone else, and that, immediately. What does that do to your faith? Is your faith influenced by time and your vision set on the watch and what you are seeing going on around you, or on Jesus Himself? Time is not the determinant of your prayer being answered.

If this resonates with you, it's alright - God knows what He is doing and He has everything under control. Which is just as well, because now Jairus, despite doing all the right things, having faith, showing honour, waiting patiently, will receive the worst medical report that you can possibly receive - his daughter has just died. Just because you receive a bad report doesn't mean that you don't have faith.

> **Mark 5:35** *While He was still speaking, some came from the ruler of the synagogue's house who said, "Your daughter is dead. Why trouble the Teacher any further?"*

The implication is that Jesus can do so much but no more - He can heal but it's not even on their radar that He can raise the dead. It's good to ask yourself "Have I placed any limits on what God can do in my life?" Is it "I can believe for this much but certainly not that?" Are there aspects of God, revealed in His Word that aren't even on your radar: His healing promises; His covenant with you; His faithfulness; His ability to do the impossible. These things need to be 'on your radar', firmly fixed in your vision to keep you strong in the midst of delays, disappointments and challenges.

> **Mark 5:36** [36] *As soon as Jesus heard the word that was spoken, He said to the ruler of the synagogue, "Do not be afraid; only believe."*

The temptation to get off track from believing to fear, doubt or discouragement has come, and Jesus moves immediately to make sure that the man stays in his position to receive, guarding his heart.

What is amazing is what Jesus didn't say. He didn't say "I'm here in the flesh; it doesn't matter what you believe, I'll heal her anyway". He didn't give Jairus an explanation of what He was about to do so that he would understand and not be tempted to fear. He didn't say it didn't matter if Jairus 'fell apart', complained, despaired and gave himself permission to get angry with God, as many in a dishonouring manner give themselves permission to do. He told him to believe, despite the circumstance.

As soon as Jesus heard the problem being spoken out, He says "Do not be afraid; only believe". This tells me that even though the right prayers have been prayed and God is right there with you, it still matters that you believe and don't go to fear and anxiety, but keep your eyes fixed on Jesus. The mustard seed or measure of faith given to all (Romans 12:3) is enough to see a miracle done (Matthew 17:20). So, it's not about the greatness of your faith or that you know everything but that your measure of faith is placed in Jesus with a simple childlike trust.

> **Mark 5:37-42** [37] *And He permitted no one to follow Him except Peter, James, and John the brother of James.* [38] *Then He came to the house of the ruler of the synagogue and saw a tumult and those who wept and wailed loudly.* [39] *When He came in, He said to them, "Why make this commotion and weep? The child is not dead, but sleeping."*
>
> [40] *And they ridiculed Him. But when He had put them all outside, He took the father and the mother of the child, and those who were with Him, and entered where the child was lying.* [41] *Then He took the child by the hand, and said to her, "Talitha, cumi," which is translated, "Little girl, I say to you, arise."* [42] *Immediately the girl arose and walked, for she was twelve years of age. And they were overcome with great amazement.*

There are a few things that Jesus did here, that are important for us to apply. Firstly, He brought people with Him who could believe, who were mature in the faith. In His earthly ministry, Jesus was God on Earth, full of faith and He had the Spirit without measure, and yet, even He is careful as to who He brings into a faith or ministry moment. Answered prayer isn't based on how many people know about the problem nor on how many people pray. It involves faith and so a few who will steadfastly believe with you is better than a multitude who may doubt.

Jesus removed the unbelief from the room - there will be people and your own head telling you it's nonsense, but you need to remove unbelief and not allow it to occupy the room. Unbelief shuts down the manifestation of the power of God. Choose to believe God.

Then Jesus didn't give voice to the problem. He says, "The child is not dead but sleeping". The more you voice the problem the more its challenge is embedded in your heart; the more it is empowered and the more it is enforced in the situation, as our words have creative power. Proverbs 18:21 tells us that 'death and life are in the power of the tongue and those who love it will eat its fruit'. Faith comes by hearing but so does unbelief.

This doesn't need to become weird, as many believers refuse to face the problem or call it a 'lie', as a way of not talking about the problem. You can still acknowledge the problem, when necessary, to those who are praying for you and you can face its reality, but like Jairus, one can acknowledge the issue, and also declare faith in Jesus to deal with it. The death of Jairus' daughter was real, not a lie. However, the truth is that Jesus and His finished work are enough to overcome the problem.

Jesus knows the situation, and isn't in denial, but He speaks according to what He is about to do. We speak according to what He has already done.

If we want the results of God, then we have to do things His way. He *'calls those things which do not exist as though they did'* (Romans 4:17). He is well aware of the problem, but to overcome it, He calls forth the answer that does not yet exist in the physical realm as though it already did (past tense), and in so doing, shows us to do the same.

Speak life into the situation. Speak the Word of God which carries His power. Jesus' words are Spirit and life (John 6:63) - they carry His Spirit, His power and His life.

We call the healing and promises of God which do not yet exist in our circumstances as though they did. Choose to believe despite the circumstances, choose to see God's promises fulfilled in your life before you see

THE LORD WHO HEALS YOU

them physically and choose to speak His Word as though it has been done. "I thank you Lord that You are the Lord who heals me; Jesus that You bore my sicknesses and carried my pains and by Your stripes I was healed."

Reading:

- Mark 5:21-24; 35-43
- Isaiah 41:10
- Isaiah 43:1,2
- 2 Timothy 1:7

Thought for the day: God is with you and in light of all He has done for you, He says "do not be afraid; only believe".

Reflection: Ask yourself whether time or circumstances have allowed doubt, frustration or anger to creep in? Have you lowered your expectation of what God can do in attempting to protect your heart from disappointment? Would you dare to take a stand of faith again?

_____
_____
_____
_____
_____
_____
_____

Write down 3 Scriptures that will strengthen your heart in your stance of faith:

Scripture 1:

Scripture 2:

Scripture 3:

Now choose to believe and declare these Scriptures as being done over your life.

20

FAITH THAT TOUCHES GOD

Mark 5:34 *And He said to her, "Daughter, your faith has made you well. Go in peace, and be healed of your affliction."*

Mark 5:25-34 [25] *Now a certain woman had a flow of blood for twelve years,* [26] *and had suffered many things from many physicians. She had spent all that she had and was no better, but rather grew worse.* [27] *When she heard about Jesus, she came behind Him in the crowd and touched His garment.* [28] *For she said, "If only I may touch His clothes, I shall be made well."*

[29] *Immediately the fountain of her blood was dried up, and she felt in her body that she was healed of the affliction.* [30] *And Jesus, immediately knowing in Himself that power had gone out of Him, turned around in the crowd and said, "Who touched My clothes?"*

[31] *But His disciples said to Him, "You see the multitude thronging You, and You say, 'Who touched Me?'"*

³² *And He looked around to see her who had done this thing.* ³³ *But the woman, fearing and trembling, knowing what had happened to her, came and fell down before Him and told Him the whole truth.* ³⁴ *And He said to her, "Daughter, your faith has made you well. Go in peace, and be healed of your affliction."*

According to John 21:25 Jesus did so many things, that all the books in the world would not be enough to contain them. Yet, the Holy Spirit in inspiring Scripture, chose a few encounters to be recorded for all time for our instruction (2 Timothy 3:16). This is, I believe, because they contain important aspects that He wants to highlight to us, to apply to our own lives.

In reading these stories, it is good to stop and really think about the person and their situation. In the above passage from Mark 5, this woman with 'the issue of blood' as she is called, had a prolonged condition that would have, most likely, caused anaemia, and with it, weakness, dizziness, shortness of breath and chest pain. The medical procedures for such a condition in those days would have been humiliating. She has now spent all that she had on doctors and is no better, but rather, worse.

This would open the door for a lot of discouragement, disappointment, hopelessness and perhaps, anger.

Under the Mosaic law of the Old Testament, everything she touched became ceremonially unclean -people, money, food and whatever she sat on. This would have lead to isolation from people, and from the house, whether her father's or her husband's – and that isolation goes on for twelve years. This would bring shame, impact on her mental health and very likely, depression.

She would not be allowed to go into crowds or go to the temple - so she is removed from the gathering of God's people and the place of God's presence (though omnipresent, His encounterable presence, at that time, was in the Holy of Holies, in the temple, before the tearing of the curtain at Jesus' death). She is probably feeling as low as you can go - sick, weak, isolated, discouraged, disappointed and feeling rejected by God and man.

So, she hears about Jesus and makes a radical, bold choice and one that carried great risk. To go into the crowd under the law meant that she would make every person she touched ceremonially unclean including Jesus *if* He were merely a man. However, the moment she touches Jesus He reverses that - He is not made unclean, but rather, He makes her clean.

It was risky and perhaps she crawled through the crowd because Luke's account says that she touched the hem or border of His garment (Luke 8:44), suggesting she may have been crouching low. She would have been ready to sneak off and not give her testimony, because, even healed, she is now meant to wait another seven days, do a ritual cleansing and offer a sacrifice. She was probably terrified when Jesus identified her, expecting judgement, but instead, she receives mercy and a public restoration. Contact with His Person and power cancels the curse of sickness that was upon her, removes the curse of the law (Galatians 3:13) and makes her clean, not just ritually but completely. Then, Jesus is the sacrifice she requires, and He restores her identity as His daughter. Jesus is everything that is needed!

There is so much in this story but the following highlights just three aspects from it, and with each of these comes a personal challenge.

Firstly, in the midst of all that was going on, this woman made a decision to step over the pain, the disappointment and discouragement and to trust God again. There are many things in life that we don't want to just ignore, and we do need to process well, but sometimes, we just have to step over some things. That means not having answers all the time as to what has taken place, not necessarily seeing everything neatly resolved before moving on, not arguing back with "But what about..." - but rather, the need to step over all that's gone before and, with 'a line drawn in the sand' moment, believe again.

Many years ago, my wonderful pastor at the time, Dr Phil Pringle, prophesied over me, after praying for a healing that didn't happen and the words were so clearly from the Holy Spirit because they still speak loudly and clearly to me today. They were, "Step over the disappointment; step over what didn't happen and believe again. Believing releases the power of the Holy Spirit."

Many emotions like disappointment, discouragement and other forms of pain unconsciously cause our hearts to take a step back from believing and trusting God. Even with a heart that has faith, these negative emotions can crowd around that seed of faith and hinder it pressing in to touch God and to receive all that He provides. In Hebrews 10:38-39, while the author is talking about salvation faith and the decision that determines one's eternal destination, there is also a principle that applies to the other areas that we trust God for. If we shrink back, in protecting ourselves and our hearts from further pain, we pull back from all that God wants to bring us into. Faith, however, presses in closer to God.

> **Hebrews 10:38,39 ESV**[10] 38 *but my righteous one shall live by faith, and if he shrinks back, my soul has no pleasure in him."* 39 *But we are not of those who shrink back and are destroyed, but of those who have faith and preserve their souls.*

We are to take that mustard seed of faith that we have all been given, place it in Jesus, press in closer to Him and trust Him without reservation. Believing releases the power of the Holy Spirit.

So, it's good to ask yourself "Is there anything that I need to just step over; leave behind so that I can freely believe again?" It may be disappointment; it might be confusion as to why certain things happened or didn't happen; it may be offense - even with God. Whatever it may be, could you decide to hand it over to God, leave it with Him and step into trusting Jesus wholeheartedly?

The second thing to highlight is that when you are specific about what you are believing God for, it focuses and hones your faith, bringing with it a clarity of spiritual vision. Faith has vision and focus allows you to see details clearly. You see what you are believing for. It's not just "Oh God, I need some healing" but it's specific, focused and clear to the point where you can see it. The woman with the issue of blood in the story is very specific - "If only I may touch His clothes, I shall be made well".

Now women in that era weren't taught the way that men were, and this woman has been kept out of the house of God and isolated from others for twelve years - so she may not have had all her doctrine correct. This is encouraging that, as important as having correct doctrine is, she didn't need to know everything in order to receive her healing. It was actually a superstition of the time that someone's power was on their garments and probably what inspired her to reach out to Jesus in the way that she did. However, because of the anointing of the Holy Spirit upon Jesus, it is not just superstition in this case, but a reality.

The anointing is the substance and presence of the Holy Spirit, and with Him, the demonstratable power of God. His presence and power are tangible and transferrable, for example through the laying on of hands, but also, here, transferrable through an inanimate substance such as a garment. Her touching of Jesus' garment inspires others later on in the sixth chapter of Mark, where the multitudes come, and as many as touched His garments were made well. It is important, however, to note that we don't make the method what we focus on, but rather, Jesus Himself.

> **Mark 6:56** [56] *Wherever He entered, into villages, cities, or the country, they laid the sick in the marketplaces and begged Him that they might just touch the hem of His garment. And as many as touched Him were made well.*

It continues later on, with the outpouring of the Holy Spirit, and Peter's shadow just passes over people, and they are healed, and with Paul, cloths are taken from his body and laid on the sick and they are healed.

> **Acts 5:15,16** [15] *so that they brought the sick out into the streets and laid them on beds and couches, that at least the shadow of Peter passing by might fall on some of them.* [16] *Also a multitude gathered from the surrounding cities to Jerusalem, bringing sick people and those who were tormented by unclean spirits, and they were all healed.*

> **Acts 19:11,12** [11] *Now God worked unusual miracles by the hands of Paul,* [12] *so that even handkerchiefs or aprons were brought from his body to the sick, and the diseases left them and the evil spirits went out of them.*

Going back to the story in Mark 5, the woman believes specifically, declares it, sees it - but now, she had to act. If she hadn't acted on what she believed, remaining beyond the crowd, then nothing would have happened. She would have had to push her way through the crowd, acting as a healed woman because focused believing gave her vision, ignited her faith and brought an impulsion and determination to act.

It's good to ask yourself, "What do I believe and see?" Do you believe and see something specific that you want from God? Does it align with His character and promises? Are there promises around it to further clarify your faith? Can you allow that focus to bring a clearer vision and expectation into your spirit?

The third aspect of this story is how her faith drew healing power from Jesus. Jesus felt her touch of faith, different to the touch of all the others around Him and said, *"Who touched My clothes?"* Note, He didn't say, "Who touched Me" but specifically identifies the person as the one who touched His clothes. Probably, only one person was there to consciously touch His clothes. She would know that He was speaking of her.

Many people want to touch Jesus; many come into His presence; but it is her touch of faith, her focus and determination to be healed and bold sacrificial faith that draws on His presence. It's not a casual contact, as with the crowd. She presses in to touch God at a potentially great personal cost.

It is good to ask yourself, what are you prepared to do to touch Jesus in a way that connects with Him? What would you sacrifice to take up more of Him? Would it be time, increased prayer, attention to the Scriptures or laying down some things? What does it look like for you?

It's not of works that we are healed, but the receiving of God's grace through faith. However, that receiving of grace often involves a drawing near to God in prayer, sometimes fasting, digging into the Scriptures, letting them become part of you, and allowing God to mould and transform you. The healing is free but, at the same time, a level of self-sacrifice is often required to receive it. We often need to lay something down of ourselves in order to take up more of what God has for us.

In reflection is there anything you need to step over to freely believe God? Do you need to be more specific in what you are asking from Him? Then, will you do what it takes to press in deeper and really touch Him?

Reading:

- Mark 5:25-34
- Matthew 9:20-22

Thought for the day: Jesus often said to people "Your faith has made you well".

Reflection:

1. Ask yourself "Is there anything that I need to just step over; leave behind so that I can freely believe again?" List them below.
   _____
   _____
   _____

2. Do you believe and see something specific that you want from God? Does it align with His character and promises? Are there promises around it to further clarify your faith? Can you allow that focus to bring a clearer vision and expectation into your spirit? Write what you are believing God for and any promises to support it.
   _____
   _____
   _____

3. What are you prepared to do to touch Jesus in a way that connects with Him? What would you sacrifice to take up more of Him? Would it be time, increased prayer, attention to the Scriptures or laying down some things? What does it look like for you? Write them below and reflect on how you may implement them.
   _____
   _____
   _____

21

THE HONOUR OF GOD

Matthew 8:8 *The centurion answered and said, "Lord I am not worthy that You should come under my roof. But only speak a word and my servant will be healed"*

Matthew 8:5-10 *⁵ Now when Jesus had entered Capernaum, a centurion came to Him, pleading with Him, ⁶ saying, "Lord, my servant is lying at home paralyzed, dreadfully tormented." ⁷ And Jesus said to him, "I will come and heal him."*

⁸ The centurion answered and said, "Lord, I am not worthy that You should come under my roof. But only speak a word, and my servant will be healed. ⁹ For I also am a man under authority, having soldiers under me. And I say to this one, 'Go,' and he goes; and to another, 'Come,' and he comes; and to my servant, 'Do this,' and he does it." ¹⁰ When Jesus heard it, He marveled, and said to those who followed, "Assuredly, I say to you, I have not found such great faith, not even in Israel!

The account of the Centurion coming to Jesus, on behalf of his servant, is an outstanding example of the attitude with which to approach God, with honour, faith and with the revelation of how authority works. There are only two places in Scripture where it says Jesus marvelled. People marvelled many times at the works of God but twice Jesus marvelled. Marvelled means 'something that causes wonder, admiration, or astonishment; a wonderful thing; a wonder or prodigy'.

One example is where He marvelled at the unbelief of the people (Mark 6:6) in Nazareth, who should have believed and didn't. We don't want God to be marvelling at our unbelief!

With the Centurion, however, Jesus marvels at one who didn't have all the teaching and background, who had much to lose, and yet, did believe. The Centurion is the only person in Scripture who caused Jesus to marvel in a positive way and so, we really need to take note of what caused that to happen.

A Centurion was a person of high esteem in the Roman army, a leader over at least a hundred men and a man of valour. Not only is he a man of eminence, but he is positioned as a leader of the occupying power over Israel at the time. Positioned under Rome at the time of Augustus, his understanding of the word 'Lord' was a title now given to the Roman Emperor to honour him as a deity and thus acknowledging him as being the only connection between the 'gods' and man, hence the Roman declaration "Caesar is Lord".

The Centurion could have come to Jesus and just asked for his servant to be healed and no doubt, Jesus would have healed him, as He did others. He could have come with a sense of entitlement and claimed his rights as a leader of the occupying army for Jesus, in appearance to many as a religious leader, to come and heal his servant. However, this man would not approach Jesus so cheaply.

He comes to Jesus and the first word recorded as him saying is "Lord". Lord is the Greek word 'kyrios' which according to Strongs[3] definition means 'supreme in authority; by implication, Master (as a respectful title); God, Lord, master, Sir'. Its biblical usage is 'the owner; one who has control of the person, the master; the sovereign, Prince, chief, the Roman Emperor; a title of respect and reverence with which servants greet their master and the title is given to God, the Messiah'.

The Centurion comes to Jesus with honour and not just respectful words, but an honour that implies that Jesus is Lord and Master, positioned under God; an honour expressed by a servant to his Master. This could be so costly to one in his position to be calling Jesus "Lord", to be approaching Jesus as Master and recognising that here is One who is positioned under God, the connection between God and man, exercising the authority of God to man. He could have come safely, but instead, he came with an honour that could cost him everything.

This is such a lesson for us all. Many come to God just asking for things. Many come with a sense of entitlement as the child of God with the promises demanding their God given rights. You can definitely demand your rights over the devil, but is this the right way to approach God? He is Lord, and we should come first and foremost to Him with the honour that He deserves.

Honour is a heart-felt appreciation and recognition of someone's worth and position, that should then be expressed through words, respect and action. It is not just putting on a veneer of honour and saying honouring words in order to get what one wants - that is just flattery. The Bible has much to say about the peril of flattery and none of it is good. In Matthew 15:8 and Mark 7:6 Jesus draws on Isaiah 29:13 to speak of those who say the right words but their hearts are far from Him. True honour is sincere from the heart.

Many think that Jesus marvelled at the Centurion's faith and understanding of Jesus' authority, but there was also the honour and extravagant value that he placed on Jesus. He risked so much for no other reason than to express the honour that was due to Jesus.

> **1 Samuel 2:30** …..*for those who honour Me I will honour and those who despise Me shall be lightly esteemed.*

When people genuinely honoured Jesus for who He was, the power of God was released into their lives. Where He was dishonoured His release of power was hindered and people failed to receive what God really wanted to give them. Matthew 13:57,58 and Mark 6:5,6 record the incident in Nazareth where the people of Jesus' hometown refuse to honour Him for who He is and what He is doing. They try to 'bring Him down' by their words about Him but the result is that few people get healed as opposed to multitudes in other regions.

> **Matthew 13:57,58** [57] So they were offended at Him. *But Jesus said to them, "A prophet is not without honour except in his own country and in his own house."* [58] *Now He did not do many mighty works there because of their unbelief.*

> **Mark 6:5,6** [5] *Now He could do no mighty work there, except that He laid His hands on a few sick people and healed them.* [6] *And He marvelled because of their unbelief. Then He went about the villages in a circuit, teaching.*

In Mark 6, this incident is recorded immediately after the raising of Jairus's daughter from the dead. The outstanding difference is that Jairus approached Jesus with honour (Mark 5:22,23) and faith.

When we honour God, we open ourselves to His kingdom and its power. It's there; it's available and honour is one of the attributes that opens us to it. When we dishonour Him, we close ourselves off from what He would do in us.

There are many ways that we can dishonour God as believers: by not trusting Him as if He were not faithful; by words that express doubt at what He has declared He has done, such as "I'm waiting for God to do something"; "Come on God You need to move" or saying that God doesn't heal everyone. Not all may receive their healing, including those of sincere faith, but healing has still been provided for all. To say otherwise is to dishonour the work of the Cross, suggesting that God is a respecter of persons, providing salvation for some and not others or to imply that what Jesus did was somehow insufficient or incomplete.

Gleaning from Matthew Chapter 8, genuine honour leads to heartfelt worship. Worship and the study of the Scriptures, position you to receive Holy Spirit inspired revelation. Revelation brings insight and understanding. Insight (seeing what the Holy Spirit is saying either through the Bible or through His impression in your heart) brings faith. Genuine faith leads to works of obedience. Obedience brings the blessing.

Reading:

- Matthew 8:5-13
- Luke 7:1-10
- Isaiah 40:25-31

Thought for the day: 1 Samuel 2:30 …..for those who honour Me I will honour

Reflection: Write down any insights or revelations that you have had as you reflect on the honour of God.

_____
_____
_____
_____
_____
_____
_____
_____
_____
_____
_____
_____
_____
_____
_____
_____
_____

Write out the Scriptures below and express them in prayer to God:

Revelation 4:11

Revelation 5:12,13

Revelation 7:12

22

JUST SAY THE WORD

> **Matthew 8:8 NIV²** ...... *But just say the word, and my servant will be healed.*

> **Matthew 8:8** *The centurion answered and said, "Lord, I am not worthy that You should come under my roof. But only speak a word, and my servant will be healed.*

I like how the NIV² puts it - "just say the word, and my servant will be healed". This Centurion was commended by Jesus for his great faith and he also revealed his understanding of how authority works, and by association, the power of God's Word when spoken - leading to his servant being healed 'that same hour' (Matthew 8:13).

> **Matthew 8:9** *For I also am a man under authority, having soldiers under me. And I say to this one, 'Go,' and he goes; and to another, 'Come,' and he comes; and to my servant, 'Do this,' and he does it."*

As a leader positioned under Caesar, the Centurion understood, that when he spoke, it carried the authority of the one he was under, and therefore, the command would be done. From this perspective, he acknowledged that Jesus was positioned under God (for the time He was on earth, but now is restored to His position as God after His resurrection, at the right hand of the Father). As such, when Jesus spoke, it would carry the power of God and hence, just His spoken Word was required for a healing to be done.

> **Hebrews 1:3** *who being the brightness of His glory and the express image of His person, and upholding all things by <u>the word of His power</u>, when He had by Himself purged our sins, sat down at the right hand of the Majesty on high.*

Jesus upholds all things by the Word of His power - not just the power of His Word. This wording suggests that His Word doesn't just have power, but it is His power.

> **Romans 1:16** *For I am not ashamed of the gospel of Christ, for <u>it is the power of God to salvation</u> for everyone who believes, for the Jew first and also for the Greek.*

The gospel, God's Word, contains His power to bring itself to pass, and is as a seed that opens and releases its potential when faith is applied to it, and this power is unto salvation which includes our healing. Inherent in that faith is the speaking of the Word, aligned with a heart that believes. What we believe is revealed through what we speak, for "out of the abundance of the heart the mouth speaks" (Matthew 12:34; Luke 6:45).

> **2 Corinthians 4:13** *And since we have the same spirit of faith, according to what is written, "I believed and therefore I spoke," we also believe and therefore speak...*

> **Hebrews 11:3** *By faith we understand that the worlds were framed by the word of God, so that the things which are seen were not made of things which are visible.*

The things which were made, were not made of nothing but things not visible. God spoke His Word; the Holy Spirit then moved in response to that Word, creating a world that was declared to be good. This set a precedence - that the Holy Spirit moves on the Word of God to create and release God's will.

> **Genesis 1:1-4** *¹In the beginning God created the heavens and the earth. ² The earth was without form, and void; and darkness was on the face of the deep. And the Spirit of God was hovering over the face of the waters.³ Then God said, "Let there be light"; and there was light. ⁴ And God saw the light, that it was good; and God divided the light from the darkness.*

God spoke to an earth without form and void, where darkness was on the face of the deep. He didn't speak according to what was visible to the natural eye, or only because the circumstances were good. He spoke to release His will.

There are so many challenges that one can face in life where life can look without form and empty; where you may feel you don't have hope, or can't see a way through, or a way out of those things placing limits on you. People or circumstances can speak to you that you can't make it, that you can't be healed, can't have that miracle or breakthrough.

It might seem like darkness is on the surface of your life - that too many bad things have happened, affecting emotional or mental well-being, and you may not be able to see a way of leaving them behind or be able to envisage a life with God's blessing or healing in it.

However, as God creates the visible from the invisible, by the power of His words, so too, we, who have been created in His image and who thus also have power in our words, need to align with Him and speak His Word to see His will, including healing, released.

> **John 6:63**... *the words that I speak to you are spirit and they are life.*

> **Proverbs 18:21** *Death and life are in the power of the tongue, and those who love it will eat its fruit.*

Due to the Fall, we as humans, also have the potential to release 'death' in our words and so, we need to be disciplined to not only speak God's words, but to refrain from speaking negativity, complaining or excessive rehearsing of the problem, which just further strengthens it in our life. James chapter 3 reveals the power of the tongue- that, as a rudder is to a great ship or a bit in a horse's mouth, it has the power to direct the course of our lives and to defile the whole body.

> **James 3:6** *And the tongue is a fire, a world of iniquity. The tongue is so set among our members that it defiles the whole body, and sets on fire the course of nature; and it is set on fire by hell.*

> **James 3:2** says *'For we all stumble in many things. If anyone does not stumble in word, he is a perfect man, able also to bridle the whole body.'*

THE LORD WHO HEALS YOU

We may not master this perfectly, but with so much evidence about the power of words, let us be mindful of what we are speaking over our health, lives and the lives of others.

In Acts 14:8, Paul speaks healing to a man and a miraculous healing from God is released. Speaking in alignment with God's will, brought the release of God's miraculous power. Paul didn't lay hands on him or pray for him, but he spoke healing to him.

> **Acts 14:8-10** [8] *And in Lystra a certain man without strength in his feet was sitting, a cripple from his mother's womb, who had never walked.* [9] *This man heard Paul speaking. Paul, observing him intently and seeing that he had faith to be healed,* [10] *said with a loud voice, "Stand up straight on your feet!" And he leaped and walked.*

In Daniel 10, the angel that appears to Daniel speaks strength and peace to him, and obviously being in line with God's will, supernatural strength and peace is released to Daniel.

> **Daniel 10:18-19** [18] *Then again, the one having the likeness of a man touched me and strengthened me.* [19] *And he said, "O man greatly beloved, fear not! Peace be to you; be strong, yes, be strong!" So when he spoke to me I was strengthened, and said, "Let my lord speak, for you have strengthened me."*

Psalm 103:20 reveals that the angels respond to the spoken Word of God; that they 'heed the voice of His Word'.

> **Psalm 103:20** *Bless the Lord, you His angels, who excel in strength, who do His word, heeding the voice of His word.*

So, whether it is God speaking, an angel communicating the word, as with Daniel, or a believer speaking Scripture or declaring healing, strength or peace - the power of God is released when words that align with God's will are spoken.

So, there on the coffee table, bedside table, or wherever your Bible resides, is the resource to see God's power released in your life - but you have to pick it up, put it in your heart and declare that Word that has the power to change your circumstance.

Speak healing Scriptures over yourself and those you pray for; speak strength; speak peace - speak the Word!

Speaking God's Word is not just a religious or faith work, or ritual. It is God's way of releasing His power or will. When we speak the Word, we are not doing it to make God's will happen; we are aligning with Him in faith and speaking what He sees over the situation. His Word reveals and releases His already accomplished will, that we are declaring to 'be done on earth as it is in Heaven'.

As Jesus was positioned under the Father in His earthly ministry, we are now positioned under Jesus. When we speak in alignment with His will, as the Centurion understood, we can speak with the authority from the One we are under. We can tell sickness and pain to "go"; God's healing power to "come" and tell bodies "to do this" and align with God's original intention of health for them.

> **Isaiah 55:10,11** [10]*"For as the rain comes down, and the snow from heaven, and do not return there, but water the earth, and make it bring forth and bud, that it may give seed to the sower and bread to the eater,* [11] *So shall My word be that goes forth from My mouth; It shall not return to Me void, but*

it shall accomplish what I please, and it shall prosper in the thing for which I sent it.

I know it says when God's Word goes forth from His mouth, but when we align with Him and speak Scripture, His Word going forth from our mouths will still prosper and accomplish what He pleases. In John 17:18, Jesus says "As You sent Me into the world, I also have sent them into the world". In Acts 1:1 Luke starts with alluding to the book of Luke and all that Jesus began to do and teach - Jesus is continuing 'to do and teach' via the ministry of the Holy Spirit operating through believers. As Jesus spoke healing, so Paul spoke healing and miracles took place. As they spoke healing, so too are we to speak healing - and God's Word will prosper in the thing for which it was sent.

Isaiah 57:19 *"I create the fruit of the lips: Peace, peace to him who is far off and to him who is near," Says the Lord, "And I will heal him."*

Reading:

- Acts 14:8-10
- Luke 4:33-37
- Romans 10:6-10
- Proverbs 15:4; 18:21; 21:23
- Psalm 119:172
- Psalm 45:1
- 2 Kings 2:19-22

Thought for the day: Hebrews 4:12 *For the word of God is living and powerful, and sharper than any two-edged sword, piercing even to the division of soul and spirit, and of joints and marrow, and is a discerner of the thoughts and intents of the heart.*

Reflection: Write down any insights or revelations that you have had as you reflect on the power of words; the words you speak over yourself or others and how that may need to change.

23

POWER IN THE NAME OF JESUS

Acts 3:6 *Then Peter said, "Silver and gold I do not have, but what I do have I give you: In the name of Jesus Christ of Nazareth, rise up and walk."*

In Acts 3, we have the story of a man, who had been lame from birth (that being over forty years), being healed through the name of Jesus. At this point, Jesus has returned to Heaven and is seated at the right hand of the Father, and the Holy Spirit has been poured out on believers to ensure Jesus' ministry is continued through the church. Having already received this grace of God, Jesus' disciples Peter and John come upon a lame man begging at the temple when they are going for prayer.

Acts 3:1-10 *Now Peter and John went up together to the temple at the hour of prayer, the ninth hour.* ² *And a certain man lame from his mother's womb was carried, whom they laid daily at the gate of the temple which is called Beautiful, to ask alms from those who entered the temple;* ³ *who, seeing*

> *Peter and John about to go into the temple, asked for alms.* ⁴ *And fixing his eyes on him, with John, Peter said, "Look at us."* ⁵ *So he gave them his attention, expecting to receive something from them.* ⁶ *Then Peter said, "Silver and gold I do not have, but what I do have I give you: In the name of Jesus Christ of Nazareth, rise up and walk."* ⁷ *And he took him by the right hand and lifted him up, and immediately his feet and ankle bones received strength.* ⁸ *So he, leaping up, stood and walked and entered the temple with them—walking, leaping, and praising God.* ⁹ *And all the people saw him walking and praising God.* ¹⁰ *Then they knew that it was he who sat begging alms at the Beautiful Gate of the temple; and they were filled with wonder and amazement at what had happened to him.*

Peter reveals that believers have the right to use the name of Jesus to release His will to be done, in His place, in this case miraculous healing. He states, "What I do have I give to you: In the name of Jesus Christ….". What did he have? He had the name of Jesus and authority in His name - as do we! The man was healed through the name of Jesus in the same way as if Jesus Himself had prayed for him.

> **John 14:13,14 AMPC**[8] *And I will do [I Myself will grant] whatever you ask in My Name [as presenting all that I Am], so that the Father may be glorified and extolled in (through) the Son. [Yes] I will grant [I Myself will do for you] whatever you shall ask in My Name [as presenting all that I Am].*

When we pray in the name of Jesus, we are presenting all that He is and what He has done, to the sickness or situation and that is more than enough to deal with any problem! Then in addition, Jesus assures us that He will do it - obviously this would require the prayer offered to be in alignment with His will and Scripture assures us that healing is His will.

Peter spoke healing to the man in the name of Jesus, presenting all that Jesus is and what He had done to that man's disability, which brought about his healing. Note that Peter did not ask God to do the healing but commanded the release of healing in Jesus' name. If we are praying for something that God has already made provision for, we are to command its release in Jesus' name. If it is something not guaranteed by the finished work of the Cross e.g., whether you will get that job, then you ask the Father, also in the name of Jesus (John 16:23).

> **Philippians 2:9-11** *Therefore God also has highly exalted Him and given Him the name which is above every name, that at the name of Jesus every knee should bow, of those in heaven, and of those on earth, and of those under the earth, and that every tongue should confess that Jesus Christ is Lord, to the glory of God the Father.*

'Therefore' follows on from the revelation that Jesus had laid down His rights as God to come and represent fallen mankind as 'the Son of Man', our Champion. He was declared to be the Son of God with power by His resurrection from the dead (Romans 1:4); He redeemed us from all sin, sickness, the curse and even death itself; and, to those under the earth, 'He disarmed the principalities and powers, making a public spectacle of them, triumphing over them' in the Cross (Colossians 2:15).

Jesus now, is not only restored to His rightful position as God, but His name is declared to be the name above all names, to which everything must bow - in the angelic realm, the earthly realm and the demonic realm.

Sickness must bow to the name of Jesus; pain must leave in His name; cancer must bow and even death bows to the name of Jesus.

> **Romans 8:37** *Yet in all these things we are more than conquerors through Him who loved us.*

We are victorious over things to the extent that we know and are convinced that Jesus is victorious over them. Our faith and conviction in His victory causes us to be more than conquerors and to live in the victory that He won. Believe in the sovereignty and power in Jesus' name! It is not our great prayers that minister the power but the ministry of the spoken name of Jesus.

Jesus' name represents Him, so speak His name specifically - "in the name of Jesus" and not, as many believers seem to pray, "in Your name". At times, it can seem like His name is thoughtlessly added to the end of prayer as a religious practice, like signing off a letter with 'yours sincerely', or neglected altogether. We must realise that the prayer is being heard and answered because of Jesus, not because of us, our eloquent words, our works or even our need.

> **Acts 3:12** *So when Peter saw it, he responded to the people: "Men of Israel, why do you marvel at this? Or why look so intently at us, as though by our own power or godliness we had made this man walk?*

All the power is from Jesus and the authority to see its release is in the name "Jesus". So, let's declare "Jesus" over every sickness and situation where we want to see His power demonstrated. Let's honour Him always; be so thankful for the privilege given to us to use His name and be so aware that when we declare the name of Jesus, we are presenting Jesus and His power to the situation. It's all because of Him and all the glory goes to Him.

Acts 3:16 *And <u>His name, through faith in His name</u>, has made this man strong, whom you see and know. Yes, <u>the faith which comes through Him</u> has given him this perfect soundness in the presence of you all.*

In Acts 3:16, Peter brings out the link between faith in Jesus and faith in His name. When we have faith in His name, we are having faith in Jesus Himself, what He has accomplished and relying on His authority and power to see His will done. Again, this is highlighted in Acts 4:10, *"let it be known to you all, and to all the people of Israel, that <u>by the name of Jesus Christ</u> of Nazareth, whom you crucified, whom God raised from the dead, <u>by Him</u> this man stands here before you whole."*

In the book of Acts we see salvation, baptism, healing and deliverance being ministered and received through the name of Jesus, with Jesus' power being manifested to realise these precious gifts into lives.

Acts 4:12 *"Nor is there salvation in any other, for there is no other name under heaven given among men by which we must be saved."*

Acts 19:5 *When they heard this, they were baptized in the name of the Lord Jesus.*

Acts 4:30 *"by stretching out Your hand to heal, and that signs and wonders may be done through the name of Your holy Servant Jesus."*

Acts 16:18 *…But Paul, greatly annoyed, turned and said to the spirit, "I command you in the name of Jesus Christ to come out of her." And he came out that very hour.*

We have been commissioned by God to heal the sick in Jesus' name.

Mark 16: 17,18 [17] *And these signs will follow those who believe: <u>In My name</u> they will cast out demons; they will speak with new tongues;* [18] *they will take up serpents; and if they drink anything deadly, it will by no means hurt them; <u>they will lay hands on the sick, and they will recover.</u>"*

To administer the will of another on their behalf, one needs an authority, right or a power of attorney (in the human sense) to do so. The religious leaders ask Peter and John in Acts 4:7 "By what power or by what name have you done this?" The religious leaders recognised that the miracle had to come by someone's power or name. It was both, the power of God ministered in the name of Jesus.

Scripture also makes note of Peter being filled with the Holy Spirit (Acts 4:8) and the impact of him spending time with Jesus. *'Now when they saw the boldness of Peter and John, and perceived that they were uneducated and untrained men, they marvelled. And they realized that they had been with Jesus'* (Acts 4:13). So, it is for us - we are not just praying a religious formula, but we are called to a lifestyle of being filled with the Spirit and spending time in God's precious presence. In that place, we discern and align with what He wants us to do, where He wants us to go and who He wants us to minister to, and how. From that position, we speak His will in the name of Jesus and then, His power is demonstrated.

Jesus, having been given all authority in Heaven and on Earth, has commanded the church to continue releasing His accomplished will in His name, and to teach others to do the same (Matthew 28:18-20). Jesus has already secured the provision for us of salvation, the forgiveness of sins, healing, complete authority over the powers of darkness and the securing of

God's covenant promises for us. Then He has given us the right to use His name to release His will to be done on Earth as it is in Heaven.

As with faith, this is demonstrated through a person submitted to Christ in obedience and aligned with doing His will. It is not to be used to glorify self or see our own will done.

So, we pray and declare God's will and promises in Jesus' name, thereby presenting all that Jesus is and what He has done, and Jesus has declared that He will do it.

Reading:

- Acts 3:1-16
- John 14:13-14
- Mark 16:15-18
- Matthew 28:18-20

Thought for the day: When I pray or declare in Jesus' Name, I am presenting all that Jesus is and all that Jesus has done to the situation and then, in addition, Jesus said He will bring it to pass.

Reflection: Write down any insights or revelations that you have had as you reflect on the power of the Name of Jesus and the fact that you have been given the right to use His Name to release His will in your life.

_____
_____
_____
_____
_____
_____
_____
_____
_____
_____
_____
_____
_____
_____
_____
_____
_____

24

HEALING IN COMMUNION

1 Corinthians 11:26 *For as often as you eat this bread and drink this cup, you proclaim the Lord's death till He comes.*

1 Corinthians 11:23-30 [23] *For I received from the Lord that which I also delivered to you: that the Lord Jesus on the same night in which He was betrayed took bread;* [24] *and when He had given thanks, He broke it and said, "Take, eat; this is My body which is broken for you; do this in remembrance of Me."* [25] *In the same manner He also took the cup after supper, saying, "This cup is the new covenant in My blood. This do, as often as you drink it, in remembrance of Me."* [26] *For as often as you eat this bread and drink this cup, you proclaim the Lord's death till He comes.* [27] *Therefore whoever eats this bread or drinks this cup of the Lord in an unworthy manner will be guilty of the body and blood of the Lord.* [28] *But let a man examine himself, and so let him eat of the bread and drink of the cup.* [29] *For he who eats and drinks in an unworthy manner* *eats and drinks judgment to himself, not discerning the Lord's body.* ³⁰ *For this reason many are weak and sick among you, and many sleep.*

There are three main sacraments that God Himself has instituted for the church - water baptism, baptism in the Holy Spirit and Communion. When something is instituted of God, and not of man, it has a divine purpose and then, divine power is attached to it, to bring that purpose to pass. God is not interested in just having religious rituals or ceremony. He brings His power to fulfil His will and purpose.

In water baptism, God's purpose is that we will leave behind our old life and be raised up out of the water, as Christ came up out of the earth, empowered by the Holy Spirit to live in 'newness of life' (Romans 6:4). When done in faith, that is exactly what happens, and people find the power to leave behind the things of the past, sin and afflictions. With the decision to follow Christ and leave behind the old way of life, one is born again, but there is divine power to live out that decision that comes at water baptism. We can't live this Christian life in our own strength- we need power to break off the 'old man' and power to 'put on the new'.

With the baptism in the Holy Spirit, God's purpose is that you will receive power to be His witness (Acts 1:8), power to obey His word and live for Him and for all believers to receive power for ministry. When done in faith, the Holy Spirit comes to immerse one in divine power to do just that.

In Communion, God's purpose is that you will receive the benefits of the Cross, notably forgiveness, healing and deliverance, and when taken in faith, His power comes to do just that. We continually need access to God's forgiveness, healing and release from spiritual opposition throughout our years here on Earth and, while these can be received through faith and prayer, God has also given us Communion as a moment of great power for

His accomplished will to be released and received. There can be a greater power released when we do it with the elements of the bread and juice/wine than just standing in faith alone for a breakthrough.

As we identify the symbols of the bread and juice/wine with Christ, His body and blood, and acknowledge that He was our substitute, we align with God's 'divine transfer', thereby positioning ourselves to receive His power. His power comes to confirm and actualise the removal of sin, sickness and spiritual opposition from us and the release of forgiveness, healing and deliverance to us. Just to clarify a point here, the elements do not physically change into Christ's body and blood, and nor do they need to, as if He needed to be sacrificed or 'broken' again. They point back to what has already been done on the Cross of Calvary; a finished work that does not need to be repeated by Christ but a work that we need to continually receive, by His grace.

> **Hebrews 9: 25,26** [25] *not that He should offer Himself often, as the high priest enters the Most Holy Place every year with blood of another -* [26] *He then would have had to suffer often since the foundation of the world; but now, <u>once</u> at the end of the ages, He has appeared to put away sin by the sacrifice of Himself.*

The following passage can be difficult and sounds very harsh, but I hope that with explanation, you will see it in another perspective.

> **1 Corinthians 11:29-30** *For he who eats and drinks in an unworthy manner eats and drinks judgment to himself, not discerning the Lord's body. For this reason many are weak and sick among you, and many sleep.*

Paul, in context with this passage, is talking about the correct attitudes for taking Communion, they being faith and love. In it there seems to be a sense of frustration in him that goes like, 'If you only knew the power in what Jesus did for you on the Cross, that is received through Communion, then you wouldn't be sick or for some, have died prematurely'. He says that failing to discern the body of the Lord will leave you weak, sick, or even result in premature death. It's not a judgement on those who haven't received healing, but it is an exhortation to all of us, to apply ourselves to understand what incredible power God has made available to us.

If you take Communion without understanding it, then you don't receive the benefits it provides. You don't earn God's promises by taking Communion properly and God is certainly not bringing judgement on anyone, despite how it may sound from this Scripture. We must read a Scripture, not only in its own context, but within the context of the whole Bible.

John 3:17 *For God did not send His Son into the world to condemn the world but that the world through Him might be saved.*

God did not go to the incredible lengths that He did to save us from our sins and resultant judgement, placing them all on Christ, to then act as if it hadn't happened and judge us for where we still lack understanding.

The benefits of the Cross are received by faith. So, if you are in need of forgiveness or healing, and you are not in faith, not discerning what Christ has done for you, then, you don't receive to yourself the forgiveness and healing that you require and, hence, remain in a place of need. It is not a case of God judging you for not taking Communion properly but, you are not receiving its benefits through taking it properly.

So, Paul is saying that if we receive Communion in the proper manner, discerning the Lord's Body; seeing what Jesus has done for us and receiving the benefits through faith, with an attitude of walking in love, then we need not remain sick.

Communion is a great opportunity to receive healing because the bread and juice help us to focus our faith on the body and blood of Jesus and what He has done for us, as well as being a God ordained moment of power.

> **1 Corinthians 11:23-26** [23] *For I received from the Lord that which I also delivered to you: that the Lord Jesus on the same night in which He was betrayed took bread;* [24] *and when He had given thanks, He broke it and said, "Take, eat; this is My body which is broken for you; do this in remembrance of Me."* [25] *In the same manner He also took the cup after supper, saying, "This cup is the new covenant in My blood. This do, as often as you drink it, in remembrance of Me."* [26] *For as often as you eat this bread and drink this cup, you proclaim the Lord's death till He comes.*

Jesus' body was 'broken' with sin, sickness and disease, and every time that we take the bread in Communion we are to remember, or meditate on the fact that 'surely He bore our sicknesses and carried our pains' (Isaiah 53:4), and receive by faith the healing that He has provided for us.

> **Isaiah 53:4,5 AMPC**[8] *Surely He has borne our griefs (sicknesses, weaknesses and distresses) and carried our sorrows and pains (of punishment), yet we (ignorantly) considered Him stricken, smitten, and afflicted by God (as if with leprosy). But He was wounded for our transgressions, He was bruised for our guilt and iniquities; the chastisement (needful*

to obtain) peace and well-being for us was upon Him, and with the stripes (that wounded) Him we are healed and made whole.

1 Peter 2:24 ...*by whose stripes you <u>were</u> healed.*

Many Christians believe that Communion is solely for us to remember that Jesus died for our sins but, if that were the case, there would be no need for us to take the bread. Only the shedding of blood can atone for sin, represented by the juice/wine and, so, if sin were the only issue in Communion, we would only need to take the juice/wine and not the bread.

Please note that it is important that the bread is unleavened and not just any bread or biscuit. Leaven in Scripture is symbolic of sin and unleavened bread had to be used in Communion (and the earlier Passover meal that preceded it) to symbolise Jesus' sinless life - the Bread of life who had no sin. To use bread with yeast in it, in the context of the Communion meal, would be communicating the idea that Jesus had sin. Again, let us be careful to honour God as we approach Him.

The wine or juice represents Jesus' blood shed for the forgiveness of our sins, the establishing of the New Covenant with all of its promises and protection from all the power of the devil, whose power over mankind was through sin. It is also His blood that redeemed us from the curse of the law (Galatians 3:13; Deuteronomy 28:15-68) the curse not only including an extensive list of sicknesses and afflictions but *'every sickness and every plague, which is not written in this Book of the Law'* (Deuteronomy 28: 61), thus including all sickness under the curse. We are redeemed from all sickness through the blood of Jesus as well as through His body!

In receiving Communion, we are to rightly discern the Lord's body, see what He has done and speak it out in faith and then, simply receive His power that flows in this moment.

I would encourage you to take some unleavened bread and grape juice and look to Jesus and declare your faith in what He has already done for you.

> **1 Corinthians 11:26** says *'For as often as you eat this bread and drink this cup, you proclaim the Lord's death till He comes.'*

The spirit of faith believes, sees, and speaks (or proclaims as in speaking out loud), proclaiming the benefits of the Lord's death and resurrection. You might pray something like this, "Lord God, I thank you for all that You have done for me through Jesus Christ, His death and His resurrection. I receive this bread as Jesus' body, broken with sickness and pain as He took it all on my behalf. I believe that 'by His stripes I have been healed' and I receive your healing power into my body right now. I take this cup of juice representing the blood of Jesus that has provided forgiveness for all sin, release from all judgement, the breaking of every curse and deliverance from all the power of the devil. I receive your forgiveness and release from every curse and bondage in Jesus' name. I thank You for forgiving me, healing me and setting me free; I receive Your power now in Jesus' name. Amen."

The Lord's Supper must never become simply a ritual, but it is a divinely appointed moment of power by which you may appropriate today all that Jesus has provided through the work of the Cross.

Reading:

- 1 Corinthians 11:17-34
- Matthew 26:26-28,
- Mark 14:22-24
- Luke 22:14-20

Thought for the day: Communion is a God ordained moment of power to receive forgiveness, healing and freedom.

Reflection: Write down any insights or revelations that you have had as you reflect on the power that God has made available to you through the Communion meal.

25

WHAT ABOUT JOB?

Job 19:25 *For I know that my Redeemer lives…*

Whenever the topic of divine healing comes up, there is always someone who will ask "Well, what about Job?" suggesting that God put sickness on Job or refused to heal him. To be clear, it was the devil who brought the calamity and God did heal Job, but questions have confounded many as to how much God allows in suffering and the testing of our faith. How do we understand suffering in the light of God's goodness and salvation?

Suffering is a complex topic and this discussion doesn't seek to provide all the answers to that, but rather, to glean some wisdom to apply to our own lives. Let's start with three foundational truths to undergird the understanding we want to receive and apply for ourselves from Job.

In the first chapter of the book of Job, we see Job, described as a very righteous man, who honoured God and regularly offered up sacrifices, finding himself in a place of extreme trial, loss of family and all his possessions, and afflicted in his health. Job, living before the time of the law, would have been following a pattern of worship of God, which though being good in the sense of works, did not necessarily point to a revelation of Christ.

So, firstly we see the issue that has faced all of mankind. No matter how good we are, no matter how many good works we do and sacrifices we make and, even if we love and honour God, there is nothing in all of our human fleshly efforts that can protect us from the devastating impact of the Fall with its resultant curses and the works of the devil.

So, Job reveals to us that being good in ourselves is never enough. We all need a Saviour, our Redeemer Jesus. His shed blood for us is the only power in the universe to deal with the impact of sin and the curse. The enormity of sin, its offense to the holiness of God and its devastating impact needs to be seen, so that the enormity of what Jesus accomplished for us can be appreciated. There is no hope without Jesus.

Secondly, we do need to recognise in studying Job that those of us today who walk with Jesus, live under a different covenant (Hebrews 8:6); in a different kingdom (Colossians 1:13,14) with better promises and blessings; we have been redeemed by Jesus' shed blood from all the curses and we have been privileged with access to a far greater revelation of God through the Scriptures. Job lived before the written Word and had to operate from his own understanding and what God would reveal directly to him. His statement, that came from his initially wrong perspective, that "The Lord gave and the Lord has taken away" is quoted by so many Christians despite the fact the Bible reveals that Satan did the taking.

All of Job's sufferings are listed under the curse of the law (Deuteronomy 28:15-68), even though he lived before the law. I would have the view that the curses were the impact of sin and the Fall, that God was trying to protect His people from, through obedience to His ways and the covering offered by the sacrifices, rather than a direct punishment for disobedience to the law. We see that these curses have always been present in the Earth since the

Fall and we need God's protection from them. Christ has redeemed us from the curse of the law (Galatians 3:13) and in redeeming us from sin itself, He also provided redemption from its terrible consequences. So, while there are things to learn from Job, we do live in place of greater provision of blessing. Many are tempted to embrace suffering as their story and even identity, identifying themselves with Job's story and in extreme trial, it can be tempting to do so. However, in all adversity, we are rather, to embrace Jesus and His story, in order to find healing and redemption.

Thirdly, Job was an upright man who sought God, which shows that adversity or sickness does not mean that someone has some hidden sin in their life as Job's friends, and some Christians, wrongly imply. Sickness or adversity are present in the Earth because of the Fall and Satan's presence in the Earth; and find their healing or deliverance through the Person of Jesus Christ, who has defeated sin, the curse and all the powers of darkness for us in His magnificent salvation. His finished work, when we receive it, is enough to combat sin, sickness and the devil.

We don't have all the answers as to why good people suffer, nor how much God allows when our faith is tested. All theology can suddenly seem unclear in the 'baptism of fire' seasons that bring the death of self, in order that the life of God would be revealed through us. We can know, however, that in the worst case of suffering, God was there and redeemed the situation.

> **James 5:11** *Indeed we count them blessed who endure. You have heard of the perseverance of Job and seen <u>the end intended by the Lord</u> - that the Lord is very compassionate and merciful.*
>
> **Job 42:10** *And the Lord restored Job's losses when he prayed for his friends. Indeed the Lord gave Job twice as much as he had before.*

WHAT ABOUT JOB?

It is interesting to note that while Job's suffering was not the judgement of God, repentance for his attitudes and the release of forgiveness towards those who had been unkind to him, were still part of the answer. Prior to this, the Lord rebukes Job's friends for speaking out of their limited understanding and thus, not speaking rightly of Him. Job was also corrected by God for trying to justify himself, and in so doing, accusing God.

Job 40:2 NLT[5] *"Do you still want to argue with the Almighty? You are God's critic, but do you have the answers?"* [6]

Job 40:8 NLT[5] *"Will you discredit My justice and condemn Me just to prove you are right?"* [6]

So, we all need to remain humble and not seek to justify ourselves; we, and all our friends, don't have all the answers but our Almighty God does if we will continue to seek Him with a pure heart.

In the story of Job, there is yet another display of the natural versus the supernatural response. Job's poor wife responds with the natural human reaction of the 'flesh' nature, which we are all vulnerable to do. She despairs and tells Job to 'curse God and die'. Let's understand here, that this poor woman has just lost ten children, and yet even in this worst of circumstances, the natural reaction of the flesh still does not bring about the response and redemptive power of God. God has ways for us to respond - it's not just because He is compassionate, and we are suffering, that He responds. We also need to align ourselves with Him and His ways, in order to see the supernatural redemptive power of God.

Job's response, even with his limited understanding of God, and thinking that He is behind the suffering, is extraordinary and, by so doing, he aligns himself with God and His redemptive power. Job's first reaction to the devastation and suffering is to bow down and worship God and to attribute no blame to Him.

Job 1:22 *In all this Job did not sin nor charge God with wrong.*

Job 13:15 *Though He slay me, yet will I trust Him.....*

It is a supernatural response to keep trusting God when you feel He is behind your suffering. A foundation in the character of God and knowing the good end He intends for us, helps us to stand in the day of trial and to reach out to God and not step back from Him. It can be so challenging when the circumstances don't align with what we see in the promises of God, but we need to keep honouring God, knowing His love and good intention for us, keep pressing in to access His grace to help us stand and to endure with patience. We need to lay all the unanswered questions at His feet while holding firm to what we know of Him.

Many will refer to Job's statement in Job 3:25 *"For the thing I greatly feared has come upon me, and what I dreaded has happened to me"* as evidence of his sacrifices being offered in fear of judgement, rather than in faith, resulting in the calamity that he suffered. While this is possible, it is also not the whole picture, as his yielded trust in God in adversity reveals another aspect of great faith.

I will, however, throw in here a cautionary note on 'fear-filled' prayers that many believers offer up when sickness or calamity come, or when a loved one is going for appointments or embarking on travel. Many feel the need that every point in a journey or process has to be prayed over: the appointments, the desired outcomes, protection on a journey, 'covering all the prayer-points'. After praying for some for healing, they feel the need to give you every detail to pray over, as if God won't manage the process otherwise. Job challenges us to have faith-filled prayers that rather just trust God in all the process.

So, I don't need to pray "God please protect my family" when He has already declared Himself to be their Lord and Protector. I am, rather, to acknowledge who He is, thank Him for protecting them, for sending His angels and then, declare His Word to release His will and rest in faith.

Scripture reveals to us the character and promises of God not so that we will pray for Him to be who He has already declared Himself to be, nor pray for what He says He has already done. The revelation is so that we can see who He is and what He has done and then simply trust Him, align with Him in faith and thank Him for it. We do need to apply and declare the Word, though it's not to try and make something happen, but rather, it is a finished work of God's power to apply to the problem.

Job stayed faithful to God in the midst of so many unanswered questions. It is interesting to note that God didn't answer the questions or challenges but rather, gave Job a greater revelation of Himself. Job knew God as El Shaddai, the Almighty but God reveals to him that He is also the Redeemer and the Healer.

He progressed from having a certain understanding of God to, over the course of the trial (around 9 months), having a revelation of Him. In Job 19:25 he declares "I know that my Redeemer lives". He now knew his saving God was real and would redeem him. How did he know this? It came as a God given revelation.

In the same way, when Jesus asks the disciples "Who do you say that I am?", Peter's response is not from human understanding, but is a God given revelation.

Matthew 16: 16,17 [16] *Simon Peter answered and said, "You are the Christ, the Son of the living God."* [17] *Jesus answered* *and said to him, "Blessed are you, Simon Bar- Jonah, <u>for flesh and blood has not revealed this to you, but My Father who is in heaven.</u>*

A greater revelation of God precedes the receiving of what that revelation speaks of. God was already Job's Redeemer, but when he saw this from a God revealed perspective, it brought the release and receiving of all that God had for him - healing, blessing and restoration. God is the Redeemer of all the curse, suffering and sickness, and not the author of it.

In **Job 42:5**, Job says *"I have heard of You by the hearing of the ear, but <u>now my eye sees you.</u>"*

He didn't see God with his physical eyes as his encounter with God was through the Lord speaking to him out of a whirlwind. He had a revelation of God and was seeing Him from a new perspective. This highlights the importance of having an encounter with God rather than just seeking Him to answer all your questions.

Job 32:8 *But there is a spirit in man, and the breath of the Almighty gives him understanding.*

It is the same for us. So, when approaching a trial or sickness, rather than asking questions, thinking, "Why me", or challenging God, seek Him for a greater revelation of who He is. The revelation will precede the healing or blessing, even though the promise is already there.

Hebrews 11:6 *But without faith it is impossible to please Him, for he who comes to God must believe that he is, and that He is a rewarder of those who diligently seek Him.*

WHAT ABOUT JOB?

There is both a believing of who He is and a drawing near. It's not just I believe He is God, but I believe who He has revealed Himself to be in Scripture. So, I believe He is with me; I believe His righteousness has been given to me; He is my peace, my Healer, my Provider, my victory in all circumstances and my Shepherd who leads me. I am to stand in my belief of who He is and who He is to me.

God did not leave Job in his state of suffering, but redemption doesn't necessarily look like a reversal and a return to, or of, what was lost. It wasn't like God raised his ten children from the dead, but He gave Job twice as much as he had before, in all areas. So, it may look a bit different, but it is good and there is a hope. Nothing is too great for God to redeem.

Reading:

- Job 40:1-8
- Job 42

Thought for the day: I can trust and keep honouring God in the midst of unanswered questions because He is my Redeemer and has good intended for me.

Reflection: Write down any insights or revelations that you have had as you seek God for a greater revelation of Himself, and who He is to you.

_____
_____
_____
_____
_____
_____
_____
_____
_____
_____
_____
_____
_____
_____
_____

Write down three Scriptures below that reveal who God is to you:

Scripture 1:

Scripture 2:

Scripture 3:

26

PAULS' THORN

> **2 Corinthians 12:9** .... *"My grace is sufficient for you, for My strength is made perfect in weakness."* ....

Invariably when healing is taught, someone will bring up 'Paul's thorn' with the assumption that God either brought him the affliction; refused to heal it or that God was using a sickness to teach him something. It is always good to study a Biblical text in context and not just receive reasonings that are not grounded in the Scriptures, and which are generally birthed out of disappointment or human reasoning to explain a contrary circumstance.

When followed to their conclusion, the reasonings that challenge divine healing, end up challenging God, questioning or contradicting His revealed character and contradicting what the Scriptures reveal about Jesus and what He did for us at the Cross of Calvary. Once believed, they lower a person's faith in God and expectation of what He can do. They bring what becomes a humanly sourced addition to His Word, causing a sense of caution in trusting God, a reservation of heart and a preparation to be disappointed by Him. This is so dishonouring to Him and so destructive for us. We need to be very careful about embracing these reasonings as they actually hinder us receiving what God has for us, His grace being received through faith.

> **2 Corinthians 12:7-10** [7] *And lest I should be exalted above measure by the abundance of the revelations, a thorn in the flesh was given to me, a messenger of Satan to buffet me, lest I be exalted above measure.* [8] *Concerning this thing I pleaded with the Lord three times that it might depart from me.* [9] *And He said to me, "My grace is sufficient for you, for My strength is made perfect in weakness." Therefore most gladly I will rather boast in my infirmities, that the power of Christ may rest upon me.* [10] *Therefore I take pleasure in infirmities, in reproaches, in needs, in persecutions, in distresses, for Christ's sake. For when I am weak, then I am strong.*

In 2 Corinthians 12:2-6, Paul tells of how he was taken up to heaven, either bodily or in a vision, he doesn't know which. He receives an abundance of revelations from God. Verse 4 is translated in the NIV[2] as '*was caught up to Paradise and heard inexpressible things, things that no one is permitted to tell*' and in the Amplified Bible (AMPC[8]) as '*was caught up into Paradise, and he heard utterances beyond the power of man to put into words, which man is not permitted to utter*'.

However, many of the revelations Paul received were expressed and written down as New Testament Scripture, that we may know, at least in part, the mind of Christ. The revelation of God's grace, the promises of the New Covenant, the revelation of the church and how we are to relate to God and each other have been revealed to us.

Whenever a word or revelation comes from God, you find that the enemy will also come with a challenge to contradict it. The Father speaks to Jesus *"You are My beloved Son; in You I am well pleased"* (Luke 3:22) and Satan shortly afterwards comes to Jesus with *"If you are the Son of God, command this stone to become bread"* (Luke 4:3).

Scripture records in Genesis 2:16,17, *[16] And the Lord God commanded the man, saying, "Of every tree of the garden you may freely eat; [17] but of the tree of the knowledge of good and evil you shall not eat, for in the day that you eat of it you shall surely die."* In the very next chapter Satan comes with *"Has God indeed said, 'You shall not eat of every tree of the garden'?"* and *"You will not surely die"* (Genesis 3:1-4).

Mark 4:15 reveals that if we do not carefully heed and receive the word God brings us, then Satan will come immediately and take away the word. How does he do this? Contrary circumstances might arise; doubt, disappointment and deception can come into the mind, and what was sown of God in the heart, can be uprooted by heeding the deafening roar that comes to challenge it.

Paul experienced the impact of that roar of the enemy, articulating in 2 Corinthians 11:22-33 the extraordinary challenges that he faced, many of which would seem to contradict the revelations of victory, authority and power in Christ that he received and recorded. Interestingly, he doesn't mention any sickness in those many trials that he went through.

Paul states in 2 Corinthians 12:7 that the 'thorn in the flesh' was a 'messenger of Satan' - 'angelos' in the Greek. This word is used 176 times in the New Testament and is translated 'angel' or 'angels' (147), 'angel's' (2), 'messenger' or 'messengers' (6) and 'spies' (1). It is a personality and not a sickness. Paul was 'buffeted' by demonically inspired opposition everywhere that he went with the gospel of Christ. Buffet means 'to strike repeatedly and violently; 'batter'; 'knock someone off course' or 'afflict someone over a long period'[11].

Many will quote Galatians 4:13 where Paul says, '*You know because of physical infirmity I preached the gospel to you <u>at the first</u>*'. Vine's dictionary[12] translates 'infirmity' as 'weakness, want of strength or inability to produce results', as opposed to the modern use of the word for sickness. 'At the first' (Galatians 4:13) refers to Paul's first visit to Galatia which occasioned him being stoned at Lystra. When a person experienced a stoning, stones were directed at their head by many assailants, for the direct purpose of killing the victim. One would have to assume that Paul would have sustained terrible facial injuries from this (Acts 14:19-20). After prayer, he gets up and continues his journey the next day into Derbe (Galatia) where they would have been confronted with a man still demonstrating 'physical infirmity', but well enough to keep preaching.

Paul states in Galatians 4:14,15, '*[14] And my trial which was in my flesh you did not despise or reject, but you received me as an angel of God, even as Christ Jesus. [15] What then was the blessing you enjoyed? For I bear you witness that, if possible, you would have plucked out your own eyes and given them to me*'. From this, some have formed the opinion that Paul had an eye disease that God refused to heal. This is not recorded in Scripture as being the case, and it is more likely that his eyes were still looking traumatised from that stoning.

Then, many interpret 2 Corinthians 12:8-9, where Paul pleads three times for God to remove the thorn, as God saying "no". Let's look again at the passage - does God say "No"? No, He doesn't. What He does say is a statement, which seen from earlier passages discussed, He often does when He wants to highlight something we need to adjust or align to. God reveals to Paul His immeasurable power to overcome in all challenges, stating "My grace is sufficient for you". What He has already freely given by grace, through Jesus, is enough to overcome the challenges that we face. It's not "no" but rather, 'what to apply' and 'how to overcome'.

The Lord goes on to say, *"My strength is made perfect in weakness"*. 'Strength' here is the Greek word 'dunamis' which describes the power of the Holy Spirit, being God's miracle working power. In Acts 1:8 when Jesus says that you shall receive power when the Holy Spirit comes upon you, that word for power is translated from 'dunamis'.

When you find yourself in a place of infirmity, weak and unable to produce results, then you can receive God's grace, the miraculous power of His Spirit that enables you to overcome that which you could never achieve in your own strength. This is why Paul goes on to say that he would now take pleasure in infirmities (2 Corinthians 12:10), not because he is weird but because he has discovered an access to the power of God that would accord miraculous breakthrough in the many challenges he faced.

Often, we want God to just remove the problem; remove 'the thorn in the flesh'; remove that which is troubling or buffeting us, when He wants us to apply what He has already given us, in order to see a miraculous breakthrough. We have to apply, by receiving through faith and acting on, His great and precious promises, His grace, His blood, His victory and His power in the authority which we have been given in the name of Jesus.

Once again, we can see an example of the natural versus the supernatural response. The great apostle Paul, who had great faith, was crying out in a natural reaction for the thorn to be removed, but even in the midst of his enormous challenges, God did not alter His method of receiving from Him. Just as with the Israelites in Numbers 21 (ref. Ch 10) asking for God to take the snakes away, His response is always to put the work of the Cross in. We are usually praying for Him to take the problem or the sickness away but His power rests upon our positioning ourselves in His perspective and responding by applying the finished work of the Cross to our situation.

Now, if we are to believe from some teaching, that God would use sickness to train or chastise us, then we would also have to heretically believe that He would use sin to do the same. Impossible! God chose to package sin and sickness together in the Atonement and to deal with them the same way. Once again, this is not suggesting that an individual's sickness or suffering is due to hidden sin in their life but referring to God's answer to the impact of the Fall.

He would no more use sickness than He would use sin to afflict someone. This is where these human reasonings, when followed to their conclusion, reveal how ridiculous, and how dishonouring of God they are. Their deception would have believers embrace that which God has delivered them from; have them not apply His grace, promises and power despite His instruction to do so and would remove all the necessary resistance to the onslaught of the enemy.

God did not remove the demon as Paul had requested but gave him His grace, or power, to overcome. Paul's writings after this in Ephesians and Romans reveal the revelation he got about our authority over the powers of darkness.

God's grace in the area of sin and sickness does not have the intent to enable you to bear what Jesus has already borne on your behalf, but rather to remove it - even though the Lord, also, does graciously strengthen and sustain us in the process.

Reading:

- 2 Corinthians 11:22 - 2 Corinthians 12:10
- Romans 8: 31-39
- Ephesians 6:10-18
- 1 John 5:4,5

Thought for the day: "... My grace is all you need. My power works best in weakness.... (from 2 Corinthians 12:9 NLT)

Reflection: Write down any insights or revelations that you have had as you reflect on God's provision of grace and power, and how you will receive and apply that grace to your circumstances.

27

IDOLS AROUND HEALING

Exodus 20:3 *You shall have no other gods before Me.*

The appropriation of healing can be a challenging one for many - navigating faith, daily realities that need to be dealt with, application of wisdom, knowing what to incorporate in the healing journey etc. In the midst of all of this, we can all be susceptible to unconsciously letting Jesus slip from first place in our lives, even as we pursue His healing grace, or other sources of healing.

We can receive healing in many ways, but as a believer, Jesus needs to be in first place in every area of our life and certainly needs to be if we are desiring to receive divine healing. There are also a wide range of health supports that may be utilised, so many of which are good, and as we seek Him first, we not only have access to divine healing, but the other remedies, as directed by Him, are blessed and work for us.

Proverbs 9:10,11 [10]" *The fear of the Lord is the beginning of wisdom, and the knowledge of the Holy One is understanding.*[11]

For by me your days will be multiplied, and years of life will be added to you.

Having faith does not mean that you can't apply sound practical wisdom and knowledge for your health - any more than God being your Provider would imply that you couldn't use sound financial advice and practices to apply to your financial world. However, while many healing sources may be good, it's not good when they become idols or what we seek first.

Christians can fall into traps of idolatry when they look for the healing at any cost, or from any source, more than the Lordship of Jesus and often it can seem to be such a fine line between them. So, it's good to be aware of what can be a trap for us, as idols hinder us receiving divine healing.

Here are a few to consider:

1. <u>The healing itself or chasing signs and the miraculous can become an idol.</u>

This is such an easy trap to fall into because as we are delving into the promises of God, hanging onto them and declaring them, even the promised healing itself can subtly creep into our primary focus and pursuit, leaving Jesus Himself out of first place.

David beautifully responds to God in Psalm 27:8, *'When You said, "Seek My face," My heart said to You, "Your face, Lord, I will seek."'* The call of God is to firstly seek His face, that is Himself, and not His hand or what He could do for you.

There can also be those who chase the signs and the miraculous that the Lord is demonstrating across the Earth, and while there is no problem in seeking to be in a place where God is moving, we just have to ensure that Jesus is still our primary pursuit.

Jesus' frustration is expressed in John 4:48 with *"unless you people see signs and wonders, you will by no means believe"*. John 6:2 - *'Then a great multitude followed Him, because they saw His signs which He performed on those who were diseased'*. They followed Jesus for the signs, but many would have ended up not following Him for Himself.

> **John 5:3,4** ³ *In these lay a great multitude of sick people, blind, lame, paralysed, waiting for the moving of the water.* ⁴ *For an angel went down at a certain time into the pool and stirred up the water; then whoever stepped in first, after the stirring of the water, was made well of whatever disease he had.*

We have already looked at this story earlier in chapter 9. While the people in this story would have been desperate, with no access to modern medicine, this scene can also serve as a picture of those who today, are looking primarily for the miraculous and the dramatic. Many Christians travel from place to place looking for the spectacular, and when it fades, they move on, rather than planting themselves where God would have them. God does work the miraculous and we love that; He does heal; He does do signs and wonders, but He also has the purpose that they are to lead us to seek and experience Jesus in a greater way. We must be careful, in the excitement of seeking to experience the signs which occur in different places and seasons, that they do not become our primary pursuit. Jesus can perform a sign anytime and anywhere that someone believes Him and responds to His Word.

The man's healing ended up coming about by responding to Jesus and His Word, bringing such miraculous power as to heal a man who had had an infirmity for thirty- eight years. The response of faith can look to many as ordinary, challenging rather than exciting, the diligence of feeding and training the spirit seen as tedious in contrast to the spectacular performance, but in pursuing a sign over faith, one can risk missing the amazing healing that God wants to release.

> **Mark 16:20** *And they went out and preached everywhere, the Lord working with them and <u>confirming the word through the accompanying signs</u>. Amen.*

2. <u>Medical science, though a precious gift, can still become an idol if it is exalted above Jesus and the healing He provides.</u>

Medical science is such a gift to the modern world and as a step of wisdom, I would recommend that professional medical advice is sought for any serious conditions.

God is not limited or hindered from healing you because you have sought help from a medical doctor, psychologist, physiotherapist etc.

It is not lack of faith to find out what is going on and to apply practical expertise in that area. I hear some people say "I'm believing God but I don't want to go to the doctor and be told anything negative" but that just isn't faith. Faith is not denial, but it faces the facts, and to do that, you need to know the facts in the first place. Faith then believes God and His Word and applies the promises to deal with those facts, while using wisdom and practical support and applications at the same time.

I have heard some healing ministers actually say that God would be limited or hindered from healing someone if they took chemotherapy or even other medicines. Let me tell you clearly that God is not limited! He is not falling off the throne and wondering how to help you because you are receiving medicine and it is not a lack of faith on your part. For the most part it is wisdom, a therapy that sustains you while waiting for divine healing to be experienced and keeps you safe in the process. It is also a testimony to the health professionals when divine healing is demonstrated.

I have seen so many people with cancer miraculously healed, of the magnitude that it was evidently of God, but they were also under professional medical care at the time, and most were receiving chemotherapy. I have also seen many die from cancer. Many of these either felt that it was lack of faith to receive medical care or chemotherapy, and others rejected medical science and sought inadequate alternative therapies.

However, despite how wonderful medical science can be, it is still not to be in first place for our attention and faith. We do not want to grieve God by not even acknowledging, let alone believing Him for the enormity of what Jesus did for us in bearing our sicknesses and diseases.

It is noted in 2 Chronicles 16, that Asa didn't seek the Lord first for his healing, seemingly implying that this is why he failed to receive it.

> **2 Chronicles 16:12-13** [12] *And in the thirty-ninth year of his reign, Asa became diseased in his feet, and his malady was severe; yet in his disease he did not seek the Lord, but the physicians.* [13] *So Asa rested with his fathers; he died in the forty-first year of his reign.*

Again, this is not to say, to not seek or follow medical advice. When Hezekiah did seek the Lord first, the result was that the Lord directed him to a medicine of the day. However, this was accompanied by what was obviously a miraculous healing, because presumably a fig poultice was not enough to cure a life-threatening infection or illness. The difference with Hezekiah's situation was that he sought the Lord first.

> **Isaiah 38: 1-5** *In those days Hezekiah was sick and near death. And Isaiah the prophet, the son of Amoz, went to*

> him and said to him, "Thus says the Lord: 'Set your house in order, for you shall die and not live.'" ² Then Hezekiah turned his face toward the wall, and prayed to the Lord, ³ and said, "Remember now, O Lord, I pray, how I have walked before You in truth and with a loyal heart, and have done what is good in Your sight." And Hezekiah wept bitterly. ⁴ And the word of the Lord came to Isaiah, saying, ⁵ "Go and tell Hezekiah, 'Thus says the Lord, the God of David your father: "I have heard your prayer, I have seen your tears; surely I will add to your days fifteen years."
>
> **Isaiah 38: 21** *Now Isaiah had said, "Let them take a lump of figs, and apply it as a poultice on the boil, and he shall recover."*

So, in seeking healing, go to the Lord first and acknowledge and honour Him as the Healer. Put your faith in Him and declare His promises but as well, seek Him for wisdom and guidance as you pursue professional medical help or any other healing avenues.

3. <u>Seeking healing that may have other spiritual entities behind it - for example</u> through New Age practices, or many of the 'natural' or 'alternative' therapists' who <u>are founded in other spiritual practices.</u>

The enemy tries to mimic all the works of God, including healing, and will aim to seduce people away from God through them (as with the magicians who replicated the works done through Moses and Aaron in Exodus 7:10-12).

This is not to say that all natural therapies or alternative therapists have another spirit behind them, but a great many do. Jesus said by their fruits you will know them and so, look carefully at the impact or 'fruit'. If the impact is people (or self) not drawing near to, or withdrawing intimacy from, God; taking a step back or feeling a separation from Him; calamity, afflictions or divisions start to occur in the lives of those around them (not just themselves) - then there is probably some other spiritual entity behind it. The enemy doesn't care if you get healed, but he does care about your intimacy with God.

I have seen many people experience long term pain, mental health concerns or traumatic afflictions that can be traced back to alternative therapists they have visited, divination received or psychic influence, not to mention the extraordinary amount of treatments they have to buy, with the associated cost. In addition, many have missed receiving important medical care for their original condition, having been directed to 'alternative' cures not based in sound scientific study or approved clinical trials, and not able to supply the required therapeutic response.

Another 'red flag' is people talking all the time about a perceived source of healing, be it certain foods or the natural therapies, but Jesus is not even on the radar for healing. It seems like a spiritual veil has come over their eyes that stops them seeing Jesus as Healer. This spiritual blockage can be clearly observed when praying for them, and there is a perception of the impartation of the anointing returning back to you. When Jesus is brought up in discussion as the Healer, there is an evident blockage of recognition or understanding of this.

God has given us an abundance of good foods to eat, with nutrient and medicinal properties within them. Indeed, many medications are derived from plants but just have had the additional elements removed. It is great to eat well and look after yourself in practical ways but if these things become a pursuit and passion above Jesus, then we are looking at idolatry and a stronghold. If Jesus is truly Lord, then He comes first in all areas of our lives.

IDOLS AROUND HEALING

A spiritual influence is also revealed through bringing a person into bondage - a rigid set of rules that they are so focused on adhering to, that they lose their freedom, as with many fad diets. This is not referring to those who need to use wisdom in foods that they eat while waiting for healing to take effect, for example, those with Coeliac or Crohn's disease or for those who just don't feel good after eating certain foods or who have allergies.

> **1 Timothy 4:1-5** *Now the Spirit expressly says that in latter times some will depart from the faith, giving heed to deceiving spirits and doctrines of demons,* [2] *speaking lies in hypocrisy, having their own conscience seared with a hot iron,* [3] *forbidding to marry, <u>and commanding to abstain from foods which God created to be received</u> <u>with thanksgiving by those who believe</u> <u>and know the truth</u>.* [4] *For every creature of God is good, and nothing is to be refused if it is received with thanksgiving;* [5] *for it is sanctified by the word of God and prayer.*

While this passage is about the deception of certain practices, including foods, being a requirement for holiness, much food and dietary advice today brings the same level of legalism and bondage. Following Jesus is not a set of rigid rules and regulations, but as we put Him first and follow Him, He will direct us into His healing, and into the application of wisdom and there will be a freedom in it.

The promise of healing in Exodus 23:25 is in context with obedience to the Lord and completely rejecting and removing idols and not following the works associated with them. Healing, as with all aspects of redemption, is not in isolation from a holistic Christian lifestyle.

Exodus 23:24-26 *[24] You shall not bow down to their gods, nor serve them, nor do according to their works; but you shall utterly overthrow them and completely break down their sacred pillars. [25] "So you shall serve the Lord your God, and He will bless your bread and your water. And I will take sickness away from the midst of you. [26] No one shall suffer miscarriage or be barren in your land; I will fulfill the number of your days.*

Galatians 5:1 *Stand fast therefore in the liberty by which Christ has made us free, and do not be entangled again with a yoke of bondage.*

4. Making an idol of God's instrument for healing

2 Kings 18:4 *He removed the high places and broke the sacred pillars, cut down the wooden image and broke in pieces the bronze serpent that Moses had made; for until those days the children of Israel burned incense to it, and called it Nehushtan.*

The bronze serpent had been an instrument that God used to bring healing in Numbers 23, but it wasn't the source of healing. However, the people had begun to worship it as such and Hezekiah destroyed it along with other idols of worship when he came into power.

In today's context this may look like people looking to a certain minister as being the source rather than Jesus and what He has done, with the necessity of having faith in Him. God has graciously anointed many believers to bring His healing grace to others. There are notable healing ministries that see more healings, presumably because the minister has applied faith, has sought God for His grace and anointing and has been faithful in ministering it to others. So, while the ministry of healing is available for all believers, it can often be seen in greater measure in these ministries.

However, despite this, we are not to look to these ministers as we would to the Lord, and this can be another trap of idolatry. I have heard, "If this minister comes and prays for me, then I will be healed". Now, we all like to have a person of faith, who carries the anointing, to pray for us and we don't want prayer from a person who is in unbelief. What we need to be really careful of, though, is that we are still looking to Jesus as number One and not looking to the minister. You are healed because of Jesus and what He has done, and because of the Holy Spirit who ministers His healing grace to us. The minister is a vessel for God to move through but not the Healer.

Soberingly, Jesus says of ministers in Luke 17:9,10 *9 Does he thank that servant because he did the things commanded him? I think not. 10 So likewise you, when you have done all those things which you are commanded, say "We are unprofitable servants. We have done what was our duty to do."*

Let not any minister accept the glory due to the Lord nor elevate themselves above other believers, no matter how mightily God may use them. God using us in the miraculous is just our reasonable service in response to an underserved grace, and an obedience to what God asks us to do.

A last one, is that the sickness itself, though obviously not looked to as an idol, can unwittingly assume first place. This can easily happen, especially with serious illness, as the sickness can become overwhelming with its demands. It can now direct your life, how your time is spent, the use of money, and can direct words, leading to complaining or rehearsing the issue. When this happens, it is like the sickness has become 'lord' of your life.

So, let's look at a simple way to start making an adjustment, step by step, so that this doesn't happen to you. Start the day in prayer and yield yourself entirely to the Lord and bring that affliction to the Cross. Ask the Lord what steps He wants you to take that day and then trust Him, that as you take a step towards His Word and what you thought you couldn't do, that His grace will meet you - like the man with the infirmity in John 5. This is taking a step of faith, and He won't require of you something that you cannot do or that He doesn't intend to give you the grace to do. It's not being foolish or choosing your own steps in the flesh, risking going beyond what you should in that moment, but allowing the Lord to direct the step/s for the day.

Psalm 25:5 *Lead me in Your truth and teach me, for You are the God of my salvation; on You I wait all the day.*

Reading:

- Psalm 27
- Psalm 25
- Matthew 6:33

Thought for the day: 'The fear of the Lord is the beginning of wisdom…'

Reflection: Write down any insights or revelations that you have had as you reflect on where God is in your pursuit, vision and application for healing. Is He first? This does not mean that you can't seek professional help and follow sound wisdom but is God first in your heart and pursuit regarding healing? Are there any changes you need to make to ensure that you are fearing the Lord in what you are applying or pursuing for your health?

_____
_____
_____
_____
_____
_____
_____
_____
_____
_____
_____
_____
_____
_____
_____
_____
_____
_____
_____
_____

28

FREE INDEED

John 8:36 *Therefore, if the Son makes you free, you shall be free indeed.*

Life can bring a multitude of challenges, unfair treatment, moments of great pain, extreme stress or trauma, abuse for many and a host of other issues which can bring wounding to the soul (mind, will and emotions), as surely as a physical blow can wound the body. Into the mix, we have an enemy of our souls, a demonic realm that seeks to unfairly, unlawfully and without invitation, take advantage of these moments to gain entry and cause many afflictions, including sickness, other physical afflictions and mental and/or emotional health issues. We can also experience the responses of anxiety, fear, rejection, anger, unforgiveness, grief and disappointment that lead to further access and bondage to the enemy.

I am so grateful that God's desire for us is to be completely healed and free. Jesus in His own earthly ministry brought not only physical healing but healing to the soul and deliverance from evil spirits and their works - and many physical healings were also resultant through such ministry.

> **Matthew 4:23-24** ²³ *And Jesus went about all Galilee, teaching in their synagogues, preaching the gospel of the kingdom, and healing all kinds of sickness and all kinds of disease among the people.* ²⁴ *Then His fame went throughout all Syria; and they brought to Him all sick people who were afflicted with various diseases and torments, and those who were demon-possessed, epileptics, and paralytics; and He healed them.*

Please don't read this as epileptics or paralytics being automatically tormented of a demon but rather, while these conditions usually have a physical cause, it is possible that they, at times, can also have a spiritual one, as with so many other conditions.

> **Luke 13:10-13** ¹⁰ *Now He was teaching in one of the synagogues on the Sabbath.* ¹¹ *And behold, there was a woman who had a spirit of infirmity eighteen years, and was bent over and could in no way raise herself up.* ¹² *But when Jesus saw her, He called her to Him and said to her, "Woman you are loosed from your infirmity."*¹³ *And He laid His hands on her, and immediately she was made straight, and glorified God.*

> **Luke 13:16** *So ought not this woman, being a daughter of Abraham, whom Satan has bound—think of it—for eighteen years, be loosed from this bond on the Sabbath?"*

As Jesus said, think of it, this poor woman was bent over for eighteen years. No mention is made of the origin of the injury or affliction, but Scripture does tell us that it is due to a spirit of infirmity, a demonic spirit bringing such affliction, that she is tormented, disabled and in pain for all that time. There appears to be no compassion being expressed to her by the religious leaders of the day, who are more affronted that Jesus would heal on a Sabbath, rather than rejoicing at her release from torment.

Jesus identifies that she has been bound by Satan, but the observation does not come with judgement or condemnation but, rather, great compassion. Whatever the cause of affliction Jesus has the answer, and the compassion, to bring healing. In this case He heals through speaking a word to 'loose' her.

To loose ('luo' in Greek) means 'set free, to free from restraint, to unbind, to dissolve'[3]. It refers to releasing something that has been restricted over a life by the powers of darkness.

There are many times in Jesus' ministry where to minister healing, He cast a spirit out of a person. This, however, does not mean that every occasion where those conditions occur it is due to a spirit; just that it can occur. Spirits of infirmity are not only seen in some sicknesses or some disabilities, but also in many cases of depression (once again, not in all), oppression, mental illness and adverse circumstances.

> **Acts 10:38** *How God anointed Jesus of Nazareth with the Holy Ghost and with power, who went about doing good, and <u>healing all who were oppressed of the devil,</u> for God was with Him.*

> **1 John 3:8** *For this purpose the Son of God was manifested, that He might destroy the works of the devil*

> **Revelation 12:11** *And they overcame him <u>by the blood of the Lamb</u> and by the word of their testimony.*

Satan and all his works are defeated through the blood of Jesus, that is, what Jesus did for us at the Cross of Calvary. In the context of Revelation 12:11, the testimony we give is not referring to our life testimony or story of receiving Jesus as Lord and Saviour, as powerful as that is in witnessing, but to the testimony of Jesus and what He has accomplished. The devil doesn't shake and flee because we tell our story - he is brought to nothing and flees at the declaration of what Jesus did in defeating him.

> **Colossians 1:13,14** [13]*He has delivered us from the power of darkness and conveyed us into the kingdom of the Son of His love,* [14]*in whom we have redemption through His blood, the forgiveness of sins.*
>
> **Colossians 2:15** *Having disarmed principalities and powers, He made a public spectacle of them, triumphing over them in it.* (i.e. the Cross)
>
> **Hebrews 2:14 AMPC**[8] *...that by (going through) death He might bring to nought and make of no effect him who had the power of death – that is the devil.*

As we believe, receive and declare what Jesus has done for us, the power of His blood is applied to our lives and freedom and healing are the result. As with every benefit of the Cross, God's healing, protection and deliverance does not happen automatically but we are required to apply faith to receive God's grace.

Jesus' ministry of bringing freedom was continued through the disciples, and then after Jesus' resurrection and the outpouring of the Holy Spirit upon the church, it was, and still is, continued through the ministry of anointed believers.

> **Matthew 16:19 (and similarly in Matthew 18:18)** *And I will give you the keys of the kingdom of heaven, and whatever*

you bind on earth will be bound in heaven, and whatever you loose on earth will be loosed in heaven."

We have been given authority to implement Jesus' victory over the powers of darkness in Jesus' name. What we bind (meaning, not allow) on Earth is not allowed in heaven. So, we bind the devil, sickness, poverty, confusion of mind, depression etc. We then loose (free from restraint) God's will to be done on Earth as it is in Heaven. So, we loose healing, joy, peace etc. We may also command Satan to loose those things that he has bound over a person's life.

In His death and resurrection Jesus paid the price for, and broke the power over us, of sin and all of its consequences including emotional damage or pain, mental torment, physical damage, sickness, all curses and demonic strongholds - whose entry point into mankind is through sin, trauma, pain or not being aligned with God's divine order for our lives. God wants you not just saved, but whole spirit, soul and body.

1 Thessalonians 5:23 *Now may the God of peace Himself sanctify you completely; and may your whole spirit, soul, and body be preserved blameless at the coming of our Lord Jesus Christ.*

As the touch of Jesus and His word of healing released that poor woman who had been bowed over for eighteen years, so now too, the presence of the Holy Spirit and the receiving of the Word of God bring that same release to anyone who has been bound. The following chapters will look at the ways we align with Him so that this freedom and healing of the soul can happen, but even now, just reach out to Him and ask the Lord to reveal to you any area that needs to be healed, corrected or set free. His response will come without any judgment but rather, with great compassion.

Psalm 139:23,24 *Search me O God, and know my heart; try me and know my anxieties; and see if there is any wicked way in me, and lead me in the way everlasting*

Reading:

- Luke 10:17-20
- Luke 4:31-37
- Luke 8:26-39
- Matthew 12:22-30
- Isaiah 54:17
- Isaiah 41:10-13

Thought for the day: It is for freedom that Christ has set us free… (Galatians 5:1 NIV).

Reflection: Write down any insights or revelations that you have had as you reflect on the desire and the power of God to deliver and set people free. Pray and ask the Lord if there is an any area you need freedom in; any challenge or affliction that may have a spiritual element behind it. Meditate on what Jesus has done for you in ensuring you can be set free and speak out the Scriptures that declare His victory (some of which are included in this chapter).

_____
_____
_____
_____
_____
_____
_____
_____
_____
_____
_____
_____
_____

29

WHERE THE SPIRIT OF THE LORD IS

2 Corinthians 3:17 *Now the Lord is the Spirit, and where the Spirit of the Lord is, there is liberty.*

The ministry of the Holy Spirit brings the release, freedom and healing that Jesus' finished work at the Cross of Calvary accomplished. Our part is to open our hearts to Him and allow Him to do it. The more we yield to Him and allow Him to work in our lives and the more we bring things out into the open, the more we receive of His gentle, healing grace.

> **Ephesians 2:8-10** [8] *For by grace you have been saved through faith, and that not of yourselves; it is the gift of God,* [9] *not of works, lest anyone should boast.* [10] *For we are His workmanship, created in Christ Jesus for good works, which God prepared beforehand that we should walk in them.*

This truth is applicable, not only for that initial moment of salvation when we receive Jesus as Lord and Saviour, but to everything we receive from God. Colossians 2:6 says that as we received Christ Jesus, so we walk in Him. The same pattern is applicable to receiving all the promises of God, including healing spirit, soul and body.

So, we come to God, recognising that only He has what we need and receive His grace as a free gift, with no works of our own to add. We can't fix ourselves and we can't heal our own souls, but we can have breakthrough and complete healing by receiving God's miracle working power through the Holy Spirit and the Word of God.

> **Galatians 3:3** *Are you so foolish? Having begun in the Spirit, are you now being made perfect by the flesh?*

However, we have responses that we need to make to cooperate with what the Lord wants to bring into our lives. We start by repenting and laying down our works, sins and afflictions at the Cross, renouncing formerly held spiritual beliefs or affiliations that do not align with God's way, and then receiving, in exchange, Jesus' perfect righteousness and healing - as a free gift!

We then walk out our faith in Christ through being discipled in His Word and ways, with the Holy Spirit confirming and actualising in our lives that Word we have received. The good work that God begins in us, we are assured He will carry on to completion (Philippians 1:6) if we remain steadfast in the faith. We are His workmanship, and while we are required to align with Him in obedience and cooperate with what He wants to do in our lives, it is He who does the work.

So, as it is for receiving Christ initially, it is for receiving the healing of the soul and experiencing freedom from strongholds, demonic works and afflictions. God's work in us is miraculous and, while not suggesting that other additional avenues can't be sought for support, God's power far exceeds anything psychology, a self-help programme or any other design of man can accomplish. In Him, what is deemed to be impossible to heal according to man, or seen to be only able to be managed, can be healed in Christ. He still does the impossible!

> **Matthew 19:26** *But Jesus looked at them and said to them, "With men this is impossible, but with God all things are possible."*

So, over this and the next few chapters, let's look at some keys to receiving the healing of the soul and freedom.

The starting point is a turning to God, from our own way. Repentance means 'to turn' and we find, in life there are paths that we are taking or responses we are making that are leading to 'death' and we can't continue in them if we want to experience life. We need to turn and regain the path of life.

> **Deuteronomy 30:19** *I call heaven and earth as witnesses today against you, that I have set before you life and death, blessing and cursing; therefore choose life, that both you and your descendants may live....*

> **Proverbs 12:28** *In the way of righteousness is life, and in its pathway there is no death.*

> **2 Corinthians 3:17** *Now the Lord is the Spirit, and where the Spirit of the Lord is, there is liberty.*

Where the Spirit of God is there is freedom, life and healing, and where He is not, those graces are not evident.

In Genesis 16 there is a story about Hagar, the maid of Sarai (later to become Sarah). With Sarai struggling to have a child, Hagar was given to Abrahm (later to be called Abraham), to bear a child. When Hagar became pregnant, she developed an attitude about her mistress/ leader Sarai and despised her. Perhaps it was pride; perhaps competitiveness - it is not really articulated in Scripture. Then Sarai became harsh with her. So now, there's contention with authority and Hagar flees into the wilderness with offense, fear and strife dislocating her from God's place for her.

We run into issues of the soul when we react to circumstances, pain, people etc rather than a response to God and what He has done for us - and the way back is always a response to God. We can all be tempted to react to things that happen in families, workplaces, church, leadership, public scandals or any form of abuse. This can cause people to react in the common responses of fight (contention), flight (leave, reject or step back) or freeze (inaction and a decision to not trust again). The reaction can seem so right to us but actually leads us on the wrong path of 'death' rather than the path of 'life'.

> **Proverbs 14:12** *There is a way that seems right to a man, but its end is the way of death.*

God meets with Hagar in the wilderness.

> **Genesis 16:8** *And He said, "Hagar, Sarai's maid, where have you come from, and where are you going?" She said, "I am fleeing from the presence of my mistress Sarai."*

He calls her Sarai's maid, reminding her of the place He had for her and correcting her reaction of flight from it, that would lead her towards death and not life. There were dangers in the wilderness and if she survived, there would likely be a return to idolatry in Egypt where she was headed. More often than not, when people react to conflict, offense or mistreatment it leads to a path where there is trouble and a moving away from their relationship with God. God's intended blessing and promises are not experienced on that path.

God has a place and a positioning for each one of us and His grace covers His will in that. We are called to live under His grace, and hence, obedience to God's will for us. Often, people are experiencing stress and anxiety because they are living beyond that covering of grace, through ungodly choices or reactions, or also, very commonly in church life, people saying "yes" to more than God is actually asking them to do.

God's place of grace for you may look very different to the demands people can place on you and when we say "yes" to what is more than what the Lord is asking of us, then we find we have to accomplish the additional tasks 'in the flesh' making us vulnerable to stress, burnout and anxiety. Much activity can often be a strategy of the enemy to hinder us from being fruitful in what we are meant to be giving focus to.

God is under no obligation to bless that which He didn't ask you to do.

Conversely, there are many times where we feel we are called to do that which is way beyond our capacity, but if it is the Lord's calling and will, He will supply His supernatural power and ability to enable us in that place.

Ephesians 5:17 *Therefore do not be unwise, but understand what the will of the Lord is.*

We need to wait on the Lord and understand His will for us and what He is actually asking us to do. It feels like His presence and peace is on it, even if it doesn't always make sense to the natural mind. Conversely, being outside His will feels like angst, stress, anxiety, heightened emotions and an absence of His peace.

For Hagar, God calls her to return to the place that He had for her and it doesn't look perfect, requiring her to humble herself and submit in a situation she had run from.

She would now have to confront her issues and deal with them, rather than run or justify them by what had happened to her previously, however unfair they were.

Our 'issues' can be pictured like a tree. We can focus on the multitude of leaves and be overwhelmed by all that they are 'speaking' to us. We can try and fix the problems by pulling off the leaves, one by one, but they will very soon grow back. However, that tree has roots and we need to allow the Lord to reveal those roots to us. An axe to the root automatically takes all the leaves with it. Many of the issues that we can experience have only a few roots (or even one). Submitting to the Lord's ways, laying down the issues before Him and receiving His healing grace through the Holy Spirit and the Word of God, puts an axe to the root(s). It is miraculous what the Lord will do when we respond to Him.

Submission to God's will is not always comfortable but it is essential for the working of our good. There is no resistance to the devil and what he devises against us without a submission to God first (James 4:7). This is not to be interpreted that one must return to ungodly relationships or circumstances, but rather, to seek the place that God has for you, even though it may not always be appealing to the flesh. For Hagar, the return brings life and fruitfulness as a multitude of peoples are to come from the birth of Ishmael.

Genesis 16:9,10 [9] *The Angel of the Lord said to her, "Return to your mistress, and submit yourself under her hand."* [10] *Then the Angel of the Lord said to her, "I will multiply your* *descendants exceedingly, so that they shall not be counted for multitude."*

Encouragingly, in all of this, is the evidence that God saw her, cared for her and her son and that He had a great plan for both of their lives.

Romans 8:28 *And we know that all things work together for good to those who love God, to those who are the called according to His purpose.*

So, it is with us all - God sees you; He sees all that you have gone through and any pain that you have experienced; He deeply cares and His correction or direction is not ever out of harshness or insensitivity to you, but a knowledge of how to bring you into redemption, abundant life and purpose.

Genesis 16:13 *Then she called the name of the Lord who spoke to her, You-Are- the-God-Who-Sees; for she said, "Have I also here seen Him who sees me?".*

So, we start by turning to the Lord, not only at salvation but continually through life. We turn from death to life; from our reactions to responding to Him; from our will to His will being done. We submit to God, knowing that He is good and that He intends good for us, knowing that only He has everything that we need and, in so doing, we are positioned for His redemptive power.

So, now would be a good time to quieten yourself before the Lord. Calm your mind and become sensitive to your spirit within, where God speaks to you and directs you. Wait until you sense the presence of the Holy Spirit and then wait in that holy presence. He has wisdom and understanding to bring you; you will start to sense His direction and leading and in

THE LORD WHO HEALS YOU

His glorious presence you experience His peace. He will bring release and freedom from those things that have brought such angst and anxiety. Rest in Him.

Reading:

- Psalm 91
- Psalm 34
- Psalm 92:12,13
- Psalm 81;13,14

Thought for the day: God sees you and knows all your cares - and He has healing and redemption for you.

Reflection: Write down any insights or revelations that you have had as you reflect on reactions you may have had to people or circumstances. Have those reactions led to God and 'life' or away from Him? Prayerfully consider your life and assess if it is too cluttered; are things that are additional to God's will for you, that are being done 'in the flesh', causing stress or anxiety? Are there adjustments to be made in order that you may have peace in your soul?

30

TURNING FROM DARKNESS TO LIGHT

Acts 26:18 '*to open their eyes, in order to turn them from darkness to light, and from the power of Satan to God, that they may receive forgiveness of sins and an inheritance among those who are sanctified by faith in Me.*'

I n the last chapter, we started with turning from wrong reactions and submitting to God and His will over our own. Now, we will look at our next responses, being confession, repentance and renouncing of any things that are not in line with God's will for us. Repentance is not always a popular concept and yet, it is one of the most powerful gifts that we have been given. In repentance, we are given yet another clean slate, yet another opportunity to move forward and not be held back by the things that can hinder us, and to receive again, the precious free grace that God offers us.

James 5:13-16 [13] *Is anyone among you suffering? Let him pray. Is anyone cheerful? Let him sing psalms.* [14] *Is anyone*

> *among you sick? Let him call for the elders of the church, and let them pray over him, anointing him with oil in the name of the Lord.* ¹⁵ *And the prayer of faith will save the sick, and the Lord will raise him up. And if he has committed sins, he will be forgiven.* ¹⁶ <u>*Confess your trespasses to* one another, and pray for one another, that you may be healed</u>*.*

Healing for the spirit and soul requires confession, repentance and application of the blood of Jesus, that is, to apply by faith what He has already accomplished through His death and resurrection. As already mentioned, repentance means to 'turn', and there is often a great emphasis on just needing repentance, but, while it is so important, you can turn and change direction in life and still have ongoing challenges. It is Jesus' work of salvation that removes sin and its stain, signified by His blood in Scripture, not merely repentance alone.

Scripture calls for us to firstly confess our sins and, while we are at it, also bring out the afflictions, challenges and hurts. Confession brings the dark areas of our lives out into the light where they start to lose their power. Things fester in the darkness and isolation, but speaking them out to the Lord, and often also sharing them with trustworthy and confidential counsel or a friend, brings those things to a place where the light of Christ can shine on them - not to bring condemnation or shame but rather, healing.

> **1 John 1:6,7** ⁶ *If we say that we have fellowship with Him, and walk in darkness, we lie and do not practice the truth.* ⁷ *But if we walk in the light as He is in the light, we have fellowship with one another, and the blood of Jesus Christ His Son cleanses us from all sin.*

There is no healing when we walk in darkness or deny our sin. When we bring it into the light and choose to walk in the light, the blood of Jesus is there to cleanse and heal us.

Then we repent. Repentance is a change of heart or attitude that leads to a change of direction. In repentance we are choosing God's truth and God's way, and rejecting our own former way, so that we can now receive His healing and life.

> **John 14:6** *Jesus said to him, "I am the way, the truth, and the life. No one comes to the Father except through Me".*

There is power in identifying and laying issues down at the Cross; a 'drawing a line in the sand' moment. Close your eyes and look to Jesus at the Cross. That is Him taking all your sin but also sickness, pains, grief, sorrows and the curse (ref Deuteronomy 28:15-61 for the many effects of the Fall upon mankind). There may be sins that need to be repented of, but also burdens, anxieties, sicknesses, wrong reactions to a person or circumstances etc that you want to leave behind in that moment. In bringing all these things, it is not saying that they are your fault, or due to personal sin, but they are areas that are not part of God's plan for you and that you want to leave behind. Speak them out and see yourself laying them down at the Cross; see them removed from you and placed on Jesus and, in that moment, allow a transaction to take place where you consciously receive God's forgiveness and healing grace. Repentance closes the door on these issues and removes the enemy's right of access through them.

> **1 John 1:9** *If we confess our sins, he is faithful and just to forgive us our sins and to cleanse us from all unrighteousness.*

> **Proverbs 28:13** *He who covers his sins will not prosper, but whoever confesses and forsakes them will have mercy.*

Repentance, and forsaking or leaving behind the sin or issue, is our necessary step of response towards the Lord and healing, but there is also something else to add. That is the power of the blood of Jesus and the need for a transactional and transformative moment for it to have its effect. As believers, we can often repent and rush on, and it can become little more than a religious act that brings no healing or change. While we have already been forgiven through Jesus' death and resurrection, we also have to appropriate, or receive, and apply that magnificent work in order for it to be actualised in our lives. We need to slow it down, take a moment to allow a transaction, and thereby, a transformation to take place, as we acknowledge and receive what Jesus' blood has done for us. His blood not only brings the forgiveness of sin, but it removes the stain or impact of sin and cleanses the conscience (Hebrews 9:14;10;22).

> **Hebrews 4:15,16 NKJV** *For we do not have a High Priest who cannot sympathize with our weaknesses, but was in all points tempted as we are, yet without sin.* ¹⁶ *Let us therefore come boldly to the throne of grace, <u>that we may obtain mercy and find</u> <u>grace to help in time of need.</u>*

Then, there might be some things to 'renounce'. Renounce means to 'state you no longer believe in something; state you want to give up a right' (MacMillan Dictionary[13]). If you renounce a belief or a way of behaving, you decide and declare publicly that you no longer have that belief or will no longer behave in that way; 'to give up voluntarily' (Collins dictionary[14]).

So, we renounce lies we have previously believed; renounce former spiritual belief systems; renounce former unhealthy patterns of behaviour such as people pleasing and performance; renounce curses or vows that may have been made (e.g., "I will never be like..." or "I am never going to allow anyone to hurt me like that again"). We give up our rights to keep unforgiveness or bitterness in our hearts despite what might have happened to us; give up any right for revenge and trust God to now take care of us. We also need to renounce any coping mechanisms or internal structures that we erected to protect ourselves that, though understandable and perhaps needed at a time of trauma, later become something that limits or controls us.

As we renounce these things, we instead turn to God, His way of doing things, His truth and His presence. We put our trust in Him and seek Him to find healing and restoration.

The following stories occur before Jesus' death and resurrection, and as such, the women involved did not have access to our salvation in Christ and the blood of Jesus to heal and restore them. However, they do highlight some of the reactions we can have to pain and two responses to God, involving a change in direction, that can assist in bringing healing and restoration. They both demonstrate the contrast between our natural responses and the supernatural response to God that positions us for His power.

Firstly, there is Leah in Genesis chapters 29 and 30. The story of Jacob, Rachel and Leah has all the makings of a soap opera. It has romance, deception, betrayal, conflict - and a multitude of pain.

A brief background is that Jacob is in love with Rachel. Rachel is described as being beautiful in appearance and form, while her older sister Leah is described as having delicate or weak eyes, with no other compliments about her appearance. Jacob wishes to marry Rachel, and in that culture the groom would pay a bride-price of certain goods, in this case being seven years of labour for his uncle, and father of Rachel, Laban. Jacob works the seven years for Rachel and then, on his wedding night, in the absence of lights or electricity, the veiled bride is brought in. In the morning, he discovers that he has been tricked and the woman next to him is Leah, Rachel's older sister. After another week he is allowed to marry Rachel, but he has to work yet another seven years for her.

Poor Leah has her father offloading the daughter who wasn't seen as desirable, and then, her husband doesn't love her - in fact, in the passage below, my Bible's footnote says literally 'hated' for the word 'unloved'. She would have experienced great rejection, loneliness, grief and insecurity. However, God saw her, loved her, accepted her and had a great plan for her life.

The reaction to great rejection is often people pleasing or performance, in order to try and be loved or accepted. Leah's response is to try and please her husband by having babies.

> **Genesis 29:31-35** *31 When the Lord saw that Leah was unloved, He opened her womb; but Rachel was barren. 32 So Leah conceived and bore a son, and she called his name Reuben; for she said, "The Lord has surely looked on my affliction. Now therefore, my husband will love me." 33 Then she conceived again and bore a son, and said, "Because the Lord has heard that I am unloved, He has therefore given me this son also." And she called his name Simeon. 34 She conceived again and bore a son, and said, "Now this time my husband will become attached to me, because I have borne him three sons." Therefore his name was called Levi. 35 And she conceived again and bore a son, and said, "Now I will praise the Lord." Therefore she called his name Judah. Then she stopped bearing.*

Reuben means 'See a son'; Simeon means 'heard'; Levi 'attached' and then comes Judah meaning 'praise'. Somewhere in between Levi and Judah,

Leah has shifted from people pleasing and performance to praise, with a focus on and a response to the Lord.

We have to come to a place of accepting by faith, and being rooted and grounded in, the unconditional love of God that we then operate from and don't try to earn. Only God has what we need. God loves us with an everlasting love; we are accepted in the Beloved (Ephesians 1:6) and we are holy and without blame before Him i.e., 'approved' (Ephesians 1:5) in Christ, before we have done anything.

God's provision for us is only received as a free gift, and whatever it may be for, it is every bit as miraculous as salvation, with no works or performance contributed by us. Any works are to follow out of that.

> **Isaiah 54:1** *"Sing, O barren, you who have not borne! Break forth into singing, and cry aloud, you who have not laboured with child! For more are the children of the desolate than the children of the married woman," says the Lord.*

God calls those who are barren, in this case the nation of Israel in exile, to sing and praise Him, before the breakthrough. This is generally not what one feels like doing when experiencing any form of barrenness or pain. There may be a physical barrenness, or as with Leah, one of the soul. To praise in the face of barrenness would be cruel if it were not for the fact that this is a key to receiving God's life and healing grace. If we will worship Him in the midst of our barrenness in any area, then He will turn that situation around to the place where we will be more blessed in that area than those who had not faced the same challenges (with children being the metaphor of blessing for that culture). This is the nature of God's Redemption.

Praise Him for what you don't have; praise Him in the pain; praise Him because He is faithful and true; praise Him because He is still good and He is worthy of praise despite what you are going through. Praise and don't complain! This leads to His redemptive power being released, bringing life, healing and fruitfulness.

The outcome for Leah was that Jesus was to come through the line of Judah and Leah was even more fruitful than Rachel. This came about as she turned and responded to God instead of reacting to the pain that people had brought.

Then there was Rachel, loved, beautiful and sought after, but she was physically barren, which cruelly in that culture was a source of shame. She became angry and jealous of her sister's fruitfulness, revealing anxiety, doubts of self-worth, blaming her husband and becoming competitive with her sister. This starts a great contention and strife in the family, as the sisters try and produce children for themselves by giving their maids as wives to Jacob.

> **James 3:16** *'For where envy and self seeking exist, confusion and every evil thing are there'.*

So, we can read into the story that there is a lot of unhealthy dynamics going on in the family, strife, division, hurt and according to the Holy Spirit, through James, confusion and every evil thing.

> **2 Peter 1:4** *..by which have been given to us exceedingly great and precious promises, that through these you may be partakers of the divine nature, having escaped the corruption that is in the world through lust.*

2 Peter 1:4 speaks of how we receive God's grace freely through His promises, and in so doing, escape the corruption of the world that comes as desires are sought to be met in other ways. Somewhere in the journey, Rachel presumably shifted from striving to get her desires fulfilled her way

and she called upon the Lord, for the following verse says that He listened to her.

> **Genesis 30:22-24** [22] *Then God remembered Rachel, and God listened to her and opened her womb.* [23] *And she conceived and bore a son, and said, "God has taken away my reproach."* [24] *So she called his name Joseph, and said, "The Lord shall add to me another son."*

Rachel turned to the Lord in her pain and instead of striving and wrestling she received life, release from her felt shame and the gaining of purpose. Joseph was instrumental in the salvation of Jacob's family and generations. She also received fresh vision and prophetic insight from the Lord, Joseph meaning 'He will add'. She saw that there would be another son, with Benjamin to follow.

> **Psalm 40:1-3** *I waited patiently for the Lord; and He inclined to me, and heard my cry.* [2] *He also brought me up out of a horrible pit, out of the miry clay, and set my feet upon a rock, and established my steps.* [3] *He has put a new song in my mouth— Praise to our God; Many will see it and fear, and will trust in the Lord.*

> **Psalm 30:2** *O Lord my God, I cried out to You, and You healed me.*

> **Isaiah 54:11-13** *"O you afflicted one, tossed with tempest, and not comforted, Behold, I will lay your stones with colourful gems, and lay your foundations with sapphires.* [12] *I will make your pinnacles of rubies, your gates of crystal, and all your*

walls of precious stones.¹³ *All your children shall be taught by the Lord, and great shall be the peace of your children.*

Psalm 37:3, 4 is a great passage of Scripture that has five keys to direct our hearts and keep us in a good place when in the midst of great challenges or pain.

Psalm 37:3,4 *Trust in the Lord, and do good; Dwell in the land, and feed on His faithfulness.* ⁴ *Delight yourself also in the Lord, and He shall give you the desires of your heart.*

Place your trust in the Lord and actively pursue doing good instead of reacting to the circumstance. 'Dwell in the land' means that you are to remain in God, in church and in the place that He has for you and do not allow your emotional reactions to move you away. Feed on God's promises and faithfulness and not on thoughts of bitterness or pain. Hebrews 12:15 tells us that the root of bitterness causes trouble and defiles many, not just the person who feeds on it. Feed your soul good food and keep it in a healthy place.

Then 'delight yourself' in the Lord - not as a method or a means to get what you want, but because He is worthy and prayer, worship and feeding on His Word is the place of devotion that we are all called to. As James 5:13 says, '*Is anyone among you suffering? Let him pray*'. As Isaiah says, "*"Sing, O barren, you who have not borne!"*". Then in John 15:7 Jesus tells us, *"If you abide in Me and My words abide in you, you will ask what you desire and it shall be done for you".*

This keeps our soul in a healthy place and the outcome is that, from a sincere, heartfelt response to the Lord, He gives you the desires of your heart.

So, we come with praise and prayer, laying down all our pain, sins, wrong reactions and coping mechanisms and intentionally receive in faith what He has for us. Don't rush these moments but wait on God; receive His precious promises and grace; allow Him to speak fresh insight and vision into your heart; and let a new song come out of you in praise to Him. There is great healing for the soul and often, as a result, for the physical body in these moments of encounter with the Lord.

Reading:

- Psalm 19
- Psalm 37
- Isaiah 54:4,5

Thought for the day: Delight yourself also in the Lord, and He shall give you the desires of your heart (Psalm 37:4).

Reflection: Close your eyes and look to Jesus. You may have sins that need to be repented of, but also burdens, anxieties, sicknesses, wrong reactions to a person or circumstances etc that you want to leave behind in this moment. Speak them out and see yourself laying them down at the Cross; see them removed from you and placed on Jesus and, in this moment, allow a transaction to take place where you consciously receive God's forgiveness and healing grace.

Write down anything that you feel God is showing you, giving you revelation or vision of, or any promises that He speaks into your heart.

_____
_____
_____
_____
_____
_____
_____
_____
_____
_____
_____
_____
_____
_____
_____

31

FORGIVEN TO FORGIVE

Ephesians 4:32: *And be kind to one another, tenderhearted, forgiving one another, even as God in Christ forgave you.*

Forgiveness is one of the most powerful things to bring healing to a soul, and often then to the body, and to remove access for any demonic entities. Jesus highlights it for special emphasis in the Lord's prayer in Matthew 6:14,15 and the prayer of faith in Mark 11:22-26 as a condition to answered prayer. So, we need to know how to forgive and it is my hope that the following teaching will make this a bit easier for you.

However, firstly we need to see the impact that unforgiveness has upon us. In Matthew 18:23-35 Jesus shares, in context with Peter questioning Him about forgiveness, the parable of the unforgiving servant. It presents a man, with an enormous, unpayable debt who pleads for mercy with his king and creditor. Mercy is shown to him and the debt, which would have destroyed him and his family, selling them all into slavery, is forgiven. However, to the outrage of those around him, he then goes and hypocritically accuses another of owing a debt, of a much smaller amount, and has him thrown into prison until he can pay it back.

The analogy is that we all, through sin, had a debt to God that we could never repay. All the good works that we could potentially do could not even scratch the surface of that debt. It was impossible and the sentence to us was death and an eternal separation from God and all of His goodness. Jesus' parable in Matthew:23-35 indicates that the impact of this affects our family and those dependent upon us.

However, God in His super abundant mercy, sent Jesus to take on our sin and associated punishment, thus releasing from debt those who believe in Him, and He even went far beyond forgiveness to give us the free gift of Jesus' righteousness and all of His great and precious promises.

> **Ephesians 2:4-7** [4] *But God, who is rich in mercy, because of His great love with which He loved us,* [5] *even when we were dead in trespasses, made us alive together with Christ (by grace you have been saved),* [6] *and raised us up together, and made us sit together in the heavenly places in Christ Jesus,* [7] *that in the ages to come He might show the exceeding riches of His grace in His kindness toward us in Christ Jesus.*

There is nothing that we could have done to deserve or earn this gift of salvation. However, God does require of us, in light of His generous mercy toward us, that we will show mercy toward our fellow mankind in their weaknesses. So, even the offenses that seem huge to us, are required to be forgiven and this then brings us to our challenge and how we will meet it.

The outcome in the parable for the one who wouldn't forgive was that he was delivered to torment - and torment of the soul is what unforgiveness brings.

> **Matthew 18:32-35** ³² *Then his master, after he had called him, said to him, 'You wicked servant! I forgave you all that debt because you begged me.* ³³ *Should you not also have had compassion on your fellow servant, just as I had pity on you?'* ³⁴ *And his master was angry, and delivered him to the torturers until he should pay all that was due to him.* ³⁵ *"So My heavenly Father also will do to you if each of you, from his heart, does not forgive his brother his trespasses."*

I have heard unforgiveness described as leasing the real estate of your mind to the one who hurt you, for them to occupy. It is also portrayed as being an invisible cord between you and the person who hurt you through which the devil continually feeds poison and traumatic memories into you. It has also been described as drinking poison and waiting for the other person to die – while in fact it kills you. Another would be, that it is like being trapped in a jail cell serving the sentence for someone else's crime.

In other words, the first thing we need to understand is that there is no benefit to us, in any way, in holding onto unforgiveness and in fact, it is the most destructive of all emotions, bringing us into torment.

So, let's look at how we can deal with this challenge that we will all face in life. It is not helpful to legalistically say to someone who has been through extreme trauma "Well, you just have to forgive", especially when it comes from one who doesn't understand their pain. However, forgiveness is critical and by applying the grace of the Holy Spirit to what we struggle with, we will find that what is impossible for us is possible to God in us.

> **Mark 11:25,26** *"And whenever you stand praying, if you have anything against anyone, forgive him, that your Father in heaven may also forgive you your trespasses. But if you do*

not forgive, neither will your Father in heaven forgive your trespasses."

We might read this and feel "I cannot do this!" Many people have had terrible things happen to them and feel that God is asking something of them that is impossible. It is good to remember that God asks us to be willing and obedient (Isaiah 1:19); not to be able. We were never meant to live God's way in our own strength. If we will be willing and obedient, He will provide the ability to do what He asks, through the power of His Holy Spirit.

So, the first step is to be willing. Would you be willing to let go of the offense and place it in the hands of God, potentially never seeing it avenged? This challenges our sense of needing justice but the justice of God saw our punishment placed on Jesus, ours and the offender's. God will have the say whether they are judged or released. Would you be willing to even see them released in spite of what they did – just as you would like to be released and blessed in spite of things you may have done? Challenging questions but it is essential that we decide to be willing.

Then we need to take a step of obedience. Note that this is a step and not the whole journey. This is a step of obedience and not the ability to forgive. The step is to pray and choose to speak out forgiveness to that person, naming them and what they did. See yourself release them into God's hands and entrust yourself, and them, to the Lord. Then you bless them. Why? That is because Jesus said to, and His ways always work. It may not seem fair or make sense to us at times, but when we do things His way, it not only brings healing and peace, but it also releases the offending person into the hand of God for Him to deal with, or redeem, them. He doesn't command us to do things to make it difficult for us. He does it because it works for our good. So, we take the step of obedience.

> **Matthew 5:44-45** [44] *But I say to you, love your enemies, bless those who curse you, do good to those who hate you, and pray for those who spitefully use you and persecute you,* [45] *that you may be sons of your Father in heaven; for He makes His sun rise on the evil and on the good, and sends rain on the just and on the unjust.*

Now having stepped out and prayed for the release of forgiveness, we need some ability to do what seems impossible to us. What God requires of us is not possible in our own strength - otherwise we could have just lived perfectly and not needed a Saviour. We need God's grace to forgive and He will readily supply it for the asking.

> **James 4:6 AMPC**[8] *But He gives us more and more grace (power of the Holy Spirit, to meet this evil tendency and all others fully). That is why He says, God sets Himself against the proud and haughty, but gives grace (continually) to the lowly (those who are humble enough to receive it).*

The grace of God is the only thing that can overcome our evil tendencies, weaknesses and inability to live God's way. Be humble and admit to God that you need His help and He will give you His power to overcome and to do what He asks. If you feel like you have zero ability to forgive the seemingly unforgiveable, it's okay, but ask God for more grace which is His power to meet your need. He will fill you with His love and the forgiveness that you need, as well as healing you from what you have suffered.

It is by the power of the Holy Spirit and not our own ability or 'flesh' nature that we can overcome what is insurmountable in our sight. We can't wait until we feel like it or have the feelings of forgiveness before we act and release it. That may be never and our ability never enough. By the power of the Holy Spirit and the receiving of God's love, unforgiveness is overcome and freedom is obtained.

> **Romans 8:13** *For if you live according to the flesh you will die; but if by the Spirit you put to death the deeds of the body, you will live.*

So, would you be willing to let that issue go? Would you take a step of obedience today with no pressure on yourself to perform but an utter reliance on God's free gift of grace?

That prayer might look like "God I am willing to forgive this person and now as an act of obedience I choose to forgive them, but I need Your help to do this. I choose to forgive; I release them to You and I lay down my need for justice or retribution. I ask that You bless them and Lord I ask that You release me and heal me from what occurred."

There are also two others who we often neglect to release forgiveness toward - God and ourselves. Now God is perfect and requires no forgiveness for Himself.

However, often people have blamed Him for events that have occurred, disappointments, unanswered prayers and healings that didn't happen.

We cannot go on holding the Lord to account for what we have perceived He failed to do. God has the advantage of seeing the whole picture and we see in part, and that dimly. So, we need to always be looking to His character - that no matter what has happened He is good, He is merciful, He is faithful and true and He is the Healer. Whatever unmet expectations we have need to be forgiven, for the Lord will not be debtor to us. You may not understand what happened, or didn't happen, but choose to trust God again, 'forgive' Him and give Him His due honour, in the midst of the mystery.

Then, we have ourselves. We are the hardest person for us to forgive. We can hold so much against ourselves, the mistakes we have made, the hurts we ourselves have caused and the missed opportunities. Where there has been offense caused by us, there may need to be steps taken to make things right with the offended person, but then having done that, we need to actually receive God's forgiveness and also, forgive ourselves.

Holding onto guilt is rejecting the work of the Cross and it will hinder us receiving God's healing grace and His blessing. Ruminating on past failures releases stress chemicals in the brain and body that make one vulnerable to sickness and mental and emotional health issues. God's design for the healthy functioning of our bodies didn't include carrying the heavy burdens of guilt and condemnation.

So, make amends but also honour the work of the Cross and receive grace for yourself. It may help to discuss this with trusted counsel and to confess your sins, allow them to pray God's forgiveness over you and then, receive that forgiveness and the assurance of righteousness in Christ alone.

> **James 5:16** *Confess your trespasses to one another, and pray for one another, that you may be healed. The effective, fervent prayer of a righteous man avails much.*

Reading:

- Matthew 18:21-35
- Romans 8

Thought for the day: The one who didn't forgive in Jesus' parable in Matthew 18 remained in prison - along with the one he wouldn't forgive. Unforgiveness kept them all bound and tormented. Forgiveness opens the prison doors and is the crucial step into freedom.

Reflection: Do you have someone you need to forgive? Or many? Would you be willing to release them? Are you prepared to take a step of obedience and pray for their forgiveness, trusting God in the process and receiving His grace to enable you?

_____
_____
_____

Have you been holding anything against God? Do you need to repent and release Him from judgements you have made?

_____
_____
_____

Are you experiencing guilt or condemnation? Do you need to receive God's forgiveness, honouring the work of the Cross and forgive yourself?

_____
_____
_____

Romans 8:1 *There is therefore now no condemnation to those who are in Christ Jesus, who do not walk according to the flesh, but according to the Spirit.*

32

SPIRITUAL WARFARE

James 4:7 *Therefore submit to God. Resist the devil and he will flee from you.*

In the last four chapters we have seen that in receiving healing of the soul and freedom from strongholds, we need to submit to God; we need to confess and repent from sin and renounce formerly held spiritual beliefs or affiliations that do not align with God's way; we need to forgive those who have hurt us and now, we need to implement some 'spiritual warfare' to push back the forces of darkness that come against us.

Matthew 11:12 *And from the days of John the Baptist until now the kingdom of heaven suffers violence, and the violent take it by force.*

There is a demonic opposition to what God has provided for us in Christ and we need to push back against the pushback.

SPIRITUAL WARFARE

> **Ephesians 6:10-12** *¹⁰ Finally, my brethren, be strong in the Lord and in the power of His might. ¹¹ Put on the whole armour of God, that you may be able to stand against the wiles of the devil. ¹² For we do not wrestle against flesh and blood, but against principalities, against powers, against the rulers of the darkness of this age, against spiritual hosts of wickedness in the heavenly places.*

Our battle is never with people even though the spiritual warfare is often delivered through them. Jesus has already contested and defeated the powers of darkness but, while we and they remain on this Earth, we do need to enforce that defeat and take a stand against the opposition they seek to bring. So, note we are not fighting them but rather, are enforcing their defeat and taking a stand, in Jesus' delegated authority and power, against their advance.

> **Ephesians 6:13-18** *¹³ Therefore take up the whole armour of God, that you may be able to withstand in the evil day, and having done all, to stand. ¹⁴ Stand therefore, having girded your waist with truth, having put on the breastplate of righteousness, ¹⁵ and having shod your feet with the preparation of the gospel of peace; ¹⁶ above all, taking the shield of faith with which you will be able to quench all the fiery darts of the wicked one. ¹⁷ And take the helmet of salvation, and the sword of the Spirit, which is the word of God; ¹⁸ praying always with all prayer and supplication in the Spirit, being watchful to this end with all perseverance and supplication for all the saints—…*

These are not just things we 'put on' by words in our in prayer time, as many seem to think but these are things we must implement and do. To be missing any part of these disciplines is to be exposing yourself to the enemy and spiritual attack. They are a lifestyle and not just things that you do when a trial comes.

The armour of God is both protective and offensive. Firstly, we have truth. Truth is a Person, Jesus Himself, and the Word of God is Truth. Also, the Holy Spirit is called the Spirit of Truth. The devil opposes truth and aims to bring his lies and deception, but the receiving of and firmly holding onto truth protects us against this attack.

Then the receiving of Jesus' righteousness, through faith in Him, guards your heart. Holding onto the truth that you are righteous in Christ alone, and not in any performance of self, will protect you from the condemnation the enemy seeks to bring, and from the temptation into a works or performance mentality that, in turn, would bring you into disobedience and a powerless Christian life.

The kingdom of God is righteousness, peace and joy in the Holy Spirit and holding onto these three gifts of God is essential to being positioned for God's kingdom power and to take a stand against the enemy. So, intentionally walking in peace and holding onto peace and joy in challenges, taking a stand against fear and anxiety, protects the soul from the access that the enemy seeks in such times.

We are then advised to 'take the shield of faith <u>with which you will be able</u> to quench all the fiery darts' and attacks of the wicked one. The attack is to steal what God has for you and the stand of faith in the promises of God not only resists the attack, but accesses God's power to bring those same promises to pass.

Then, the 'helmet of salvation', the renewing of the mind to the Word of God, protects against the doubts, discouragement, deception and depression that the enemy seeks to bring.

Then there are the offensive elements of the armour - the Word of God and all kinds of prayer. The Word brings faith, perspective, the power to obey, power to drive back the devil, power to believe God and power to see the will of God released in your life. Prayer brings the presence and power of God and the implementation of the other aspects of the 'armour'.

We need knowledge of the Scriptures, of what Jesus has provided for us, our authority in Him and over the powers of darkness. Then, we need to implement that authority and power.

> **Luke 10:19** *Behold, I give you the authority to trample on serpents and scorpions, and over all the power of the enemy, and nothing shall by any means hurt you.*

We use the authority we have been given by God, through Jesus' name and the Word of God, to command the devil to leave, and for people, or ourselves, to be set free.

Be careful to not give too much attention to any demonic spirit, as many have been tempted to do, researching them and giving them names. This can be a ploy of the devil to get attention onto himself. Keep your eyes on Jesus, submit to God and from that position and focus, tell the devil to go, and he must flee. The power comes as your eyes are on Jesus and not on the enemy and what he is up to.

If you are doing the praying for another, don't make it 'weird'. Many people have felt traumatised through 'deliverance prayer' poorly ministered. The power of God is not ministered through being loud, through performance or weird actions. The flesh has nothing of value to add to the power of God.

> **John 6:63** *It is the Spirit who gives life; the flesh profits nothing. The words that I speak to you are spirit, and they are life.*

For a person who knows their authority in Christ and who carries His anointing, this prayer can be, and should be, very gentle and healing, yet authoritative and powerful. Pray according to Jesus' finished work of the Cross, in Jesus' Name and pray the Word of God that carries His power. Don't rely solely on visions, even though the Holy Spirit does give beautiful visions of insight and hope in these moments. Don't use paraphrase versions of Scripture for this is a moment where power is needed, and a literal version of Scripture, spoken in faith and boldness, will deliver it.

When Jesus was tempted in the wilderness by the devil (Matthew 4:1-11), all He did was say "It is written" and quoted Scripture and the devil was overcome (although even Jesus had to do it three times before the devil would leave). The Word of God has the power of God to overcome all demonic powers. It should be noted that this power and authority In Christ operates on the foundation of a life that has first submitted to God.

We need to make sure that we are not leaving the 'house' empty but filling ourselves with the Word of God and the Spirit of God. If the enemy were to return for another attempt, he will find the 'house' filled, with no room for him.

> **Luke 11:24-26** [24] *"When an unclean spirit goes out of a man, he goes through dry places, seeking rest; and finding none, he says, 'I will return to my house from which I came.'* [25] *And when he comes, he finds it swept and put in order.* [26] *Then he goes and takes with him seven other spirits more wicked than himself, and they enter and dwell there; and the last state of that man is worse than the first."*

Galatians 5:1 NIV[2] *It is for freedom that Christ has set us free. Stand firm, then, and do not let yourselves be burdened again by a yoke of slavery.*

We need to replace lies that have taken root in our thinking with God's truth to remain free. When truth comes in, light and power come to bring change. Truth is a Person - Jesus, and the Holy Spirit is the Spirit of Truth. Ongoing struggles are usually where a person's heart hasn't first been brought into alignment with God's truth. While many need a mature believer to exercise their authority in Christ to see them <u>set</u> free, it's really truth that <u>makes</u> you free.

John 8:31;32 *Then Jesus said to those Jews who believed Him, "If you abide in My word, you are My disciples indeed. [32] And you shall know the truth, and the truth shall make you free."*

Reading:

- James 4:7,8
- 1 Peter 5:6-11
- Matthew 4:1-11
- Psalm 147:13,14

Thought for the day: And you shall know the truth, and the truth shall make you free." (John 8:32)

Reflection: Reflect on whether your thoughts about yourself and your circumstances align with God's truth.

_____
_____
_____
_____
_____
_____
_____
_____
_____
_____
_____
_____
_____

Write down three Scriptures that you will meditate on to renew your mind in an area that you have any struggle with. Some examples are below.

- **Replace not feeling loved with 1 John 4:16** *And we have known and believed the love that God has for us. God is love, and he who abides in love abides in God, and God in him.*

- Replace not feeling accepted with Ephesians 1:6 - *to the praise of the glory of His grace, by which He made us accepted in the Beloved.*
- Replace any feeling of shame with Isaiah 54:4 NLT[5] *Fear not; you will no longer live in shame. Don't be afraid; there is no more disgrace for you. You will no longer remember the shame of your youth and the sorrows of widowhood.*
- Replace any self-pity with Romans 8:37 *Yet in all these things we are more than conquerors through Him who loved us.*
- Replace any feeling of 'not good enough' with Ephesians 1:4 *just as He chose us in Him before the foundation of the world, that we should be holy and without blame before Him in love…*
- Replace guilt or not feeling 'right' before God with 2 Corinthians 5:21 *For He made Him who knew no sin to be sin for us, that we might become the righteousness of God in Him.*

Scripture 1:

Scripture 2:

Scripture 3:

33
HE RESTORES MY SOUL

Psalm 23: 3 *He restores my soul....*

Matthew 10:1 *And when He had called His twelve disciples to Him, He gave them power over unclean spirits, to cast them out, and to heal all kinds of sickness and all kinds of disease.*

This passage and Matthew 4:23 both separate the healing of sickness and the healing of disease. In our modern language, we would use these words interchangeably but a no longer used translation of the word disease is 'dis- (lack of) ease (peace)'. Long before modern psychology and psychiatry grouped and named the conditions of the soul (the mind, will and emotions), Jesus was noted to heal such conditions, described in the gospels as disease or having a lack of peace.

Jesus made provision for such healing, again through the work of His Cross, bearing all sin and affliction on our behalf, so that divine healing for the soul can be received, as much as for the body and the spirit. There is nothing impossible for Him and while it is good to be under professional care, the Word of God and the Holy Spirit can, and do, bring such healing as to be deemed impossible or incurable by medical science or any alternative practice.

> **Isaiah 53:5 NIV**[2] *But He was pierced for our transgressions, He was crushed for our iniquities; <u>the punishment that brought us peace was on him, and by his wounds we are healed</u>.*

> **John 14:27** *Peace I leave with you, My peace I give to you; not as the world gives do I give to you. Let not your heart be troubled neither let it be afraid.*

As there is supernatural healing power to miraculously heal the body, there is a supernatural peace from God that heals and restores the soul. There is nothing superficial about this peace, so that one would just cope in life, but it is a peace that reaches to the very depths of the soul, its most intimate places, its darkest places and memories and it brings a deep and lasting healing and restoration.

The Lord brings healing of the soul through the ministry of the Holy Spirit, the receiving of God's supernatural peace, and this is importantly combined with the receiving and application of His Word. The receiving and application of the Word of God will be looked at in the next chapter.

> **John 16:14** *He will glorify Me, for He will take of what is Mine and declare it to you.*

The Holy Spirit, as God on Earth, takes what is of Jesus and what Jesus has done, and He declares it to us, by bringing it into our experience. Again, the Holy Spirit moves on the Word of God, Jesus Himself and the Scriptures. The Holy Spirit takes the healing grace and peace that Jesus has already provided and He makes it tangible in our lives so that we experience it.

The Holy Spirit is pictured as a river of water of life in Ezekiel 47:1-12 and Revelation 22:1-2 with Him giving life wherever He flows, one outcome of which is healing.

> **Ezekiel 47:12** *Along the bank of the river, on this side and that, will grow all kinds of trees used for food; their leaves will not wither, and their fruit will not fail. They will bear fruit every month, because their water flows from the sanctuary. Their fruit will be for food, and their leaves for medicine.*
>
> **Rev 22:1,2** *And he showed me a pure river of water of life, clear as crystal, proceeding from the throne of God and of the Lamb.* ² *In the middle of its street, and on either side of the river, was the tree of life, which bore twelve fruits, each tree yielding its fruit every month. The leaves of the tree were for the healing of the nations.*

As we open up to Him, His life fills us and removes the darkness of sickness, pain, trauma, depression, grief and mental or emotional afflictions.

> **Romans 8:11** *But if the Spirit of Him Who raised Jesus from the dead dwells in you, He Who raised Christ from the dead will also give life to your mortal bodies through His Spirit Who dwells in you.*

The presence of God comes through seeking Him in prayer, praise and worship, meditating on the Scriptures and receiving anointed prayer through another believer. Many can solely rely on the receiving of prayer from others, and while this is powerful, we also need to be seeking the Lord for ourselves. Anointed ministry does bring healing, God's presence and His peace but the complete healing of the soul requires personal encounters with God where a transaction takes place, removing what afflicts us and replacing it with the abundant life and peace that He has for us.

Praise and worship are two of the most powerful spiritual weapons that you have. Praise and worship are more than singing a few songs or saying some uplifting words about God. They invite and attract the very presence of God Himself, and when the presence of God comes on the scene, your enemies, whatever they may be, affliction or spiritual opposition, are driven back.

> **Psalm 9:1-3** *¹I will praise You, O LORD, with my whole heart; I will tell of all Your marvelous works. ² I will be glad and rejoice in You; I will sing praise to Your name, O Most High. ³ When my enemies turn back, they shall fall and perish at Your presence.*

> **Psalm 100:4** *Enter into His gates with thanksgiving, and into His courts with praise. Be thankful to Him, and bless His name.*

We enter into God's presence with thanksgiving and praise.

> **Psalm 22:3** *But You are holy, Enthroned in the praises of Israel.*

God actually inhabits, or dwells, in praise. With His presence, comes all that He is. He is our Healer, Jehovah Rapha; He is our peace, Jehovah Shalom; He is the Lord Who is there, Jehovah Shammah. In His presence there is joy and peace that soaks into us as we praise and worship.

THE LORD WHO HEALS YOU

Psalm 16:11 *You will show me the path of life; In Your presence is fullness of joy; At Your right hand are pleasures forevermore.*

God is love and so you encounter overwhelming love when in His presence. His perfect love casts out fear and anxiety.

1 John 4:18 *There is no fear in love; but perfect love casts out fear, because fear involves torment. But he who fears has not been made perfect in love.*

Psalm 94:19 *In the multitude of my anxieties within me, Your comforts delight my soul.*

The ministry of the Holy Spirit through Jesus firstly, and then continued through the church, brings healing to the broken-hearted, comfort and freedom from things that have held one bound.

Isaiah 61:1-4 *[1] "The Spirit of the Lord God is upon Me, because the Lord has anointed Me to preach good tidings to the poor; He has sent Me to heal the brokenhearted, to proclaim liberty to the captives, and the opening of the prison to those who are bound; [2] to proclaim the acceptable year of the Lord, and the day of vengeance of our God; to comfort all who mourn,[3] to console those who mourn in Zion, to give them beauty for ashes, the oil of joy for mourning, the garment of praise for the spirit of heaviness; that they may be called trees of righteousness, the planting of the Lord, that He may be glorified." [4] And they shall rebuild the old ruins, they shall raise up the former desolations, and they shall repair the ruined cities, the desolations of many generations."*

Wrap or cover yourself in praise and it will repel the heavy spirit. As you praise, the weariness starts to lift off you and you receive strength from God. Depression (ashes) and the spirit of heaviness (discouragement) will supernaturally start to lift.

In His presence, a divine exchange takes place, bringing healing where there was pain and trauma, joy where there was sadness or grief, beauty of soul in place of depression. In His presence He plants what is of Him in our lives; He rebuilds our lives from what had been ruined, even that which has been present for generations.

Isaiah also speaks elsewhere of the anointing oil, that symbolizes the presence of the Holy Spirit, that will break the heavy and restrictive yoke of bondage, those things that have held you bound and that you struggle to deal with.

> **Isaiah 10:27** *It shall come to pass in that day that his burden will be taken away from your shoulder, and his yoke from your neck, and the yoke will be destroyed because of the anointing oil.*

> **Matthew 11:28-30 AMPC**[8] *[28] Come to Me, all you who labour and are heavy- laden and overburdened, and I will cause you to rest. [I will ease and relieve and refresh your souls.] [29] Take My yoke upon you and learn of Me, for I am gentle (meek) and humble (lowly) in heart, and you will find rest (relief and ease and refreshment and recreation and blessed quiet) for your souls. [30] For My yoke is wholesome (useful, good—not harsh, hard, sharp, or pressing, but comfortable, gracious, and pleasant), and My burden is light and easy to be borne.*

THE LORD WHO HEALS YOU

A yoke is a wooden device placed across two animals so that they will walk in step with each other and pull in the same direction. So, if we are yoked to the things of this world or past trauma, pain, bitterness etc - and such yokes are heavy - then we will be pulled in the direction of these things and be limited from stepping into the healing, peace and freedom that God has for us.

We are to take off any heavy yokes that we might have carried before (for example, bitterness, unforgiveness, pain, performance, people pleasing, an identity moulded by this world and not an identity in Christ, demands placed upon self or by others, anxiety, stress etc.), and be yoked to Jesus. His yoke is light, an easy fit and so much less demanding. He is easily pleased. He then leads us into His rest and relieves and refreshes our souls. He invites us to learn from Him, to take on His attitudes and ways. Jesus lived in perfection of thought, attitude, action, health, abundant soul life and perfect responses in all kinds of challenges, and so, He is the perfect One to learn from.

Come to God in praise, worship and prayer. Consciously lay down those heavy burdens and give them to the Lord. You may have to do this many times before you feel the release, but can I encourage you to persist. Then rest in His presence and consciously receive His peace. It is the Holy Spirit who dwells within the believer and who reveals Jesus to us. Listen to the 'still, small voice of the Holy Spirit' as He declares Jesus to you, brings revelation on Scriptures meditated on, and speaks hope into your soul.

So, He says "Come to Me...."

Reading:

- John 14:15- 21; 25-28
- John 16:5-15
- John 16:33
- Psalm 55:18
- Galatians 5:22,23
- Colossians 3:15,16
- Psalm 147:3
- Psalm 62:1; 5-8
- Psalm 46

Thought for the day: The Lord restores your soul (ref Psalm 23). Let His peace rule in your heart (ref Colossians 3:15).

Reflection: Write down any insights or revelations that you have had as you reflect on the gift of God, received through the Holy Spirit, of His peace.

Take some time to slow down and sit in His presence. Can you sense His peace? If there is still a lot of clutter in your mind and emotions you may need to pray for a while, put on worship music and praise until you feel your mind and emotions settle enough to be able to focus. Sometimes you need to speak, in the authority that you have in Jesus' name, and tell the devil, distractions and hindering thoughts to go.

Keep pushing through until you enter into God's presence and peace. Don't let your mind race or even pray for a lot of things at that point, but sit, rest and receive His peace. It will heal your soul.

Now can you sense His peace?

Do you feel any impressions in your spirit from the Holy Spirit? If so, write them down and later pray over them. There also may be things He prompts you to act on and so write them down and afterwards commit to act on them. Ensure that these impressions are consistent with the Scriptures and if you are not sure, ask a trusted church elder for counsel.

34

THE IMPLANTED WORD WHICH IS ABLE TO SAVE YOUR SOUL

James 1:21 ...... *and receive with meekness the implanted word, which is able to save your souls.*

There appears to be a great increase in suffering from anxiety, depression and other soul issues and many seek prayer for healing from such. From much observation and ministry, and personal experience, healing - from anxiety, depression, PTSD, effects of abuse in any form and trauma, or any other affliction of the soul - comes not only from prayer and God's presence, but also, the receiving of the implanted Word of God, renewing the mind to that Word and renewing 'the spirit of the mind' (how you see yourself).

John 8:31-36 [31] *Then Jesus said to those Jews who believed Him, "If you abide in My word, you are My disciples indeed.* [32] *And you shall know the truth, and the truth shall make you free."* [33] *They answered Him, "We are Abraham's descendants,*

> and have never been in bondage to anyone. How can You say, 'You will be made free'?" ³⁴ Jesus answered them, "Most assuredly, I say to you, whoever commits sin is a slave of sin. ³⁵ And a slave does not abide in the house forever, but a son abides forever. ³⁶ Therefore if the Son makes you free, you shall be free indeed.

Firstly, Jesus highlights that we are to abide in His Word, that is, we are to live there and not just visit occasionally. This leads to knowing His truth. The word used for 'know' (Greek - ginosko³), here, refers to a knowing by experience rather than the knowing of a fact. It is the experience of truth that makes us free. Prayer and an encounter can set you free but to be made free and live in freedom, one must experience, and therefore embrace and act on, God's truth.

The Jews that Jesus was talking to at the time couldn't see their issue (in their case sin that wasn't removed by merely adhering to religious law) but Jesus gets to the core of their problem. So too, He does with us and we, even as believers, can have areas in our lives that hold us 'in bondage', that is, they restrict and limit us from living in the freedom of soul that God desires us to live in, and that Jesus paid the price for us to live in. Jesus links Himself making us free, to the receiving and experiencing of His Word.

> **James 1:21** *Therefore lay aside all filthiness and overflow of wickedness, and receive with meekness the implanted word, which is able to save your souls.*

Filthiness and overflow of wickedness is that which not only comes from sin, but those things that can defile or accumulate on us from our past life or as we listen to the things of this world, anger, pride, falsehood etc. We are advised to put them off and to humbly receive the Word of God.

THE IMPLANTED WORD WHICH IS ABLE TO SAVE YOUR SOUL

The word 'save' ('sozo' - Greek) means 'to deliver or protect, heal, preserve, do well or make whole'[3]. We are to put off the negative input and receive God's Word that is able to heal, restore and bring peace to the soul. Note that this is something we do as an act of our will and not something God, or other's prayers, does for us.

The mind cannot be embracing the thoughts of the flesh or the world and have the peace of God at the same time. Thoughts are the access to the soul for strongholds to be formed. Many (not saying all) of the issues of the soul are rooted in thoughts, attitudes, responses, reflections on memories, ruminating on issues, opinions and input from the world. Without meditating on God's thoughts and renewing our minds to His way of thinking, healing of the soul is hindered.

> **Isaiah 55:8,9** [8] *"For My thoughts are not your thoughts nor are your ways My ways," says the Lord.* [9] *"For as the heavens are higher than the earth, So are My ways higher than your ways, and My thoughts than your thoughts."*
>
> **Romans 12:2** *And do not be conformed to this world, but be transformed by the renewing of your mind, that you may prove what is that good and acceptable and perfect will of God.*

The word 'transformed' here is the Greek word 'metamorphoo', from which we get the English word 'metamorphisis', meaning to be changed into a completely new and different species. It's the transformation of the caterpillar to the butterfly; immature form to mature form; the sinner to the new creation in Christ.

Healing comes as we don't just read Scripture, but we renew our minds to it, repenting of and laying down old ways of thinking, and then, taking on God's thoughts, meditating on them, which in turn, should lead us to act on them.

> **Ephesians 4:22-24** *²² that you put off, concerning your former conduct, the old man which grows corrupt according to the deceitful lusts, ²³ and be renewed in the spirit of your mind, ²⁴ and that you put on the new man which was created according to God, in true righteousness and holiness.*

To be renewed in the spirit of your mind goes even further than renewing the mind. Renewing the mind is the receiving of God's thoughts in exchange for our own.

Renewing the spirit of the mind is to meditate on the Scriptures to the place where it changes how you see yourself. Your vision of yourself starts to align with how God sees you. This passage in Ephesians highlights that this is the critical action to removing the old and putting on the new.

> **2 Corinthians 5:17** *Therefore, if anyone is in Christ, he is a new creation; old things have passed away; behold, all things have become new.*

In the Bible, God declares His intention for us and what He has made full provision for us to be – to be like Jesus - and He will provide all necessary power to get us there. However, that process of transformation involves us choosing to not be conformed to the thoughts, attitudes and ways of this world and to take on the thoughts of God.

The 'new creation' looks like Jesus, thinks like Him and acts like Him. It is full of love, joy, peace, longsuffering, kindness, goodness, faithfulness, gentleness and self- control. We have received these characteristics through faith in Christ and the infilling of the Holy Spirit, but we have to then engage with and meditate on these truths and allow them to be worked out in our lives - receiving the Word and choosing to obey it. The more we renew our minds, accept and embrace God's thoughts, which are far above our own, and align our thinking and expression with His thoughts through obedience, the more we experience what God has for us.

> **Philippians 2:12,13** [12] *Therefore, my beloved, as you have always obeyed, not as in my presence only, but now much more in my absence, work out your own salvation with fear and trembling;* [13] *for it is God who works in you both to will and to do for His good pleasure.*

We don't work for our salvation, but we do have to cooperate with God and allow what He has created us to be, provided for us and deposited in us at salvation, to be worked out into our physical and soul-life experience.

There are three ways that the Scriptures are described as being sustenance to us. They are presented as the milk of the word, as bread and as solid food, or in some translations of that, meat.

Rather than there being three different levels of teaching, I can see three different ways that we receive the same Word. We can receive it as milk, where it helps us to grow in the early stages, being drip fed in. When someone just looks at a Scripture a day from a devotional, that is the milk of the word; taking in a small portion to bring encouragement but not necessarily change.

Then when revelation comes, it is like bread that has had the fire on it. It lights us up; we can feel our soul being fed and built up by it; it excites us. We start to 'see' it and understanding comes.

Then, there is the meat of the word where that same Word becomes part of who we are. So, we can read the Bible and feel some encouragement and then we can read and pray until revelation comes but it is not to stop there. We are to meditate on it and receive it into ourselves and importantly, obey it, so that it becomes part of who we are - not just what we believe or have inspired to us but part of who we have become. Then, we know it by experience. The anointing of the Holy Spirit falls on the Word that has been 'made flesh'.

> **John 1:18** *No one has seen God at any time. The only begotten Son, who is in the bosom of the Father, He has declared Him.*

The only way that the world could see God was that the Word of God, the second Person of the Trinity, was 'made flesh' and dwelt among us (John 1:14). Jesus says in John 17:18 that as the Father sent Him, so He now sends us - to reveal the Word of God to people through the gospel but also through His Word being 'made flesh' in us. Our changed nature reveals the work of God in us and in its manifestation, there is transformation and healing to us.

So, let's look at two passages as examples of how this can be applied. Firstly, one of 365 Scriptures in the Bible that tells us to 'fear not' (one for every day of the year).

> **Isaiah 41:10** *"Fear not, for I am with you; be not dismayed, for I am your God. I will strengthen you, yes, I will help you, I will uphold you with My righteous right hand."*

Now, read it slowly. We 'fear not' not through self-talk but because of the absolute truth that God is with us; He never leaves us nor forsakes us (Hebrews 13:5). Close your eyes and meditate on the fact that God is with you; focus within, where He dwells and progressively develop an awareness of His presence. If Jesus, the One who is above all things and who is all powerful, were to be standing next to you as you do life or approach that situation, would you be afraid? The answer would be "no". Well, He is with you and in you, by His Holy Spirit, and so, focusing on Him and heightening your awareness of Him enables you to step into that place of 'fear not'.

The Scripture then expands further as to why we can 'fear not'. He is our God and He is in control; He cares for us and upholds us. So, we can lay down being dismayed, overwhelmed or confused and instead, take up the thought and awareness that God is with us and that He will strengthen us and help us, as we turn to Him and avail ourselves of His support, strength and power. We won't fall because He is upholding us with His right hand, that being a metaphor of His power.

It may take some time, but progressively make a practice of laying down the fear and mediate on this or other 'fear not' Scriptures. Think about it. What does this Scripture mean to you? Visualise it; what does your life look like with this truth in it? Speak it out over your life. This meditation on God's Word will, over time, renew your mind and you will experience the truth of it more and more.

Let's look at one more Scripture as an example in our renewing of the mind.

> **Philippians 4:6-7** [6] *Be anxious for nothing, but in everything by prayer and supplication, with thanksgiving, let your requests be made known to God;* [7] *and the peace of God, which surpasses all understanding, will guard your hearts and minds through Christ Jesus.*

There is a peace from God that will guard and protect your mind and heart, but we are advised, in context, that to lay hold of and maintain this peace, we need to choose to not be anxious, to pray and cast our cares on the Lord, to be thankful and then, to discipline and put boundaries on our thought life. So, there are things we need to engage with and act on.

Firstly, again, we read it slowly. Why will we 'be anxious for nothing?'. The reason is that God is with us and He is on the end of that prayer with supernatural peace to replace our anxious thoughts. So, as an act of will, lay down the anxiety and slow down the thoughts. Pray about it and intentionally place the issue in the hand of God (and don't take it back!). More often than not, it seems that God waits for us to relinquish the worry and leave it with Him, before He acts. As long as we hold onto it (and by so doing we are controlling it) the Lord seems to stand back and wait. We are not God and not in control - so let it go to the One who is and trust Him.

1 Peter 5:7 *casting all your care upon Him, for He cares for you.*

Practise thankfulness for all that God has done for you. This is powerful, renewing your mind, shifting your perspective from your problem onto Him and what He has done for you, and then, also brings you into His presence.

Now, intentionally receive the free gift of God's peace. His peace in your mind helps you to think clearly and His peace in your heart enables you to 'hear' or sense the leading of the Holy Spirit. You don't hear His voice with your physical ears (although on rare occasions some have) but it is rather, a strong sense of His leading in your spirit and a sensing of His words in your spirit that translates to your mind as having 'heard' those words. We don't hear His voice well in the absence of peace and so the receiving and maintaining of peace is critical in our walk with God and in dealing with all the situations of life.

The devil seeks to gain entry into our lives, and he also does this through thoughts, but these come to the mind as doubts, accusation, condemnation, fear, anxiety, discouragement or depression. Romans 14:17 reveals that the kingdom of God, which Jesus said is within us, is righteousness, peace and joy in the Holy Spirit. One of the devil's many strategies to access our souls, is to try and shift us out of righteousness, peace or joy. We are righteous in Christ alone but we can be tempted into actions of unrighteousness or unrighteous thoughts that disrupt us living according to the Spirit. The devil aims to shift us, through temptation or trouble, to take on his thoughts instead of God's or to get us to focus on the problem rather than on the Lord.

> **Romans 8:5** *For those who live according to the flesh set their minds on the things of the flesh, but those who live according to the Spirit, the things of the Spirit.*

We are to be intentional, especially in times of trial, to keep our eyes and thoughts on the Lord, to meditate on His Word and to actively hold onto righteousness, peace and joy.

> **Philippians 4:8** *Finally, brethren, whatever things are true, whatever things are noble, whatever things are just, whatever things are pure, whatever things are lovely, whatever things are of good report, if there is any virtue and if there is anything praiseworthy- meditate on these things.*

Then, having meditated on the Scriptures we are to speak them out. Speaking God's word is not 'blab it and grab it' but rather an aligning of ourselves with Him, His ways and how He releases His will.

In Isaiah 55, the Lord invites us to take on His thoughts and, in so doing, find an abundance for the soul that cannot be found any other way. For those who lack resources and think they can't access help, He says "Come"; for those who spend their resources trying to find satisfaction, He says "Come".

Isaiah 55:1-3 ¹*"Ho! Everyone who thirsts, come to the waters; and you who have no money, come, buy and eat. Yes, come, buy wine and milk without money and without price.* ² *Why do you spend money for what is not bread, and your wages for what does not satisfy? Listen carefully to Me, and eat what is good, and let your soul delight itself in abundance.* ³*Incline your ear and come to Me. Hear and your soul shall live: and I will make an everlasting covenant with you - the sure mercies of David.*

Buy usually means to purchase, especially with money, but it can also mean to accept. Here the purchase is without money. The grace of God that brings abundant life and an abundance of soul is freely given. There is a required transaction to take place, however, as we come to Him, laying down what is not of Him, so that we can take up what He offers.

To eat what is good is in context with listening carefully to God, which suggests that there is a diet of contrary words or thoughts that do not equate with eating what is good, making the soul weak and prone to sickness.

So, the Lord calls us to come, to listen and to receive the abundance of love, peace, joy, contentment and the other riches that He has for us and so, let your soul delight itself in abundance. When was the last time your soul felt full of the abundance of life and of God?

So, "Come…."

Reading:

- Mark 4:1-32
- Psalm 107:20
- Isaiah 57:19
- Psalm 119:9-11,28,50,92-93,165
- Psalm 85:8
- Psalm 19:1

Thought for the day: The word sown in your heart by believing, receiving, seeing and speaking it and then, acting on it, will produce results.

Reflection: Below are a few examples, intentionally not written down so that you can look them up and write them out for yourself, starting the process of meditating on them.

God brings healing to depression through His peace and joy, restoring that which is absent in the soul (Romans 15:13; Nehemiah 8:10; John 16:33).

He brings healing to anxiety through being rooted and established in His love that casts out all fear (Ephesians 3:14-21; 1 John 4:18; Philippians 4:6-8).

He brings a sense of safety and security, and the removal of fear and terror, with the assurance of His presence being with us, that He will help us, and to 'fear not' for those very reasons (Isaiah 41:1-14; 2 Timothy 1:7; Isaiah 43:1,2; Psalm 27:1; Psalm 34:4; Hebrews 13:5,6).

Please look up these Scriptures and receive with humility the ingrafted Word that is able to save and heal your soul.

35

THE LORD'S PRAYER FOR HEALING

Matthew 6:10 *Your kingdom come. Your will be done on earth as it is in heaven.*

The Lord's prayer reveals God's priorities in prayer and as we align with them, we align with His kingdom purposes and, I believe, we are positioned to receive of His kingdom power. It's not a formula but, having said that, Jesus did say "In this manner, therefore, pray".

Matthew 6:7-8 *"7 And when you pray, do not use vain repetitions as the heathen do. For they think that they will be heard for their many words. 8 "Therefore do not be like them. For your Father knows the things you have need of before you ask Him."*

Jesus starts the teaching with what we are not to do in prayer, that is, vain repetitions. These can be prayers that are mechanical and not heartfelt, not Spirit led and empowered, or they are prayers not connected to truth or not prayed in faith.

Hence, they are vain, meaning 'producing no result or useless'. Conversely, James 5:16 says that 'the effective, fervent prayer of a righteous man avails much' - that would be prayer that is passionate, heartfelt and full of faith.

There are many ways we can pray vain repetitions, but there is an implication from verse eight that it is when we are asking for things that He already knows we need. God already knows what you need; He has already given you all things pertaining to life and godliness through the finished work of the Cross. Jesus took His own blood into the tabernacle of heaven and secured forgiveness and healing for us forever.

Our prayers, when led by God's priorities and the Holy Spirit, presented in faith and the acknowledgement of who God is and what He has already done, release what is already established in Heaven, here on Earth.

So, we can ask, and be persistent, but it needs to be in faith and not with an incessant asking of Him to do what He has already done. For example, prayer requests come such as "I want you to pray that God will be with me at the medical appointment". Well, the Lord says that He will never leave you nor forsake you and so He will be there! Such prayer would be one of unbelief, that is, denying what He has already said. It might be "I want God to heal me from such and such". So, that is a real and valid desire but how we present it is important. From God's perspective He has already healed you in Christ, so an alignment is required to present a prayer acknowledging that, and then declaring the release of, and receiving in faith, that healing.

Matthew 6:9 *In this manner, therefore, pray: Our Father in heaven, hallowed be Your name.*

Jesus reveals that the first priority of prayer is not to rush in with our many requests but to set our eyes on God, praise Him and honour Him for who He is. Amongst so many of His divine attributes, in Exodus 15:26 He says, *"For I AM the Lord who heals you"*. He is worthy of all praise and honour, and then praise also, brings us into His presence.

This approach to God also aligns our hearts to one of honour and respect, and helps correct us from prayers that dishonour Him, for example, prayers that would doubt His willingness to heal, that would question His goodness or challenge Him when healing hasn't yet been experienced. Many healings performed by Jesus were preceded by the person honouring Him and, whether we have been healed or not, He still deserves the praise and honour for what He did for us at the Cross of Calvary.

> **Matthew 6:10** *Your kingdom come. Your will be done on earth as it is in heaven.*

Healing is God's will! So, at this point you could spend time declaring the Word of God over your and others' lives, in Jesus' name. The Holy Spirit moves on the Word of God to bring it to pass.

> **Psalm 103:2,3** *Bless the Lord, O my soul, and forget not all His benefits: who forgives all your iniquities, who heals all your diseases.*

> **1 Peter 2:24** *who Himself bore our sins in His own body on the tree, that we, having died to sins, might live for righteousness—by whose stripes you were healed.*

> **Matthew 8:17 NLT**[5] *This fulfilled the word of the Lord through the prophet Isaiah, who said, "He took our sicknesses and removed our diseases.*

Praying this way brings faith and aligns our hearts with what has already been provided for us, so that it adjusts any potential doubt filled requests. Faith, and taking Jesus at His word, preceded many of the documented healings in the New Testament.

Can you see what Jesus is doing? He's getting our eyes off ourselves and our circumstances and firmly onto Him and what He has done. He is lifting our perspective to His, before we ask for anything.

Matthew 6:11 *Give us this day our daily bread.*

Now we can pray for anything that has not already been covered. Remember, to not hold God to your specific ways and timelines, but cast your cares onto Him, put your trust in Him and allow Him to direct the way. Ask for discernment of what He is doing so that you can cooperate with Him. Ask in faith and choose to believe that you receive any prayer request that clearly aligns with the Word of God.

> **1 John 5:14,15** [14] *Now this is the confidence that we have in him, that if we ask anything according to His will He hears us.* [15] *And if we know that He hears us, whatever we ask, we know that we have the petitions that we have asked of Him.*

> **James 1:6-8** [6] *But let him ask in faith, with no doubting, for he who doubts is like a wave of the sea driven and tossed by the wind.* [7] *For let not that man suppose that he will receive anything from the Lord;* [8] *he is a double-minded man, unstable in all his ways.*

If you are not sure if a request is God's will or not, ask for His wisdom and for Him to reveal what His will is in the situation. If you desire His will above what you want, He will reveal it to you. The Holy Spirit will bring a peace in your heart for what is of God and a 'check' or a feeling of warning, unrest or discomfort, for what is not of Him.

> **Psalm 25:14** *The secret of the Lord is with those who fear Him, and He will show them His covenant.*

Then comes a helpful checklist:

> **Matthew 6:12** *And forgive us our debts, as we forgive our debtors.*

If there is any sin that we are aware of, we need to repent of it. Repentance is not just saying sorry but turning away from the sin. Jesus has already provided the forgiveness, but He is concerned that we turn and align ourselves with His ways. This is not to say that you have to be perfect before being forgiven or healed, but if sickness lingers, this can be one of the blockages to healing being experienced.

Also, God, while not bringing any sickness, can use a circumstance to compel us to turn to Him and then healing follows.

In John 5:14 Jesus says to a man He has healed from thirty-eight years of sickness *"See you have been made well. Sin no more lest a worse thing come upon you"*, indicating that his infirmity had been related to a sin.

Then we are to forgive <u>anyone</u> we have <u>anything</u> against. This is the only part of the prayer that Jesus repeats at the end and takes further, just in case we were going to brush over it.

> **Matthew 6:14,15** *"[14] For if you forgive men their trespasses, your heavenly Father will also forgive you. [15] But if you do not forgive men their trespasses, neither will your Father forgive your trespasses."*

This is clear, brutal and often really tough, for many sins can seem unforgivable to us. It is good to remember that you have to be willing and obedient, that is, choose to forgive, release the person from your judgement and into God's hands for Him to manage, and then pray a blessing over them. When we step out in obedience, even if we don't have the feelings of forgiveness at that point, then the Holy Spirit will come with His grace and provide all the ability that we need. This is important, as unforgiveness is a huge blockage to receiving the power of God and healing. Healing often comes as we forgive and release others.

> **Matthew 6:13** *And do not lead us into temptation but deliver us from the evil one. For Yours is the kingdom and the power and the glory forever. Amen.*

Looking at the first part of the verse – The New Living Translation[5] puts it as *"Don't let us yield to temptation"*. Let's be clear that God will not tempt us or lead us to be tempted to sin (James 1:13,14). This is rather, a request for God's help, His wisdom and His strength, to empower us and lead us away from areas that we struggle with, and though unspoken, into godly responses and ways.

> **Hebrews 2:17,18** [17] *Therefore, in all things He had to be made like His brethren, that He might be a merciful and faithful High Priest in things pertaining to God, to make propitiation for the sins of the people.* [18] *For in that He Himself has suffered, being tempted, He is able to aid those who are tempted.*

Jesus, having faced all temptation, and remained without sin, is both able to show mercy and understanding to the one being tempted and also, bring the power and keys to overcome.

Then 'deliver us from the evil one'. Ask yourself if there is a possibility of a spiritual component to the sickness? This can come in two different ways. Firstly, sometimes people unwittingly have allowed spiritual entities into their lives through practices that have a demonic component to them and have come under, or been impacted by that spirit, which can bring sickness or pain into their bodies, as well as deception and a hardening of the heart to what Jesus has for them. Many healings in the Bible came through Jesus casting out such a spirit.

The other impact of evil is spiritual opposition or warfare that comes against the believer, not through sin, but because that person may be progressing in their walk with God and the enemy wants to push them back. Jesus has defeated all such powers and given us authority in His name to remove them. Chapters 28 and 32 of this book looked at experiencing freedom from these forces, and can be reviewed, or you may want to get a trusted person, who is strong in their authority in Christ, to pray for you.

The prayer started on praise but ends in worship. Keep lifting up the name of God, be thankful and allow the Holy Spirit to lead you deeper into worship. Thank God for His healing before you even receive it; for His faithfulness; His goodness; and wait in the presence of the Holy Spirit for a while. He will reveal things to you in your spirit, in that place of quietness and focus. This place of fellowship with God is real prayer. He will give you wisdom; He may show you areas that need adjustment; He will give you fresh ideas and revelation, and He will speak His promises directly into your spirit, bringing faith. Take the time to allow a spiritual transaction to take place between God and yourself.

Reading:

- Matthew 6:5-15
- Psalm 23

Thought for the day: Your kingdom come. Your will be done on earth as it is in heaven (Matthew 6:10).

Reflection: Write down any insights or revelations that you have had as you reflect on God's priorities in the Lord's Prayer. How can this be implemented into your own prayer life?

36

FREELY YOU HAVE RECEIVED FREELY GIVE

Matthew 10:8 *Heal the sick, cleanse the lepers, raise the dead, cast out demons. Freely you have received, freely give.*

The next three chapters are for those who would like to develop and be able to minister healing to others, being prepared to set themselves apart and align with the Holy Spirit in continuing Jesus' own ministry.

Matthew 28:18-20 [18] *And Jesus came and spoke to them, saying, "All authority has been given to Me in heaven and on earth.* [19] *Go therefore and <u>make disciples</u> of all the nations, baptizing them in the name of the Father and of the Son and of the Holy Spirit,* [20] *<u>teaching them to observe all things that I have commanded you</u>; and lo, I am with you always, even to the end of the age." Amen.*

FREELY YOU HAVE RECEIVED FREELY GIVE

Mark 16:15-20 ¹⁵ *And He said to them, "Go into all the world and preach the gospel to every creature.* ¹⁶ *He who believes and is baptized will be saved; but he who does not believe will be condemned.* ¹⁷ <u>*And these signs will follow those who believe*</u>*: In My name they will cast out demons; they will speak with new tongues;* ¹⁸ *they will take up serpents; and if they drink anything deadly, it will by no means hurt them;* <u>*they will lay hands on the sick, and they will recover.*</u>*"* ¹⁹ *So then, after the Lord had spoken to them, He was received up into heaven, and sat down at the right hand of God.* ²⁰ *And they went out and preached everywhere,* <u>*the Lord working with them and confirming the word through the accompanying signs.*</u> *Amen.*

Jesus' final instructions to the disciples would obviously capture His heart for the development of future disciples and the church. Included in them are His compassion and provision for the sick, the importance of healing in the preaching and validation of the truth of the gospel, and the importance that believers are taught what Jesus had taught His own disciples, with healing the sick being a significant part of that.

Firstly, in this chapter, I want to look at some of our attitudes in approaching ministry and then in the next two chapters we will look at our equipping from God and our position in ministering, and finally, some practical keys for when we pray for another person. It's not a presentation of all aspects of ministering in the Holy Spirit, but rather, just a few steps to help you get started.

Matthew 10:7,8 ⁷ *And as you go, preach, saying, 'The kingdom of heaven is at hand.'* ⁸ *Heal the sick, cleanse the lepers, raise the dead, cast out demons. Freely you have received, freely give.*

For those who become disciples, the call is to release the power of the kingdom of God. To my mind, a picture of our role in ministry is found in the story of Jesus 'feeding the five thousand' (Matthew 14, Mark 6, Luke 9 and John 6).

> **John 6:10,11** [10] *Then Jesus said, "Make the people sit down." Now there was much grass in the place. So the men sat down, in number about five thousand.* [11] *And Jesus took the loaves, and when He had given thanks He distributed them to the disciples, and the disciples to those sitting down; and likewise of the fish, as much as they wanted.*

The miracle and provision were completely of God, but Jesus required the disciples to be involved in handing out the bread and fish. He could have managed without them, but He included them. The disciples would not have been so deluded to think that it was because of them, or their own godliness, position or even calling, that the miracle was taking place and there was no pressure on them to work the miracle.

However, it was essential that they handed out the miracle, in order for people to receive the provision Jesus had for them.

In releasing the power of the kingdom, including healing, we are just 'handing out the bread'. God could do it without us, but He has ordained that we be included in the process. It is essential that we do it, or people won't receive the salvation and healing that God has intended for them, but we don't carry the weight of working the miracle - and we don't get the credit or glory for it (Isaiah 42:8). We are called to minister or hand out the miraculous healing power of God, made available through the Cross and the power of the Holy Spirit's anointing upon us.

In Matthew 10:8, Jesus advises that "freely you have received freely give". The whole of salvation is free and must be freely ministered. I am going to point out, here, that you can't 'sow finance' to receive healing. You can't give a payment for what has freely and graciously been given. If a ministry asks for an offering directly connected to the receiving of healing (as opposed to appropriate Scriptural offerings) it is dishonouring the work of the Cross.

Imagine Jesus purchasing you a priceless gift that cost Him everything, with which came with all of His love, and then you feel, or are told, that you have to make a financial contribution in order to receive it. This devalues the graciousness and love in the gift. Note that this is different to the Scriptural teaching of giving tithes and offerings, a worker deserving his wages (1 Timothy 5:18; 1 Corinthians 9:13,14), the necessary support of the church ministry, offerings to support other ministries and of course, supporting those in need. The latter is God-ordained support for building His church and supporting ministers and the former is deriving money from the free gift of healing or, if on the part of the one receiving, trying to earn grace. God's healing is free, and we minister it freely.

> **John 14:12** *"Most assuredly, I say to you, he who believes in me, the works that I do he will do also; and greater works than these he will do, because I go to My Father."*

When Jesus came, He could have just ministered as God and, while still absolutely in awe of what He accomplished, we would have to stand back and say "Well, He did that because He was God and therefore, I could never minister in that way".

However, Jesus, though being the second Person of the Trinity, the Word of God, pre-existent from the beginning with the Father and the Holy Spirit, chose to lay aside all His rights as God and come to Earth in the form of a man (Philippians 2:6,7). In His earthly ministry, He ministered as a man anointed by the Holy Spirit. He did no mighty miracles until the Holy Spirit came upon Him at water baptism (Luke 3:21- 23) – noting that water baptism was not needed for Him with His perfect life, but done as an example of righteousness for us.

He showed His disciples how to minister as one anointed by the Holy Spirit and then commanded them to go and do it (Matt 10:7,8; Mark 6:13; Luke 10:1-12,17), and then, to make other disciples, teaching them to do the same (Matthew 28:20). What were they to teach them? Whatever Jesus had taught them. He not only taught theology, but also how to be a minister of the Holy Spirit.

In John 14:12, Jesus is saying that whatever He did, they could do also. So, we are talking about seeing multitudes healed, multitudes fed, the dead raised, not from an ability or sufficiency in themselves, or ourselves, but a sufficiency from God. God would not ask us to do something that He wouldn't make full provision for us to do.

> **Ephesians 3:20** *Now to Him who is able to do exceedingly abundantly above all that we ask or think, according to the power that works in us...*

This is a promise that many declare over their situations, but its manifestation comes not just from declaration but an alignment, with a life submitted to God in worship, submitted to His will and being rooted in His love (reading it in context with the passage in Ephesians 3:14-20). From that seemingly lowly and yet, powerful position, nothing is impossible, and it's demonstrated according to the power that works in us - faith in God and the miracle working power of the Holy Spirit.

The call to pray for the sick is made available to all who believe (Mark 16:17). However, not all can pray. By the nature of the call, the Christian must be in faith and living as a disciple, setting themselves apart to the Lord and His purposes. To permit those, who have not set themselves apart and pursued the Lord, to minister would be to dishonour the Holy Spirit and to treat His presence and the anointing as something common.

I would advise against the invitation for anyone in a church service to go and lay hands on and pray for the sick person next to them. There is no guarantee of the faith, the maturity or the submission to Christ of the person doing the 'laying on of hands'. That is a moment for the 'elders' of the church, although, an 'elder' can easily be a young person who is a disciple of Jesus and living for Him. It's not about age or how long someone has been in church but that they are recognised by church leadership as someone who is sound in their Christian walk, full of faith and full of the Holy Spirit. In the book of Acts, when selecting people to serve in the new church, the requirement was that they were of good reputation, full of the Holy Spirit and wisdom (Acts 6:3). This guidance still holds true today.

The Holy Spirit is just that - He is Holy and His anointing is holy and must be honoured as such. We are not to dishonour Him by thinking that just anyone can minister His holy presence. However, we are also not to limit ourselves by thinking that someone needs to be of a certain position or standing to minister His holy presence. It is all about choosing to be set apart for Him and to live as a disciple. Do not grieve the Holy Spirit by treating Him as common in any way.

> **Ephesians 4:30** *And do not grieve the Holy Spirit of God, by whom you were sealed for the day of redemption.*

Ephesians 4:30 is sandwiched in between other verses that speak of putting off ungodly behaviour. Let us live and minister in a way that is mindful of the holiness of God's presence, with which He so graciously seeks to anoint us with.

2 Timothy 2:20,21 [20] *But in a great house there are not only vessels of gold and silver, but also of wood and clay, some for honour and some for dishonour.* [21] *Therefore if anyone cleanses himself from the latter, he will be a vessel for honour, sanctified and useful for the Master, prepared for every good work.*

So, we need to be in faith, choosing to live as a disciple (with no expectation of being perfect but just being in the process), with an absolute confidence in what Jesus has done, what we have been called to do and the power that God has made available for us to do it. In the ministry of healing, one can see that believers can swing to one of two extremes, either that of fear and stepping back, or an over confidence in self and performance, whereas the place of fruitful ministry lies in between.

The first group, that many believers find themselves in, is that "I am unworthy, unequipped, not anointed enough to minister healing and that this ministry is only for the 'gifted'". This results in people always looking to someone with a 'gift' to pray for them, or they may see the sovereignty of God as a reason as to why something does or doesn't happen, which can be distorted to become a kind of fatalism.

Now, it's Scriptural for those who are sick to call for the elders of the church to pray for them (James 5:14-16) or to receive ministry from an anointed minister. The anointing of the Holy Spirit is crucial for the minister, and it should be the mature (in the faith and anointing - not age) doing the laying on of hands (see 1 Timothy 5:22 for people not being released into ministry too quickly). However, it is not Scriptural for a believer to remain in an inactive state or in immaturity of faith, but rather to progress in their discipleship journey, to become someone who carries the anointing and who can minister in some capacity. You don't have to have the call to full time ministry to be used by God in the area of healing.

The second group, on the other extreme, can present with an over confidence in self, or their accomplishments, rooted in pride or insecurity, rather than a humble, submitted position in Christ. The soul is conscious of and focused on self, be it inadequacy or pride, and the spirit is focused on and conscious of God. To minister in the power of the Spirit you need to operate from your spirit and keep the soul or 'flesh' in check.

The position of the minister is to balance out the two facts of your absolute inadequacy in self and that 'apart from Him you can do nothing' (John 15:5) and the supreme adequacy of Jesus who calls and equips you to carry out His purpose. The balance is found in a position on your knees before Him in humility, prayer, seeking Him, and utterly relying on Him every step of the way. To be able, at the same time, to recognise your insufficient humanity, but also, the all sufficiency of Christ and to receive His sufficiency to carry out what would otherwise be an impossible task.

> **2 Corinthians 3:5,6** *Not that we are sufficient of ourselves to think of anything as being from ourselves, but our sufficiency is from God,* ⁶ *who also made us sufficient as ministers of the new covenant, not of the letter but of the Spirit; for the letter kills, but the Spirit gives life.*

There is absolutely nothing in self that is sufficient to bring healing to the sick or any other manifestation of the Holy Spirit. However, you are sufficient - in what God has already given you. He has given you 'all things pertaining to life and godliness' (2 Peter 1:3) through Jesus' finished work on the Cross of Calvary and His great and precious promises, the authority to release these in Jesus' name, on Earth as it is in Heaven, and then, the power of the Holy Spirit who brings these things to fruition.

1 Peter 4:11 *If anyone speaks, let him speak as the oracles of God. If anyone ministers, let him do it as with the ability which God supplies, that in all things God may be glorified through Jesus Christ, to whom belong the glory and the dominion forever and ever. Amen.*

1 Corinthians 12:7-11 *To each is given the manifestation of the Spirit for the common good.* ⁸ *For to one is given through the Spirit the utterance of wisdom, and to another the utterance of knowledge according to the same Spirit,* ⁹ *to another faith by the same Spirit, to another gifts of healing by the one Spirit,* ¹⁰ *to another the <u>working of miracles,</u> to another prophecy, to another the ability to distinguish between spirits, to another various kinds of tongues, to another the interpretation of tongues.* ¹¹ *All these are empowered by one and the same Spirit, who apportions to each one individually as he wills.*

To each one is given a manifestation of the Spirit and so this includes you! When you minister healing, many people talk about 'your gift of healing'; or 'you are a healer' and it becomes all about a certain minister who does healing. Mark 16:17 says that 'these signs follow those who believe' and they are not limited to those in the healing ministry or church leadership.

My thoughts are it's not your or my gift. The gifts are the Holy Spirit's, but you and I have the Holy Spirit, and therefore, the potential for Him to move through us using any of His gifts. Many people see it as the Holy Spirit distributing the gifts so that one can only move in healing, another only in prophecy or another in the word of wisdom. This results in limited thinking where people get a mindset about what God can and can't do through them and they remove themselves from being used by Him in many situations. It can put a ceiling on what you can step into in God and see Him do through you.

I see the Holy Spirit's distribution of the gifts as being displayed according to what He wills in any given situation. This causes me to remain reliant on Him, to discern what He is doing and then to align with Him, with Him leading. Jesus said, "I only do what I see My Father do". Even our Lord was utterly reliant on the Father, looking to Him continually, fully aligned with and submitted to Him, and never operated independently of Him.

I have seen healing through seven of the nine gifts of the Spirit, and believe that tongues, as another, is an integral part of building your spirit and discernment, in order to operate in the other spiritual gifts. This keeps me listening to the Holy Spirit as I minister. "What are you doing here Holy Spirit; How do You want to minister to this person; How are You releasing healing to them". My role, and yours, is to discern what He is doing, to align with Him and to speak and minister the way He directs in the moment. Whether this comes through as a word of knowledge, a gift of faith, a prophetic word declared, or as a gift of healing does not limit the level of power released or the manifestation of the healing.

Things to note

- Some gifts may be seen more in one than another because it is required for their particular call; because they have focused on and really sought God to be used in that area; or because they continue to grow in an area that they have been faithful with.
- You are not limited to one type of gift. If you stay open to the Holy Spirit, He can move any of the gifts through you.

- Don't limit God through unbelief as to what He can do through you. For example, don't say 'healing is not my thing' because you have the Holy Spirit- and it's His 'thing'.
- Gifts are for giving - they operate when we focus on doing good to others. The Holy Spirit's gifts are not for self-importance or building 'our own ministry', but for serving others and building the church. It's for the profit of all. The Body of Christ misses out if each one is not allowing the manifestation of the gifts to operate through them.
- Praying for healing is not following a formula, that risks making us operate independently of God, but a cooperation with the Holy Spirit as to how He wants to release that healing. He can do this through any of His gifts and not through a prayer formula or solely through the gifts of healings.
- Our role is to discern what the Holy Spirit is doing, align our mouth, heart and actions to Him and act as a connector or translator between Him and the person being prayed for. We are the facilitator, not the dominator. We are not imposing 'our ministry' on someone but we are communicating to them what the Holy Spirit wants to do so that, they in turn can co-operate with His process.

Reading:

- 1 Corinthians 12 and 13
- 1 Peter 1:13-19
- 2 Timothy 2:14-26
- 1 Timothy 4:12-16

Thought for the day: You are sufficient as a minister of the New Covenant.

Reflection: Write down any insights or revelations that you have had as you reflect on the call for you to minister healing, as well as the call for you to live set apart for God and His purposes.

_____
_____
_____
_____
_____
_____
_____
_____
_____
_____
_____
_____
_____
_____
_____
_____
_____
_____
_____
_____
_____

37

THE WORKS THAT I DO YOU WILL DO ALSO

John 14:12 *"Most assuredly, I say to you, he who believes in me, the works that I do he will do also; and greater works than these he will do, because I go to My Father".*

When looking at the extraordinary promise in John 14:12 it is important to look at the context of the passage. Many people are just declaring the promises, without looking wider and deeper at the context of them, where you find that, the promise is often the end result of the discussed teaching being put into practice. Some promises, for example, those of salvation, come freely with the believing; grace received through faith, without any additional requirement on our part. Others, like John 14:12 are freely given but then realised through renewal, being actively positioned in Christ and the application of Scriptural truths.

Therefore, some action is required on our part in response to the promise. There is a position in Christ that we minister from and with so much insight given on this, in context with John 14:12, I would encourage you to do a study on the book of John, chapters 14 and 15.

> **Acts 1:8** <u>But you shall receive power when the Holy Spirit has come upon you</u>; and you shall be witnesses to Me in Jerusalem, and in all Judea and Samaria, and to the end of the earth."

The Greek word 'dunamis', translated power in Acts 1:8 speaks of 'great power, great strength'[3] and is used to describe God's miracle working power.

The first step is that we step into faith - to believe, see and act from God's perspective. So, we believe that the works that Jesus did, we will do also; that we have received power (Acts 1:8), God's miracle working power at that; and we are sufficient as ministers of the Spirit (2 Corinthians 3:5,6), not in ourselves but in what God has given to us in Christ Jesus. The Holy Spirit moves in response to faith.

So, we don't operate from our own perspective where we can easily focus on self, our insufficiency or the size of the problem presented before us. God's perspective is that He sees the same Holy Spirit who was on Jesus, poured out on you; you are an able minister of the Spirit. He sees the finished work of the Cross and that nothing is impossible for Him or for those who believe. His power is released when we see and minister according to His perspective and not our own.

Then, I believe that in John 14:10, Jesus gives us an insight into how He ministered, while on Earth. In this passage we find that there was a positioning, a power and a perspective to His ministry.

> **John 14:10** *Do you not believe that I am in the Father, and the Father in Me? The words that I speak to you I do not speak on My own authority; but the Father who dwells in Me does the works.*

John 14:20 *At that day you will know that I am in My Father, and you in Me, and I in you.*

As Jesus was in the Father, so we are in Jesus and this is the position that we live and minister from. We are in Jesus! So, amongst other things, we are in His righteousness; in His performance and not our own; in His peace; positioned under His authority, we have authority in His name; we are to be positioned in obedience to His commandments; and we are in His love.

Being in His righteousness, nothing is of our earning or performance, and our confidence needs to be in Him. If you are feeling condemned or inadequate you won't release the anointing. You are righteous in Christ alone.

2 Corinthians 5:21 *For He made Him who knew no sin to be sin for us, that we might become the righteousness of God in Him.*

A manifestation of the power of the kingdom of God is Matthew 10:8, '*heal the sick, cleanse the lepers, raise the dead, cast out demons. Freely you have received, freely give*'.

1 Corinthians 4:20 *For the kingdom of God is not in word but in power.*

The kingdom of God is not just theology, but it comes with an experience of God's power. Romans 14:17 reveals that the kingdom of God is righteousness, peace and joy in the Holy Spirit. Kingdom power is released through a person who is in righteousness, peace and joy in the Holy Spirit. If there is no peace or joy, or if there is hidden sin, the kingdom of God power, although available, is hindered and little or no power is released.

The enemy can't take the kingdom power from you, but he can hinder it by coming against these three areas - temptation in all forms (not just overt sin but offense, unforgiveness, criticism, judgment, pride, anger etc) and then trouble to rob peace and joy. This is why the enemy will try to get you upset or unsettled before you minister and so, in anticipation, one must keep guard, at all times, over these areas.

We have authority in the name of Jesus - we have been given the right to release His already accomplished will, in His place and in His name, with His name representing Him.

> **John 14:13-14 AMPC**[8] *And I will do [I Myself will grant] whatever you ask in My Name [as presenting all that I Am], so that the Father may be glorified and extolled in (through) the Son. [Yes] I will grant [I Myself will do for you] whatever you shall ask in My Name [as presenting all that I Am].*

The Amplified Bible brings out the fact that when we pray in Jesus' name, we are presenting all that He is. So, when I pray in His name, I am not bringing myself as the minister but rather, I am presenting Jesus and all that He has done to the problem. Not only that, Jesus said that when I do that, in faith, He would answer and fulfill the request (obviously, needing to be in line with His will, which healing is). This now lifts my faith further, knowing that nothing is of me or any performance, but I have an assurance from Jesus that He will move in response to prayer or declaration offered in His name.

It is important that we understand that Jesus' name represents Him and that we are to pray His name "Jesus" and not "in Your name", "in Your mighty name" or other ways that many Christians pray. The whole reason that prayer is being answered is because of Jesus and not us, and so, we are to put Him front and centre of that prayer and speak the name "Jesus", in faith and in honour for who He is and what He has done. Say His name - "Jesus"!

John 14:15 *If you love Me, keep My commandments.*

John 14:21 *He who has My commandments and keeps them, it is he who loves Me. And he who loves Me will be loved by My Father, and I will love him and manifest Myself to him."*

The above verse is not speaking of God's love being conditional but there is a manifestation of Jesus to the one who sets their love upon Him and who obeys Him. We need to be positioned in obedience to His will if we want to minister the power of the Holy Spirit.

Ephesians 3:19 *to know the love of Christ which passes knowledge; that you may be filled with all the fullness of God.*

In context with this verse, Paul is praying that believers would know the love of Christ. To be filled with the fullness of God is to be filled with His love. If we want to see God move through us and if we want to do what Jesus did, as in John 14:12, then we need to become more like Him. This happens when we know Him and are filled with His love.

So, the attitude for ministry is love. It is not about attaining an identity of someone who can work the miraculous; not an identity of someone who has 'claimed' and is living in all of the promises; not someone who has position, authority or power, but rather, someone who is rooted in the love of God, submitted to do His will, which is accomplished by expressing His love, through us, for others. Faith works through love (Galatians 5:6). We are to be moved with love and compassion, as Jesus was in His own earthly ministry, for the Holy Spirit to really move through us.

So, that is our positioning for ministry, in Christ, but now, we also need power. In John 14:10 Jesus said that the Father was in Him. For us, we need Jesus in us by the rich indwelling of His Word and the infilling and empowering of the Holy Spirit.

> **John 15:7** *if you abide in Me and My words abide in you, you will ask what you desire and it shall be done for you*

This verse is in context with the passage of being fruitful for God. Ministering healing is not just following a series of steps, but it is a whole lifestyle of being 'in Christ'. The Word contains the power to bring itself to pass when faith is applied to it. Meditate on the Scriptures and promises, until the Word becomes 'flesh' in you.

> **John 14:16,17** [16] *And I will pray the Father, and He will give you another Helper, that He may abide with you forever—* [17] *the Spirit of truth, whom the world cannot receive, because it neither sees Him nor knows Him; but you know Him, for He dwells with you and will be in you.*

The Greek word for another ('allos') means 'one besides, another of the same kind'[3]. Jesus' use of the word 'allos' for sending another Helper or Comforter means that He was saying, "I will send One besides Me and in addition to Me but One just like Me. He will do in My absence what I would do if I were physically present with you." Jesus has just told Philip that he who had seen Him had seen the Father (John 14:9), in other words, the Father was just like Him. Now, He tells the disciples that the Holy Spirit is also just like Him - a separate member of the Godhead but completely alike and aligned in unity of purpose and nature.

The Holy Spirit, as our Helper, is not an impersonal power, but One just like Jesus who abides with us all the time. When you receive the infilling of the Holy Spirit, also termed the 'baptism of the Holy Spirit', a Divine Person comes to live on the inside of you and He comes with His miracle working power. In Luke 5:17, Jesus is ministering and the Bible says that 'the power of the Lord was present to heal them'. This power of the Lord is the Person of the Holy Spirit who rests upon a believer and His presence brings healing.

In Luke 24:49 Jesus advised the disciples to wait until 'they were endued with power from on high'. So it is, for us. We need to receive the Holy Spirit and His inherent power and sufficiency before we can release the works of God in ministry.

> **John 16:7** *Nevertheless I tell you the truth. It is to your advantage that I go away; for if I do not go away, the Helper will not come to you; but if I depart, I will send Him to you.*

Jesus said in John 16:7 that it was better for us if He went away, because then He would send the Holy Spirit to us, who could be with each one of us all the time, unlike Jesus, who wouldn't have been able to had He remained down here on Earth.

> **Luke 4:18,19** [18] *"The Spirit of the Lord is upon Me, because He has anointed Me To preach the gospel to the poor; He has sent Me to heal the brokenhearted, to proclaim liberty to the captives and recovery of sight to the blind, to set at liberty those who are oppressed;* [19] *to proclaim the acceptable year of the Lord."*

Yes, in this Scripture, Jesus was speaking of His own ministry but the same Holy Spirit who anointed Him for ministry is the One who anoints you, to carry out the same purpose.

The presence of the Holy Spirit is also called the anointing. The anointing is the tangible substance of the power and presence of God. The anointing can be felt in both the minister and the person receiving healing. It can be felt in many ways, some of which include like a wind, like a waterfall, like fire in the hands, like a fire inside your spirit, like an overwhelming heat in the body, like a gentle warmth, like a freshness over the face, like a beautiful love-filled presence washing over you or as great peace or joy. The anointing can reside on a person and it can be transmitted in a number of ways including through the laying on of hands, the spoken word, prophecy or just 'soaking' in His presence.

The anointing is not just for the entertainment of believers. Many times believers want to just 'play' in His presence and keep the experience for themselves. While being in His beautiful presence is essential, and it is the most enjoyable of all experiences, the anointing is primarily for equipping the believer with God's presence with the purpose of work - to see the work of God done, in His mighty power.

> **Acts 10:38** *how God anointed Jesus of Nazareth with the Holy Spirit and with power, who went about doing good and healing all who were oppressed by the devil, for God was with Him.*

The anointing on Jesus translated into the works of God being demonstrated. Similarly, in Acts 5:15, the anointing on Peter is so great that even his shadow is charged with the power of God and God's healing power flowed wherever his shadow fell. The deacon Philip goes out to Samaria in Acts 8:6,7 and ministers healings and miracles because of that same anointing. Paul ministered healing and miracles again by the receiving of the anointing.

> **Acts 19:11,12** *Now God worked unusual miracles by the hands of Paul, so that even handkerchiefs or aprons were brought from his body to the sick, and the diseases left them and the evil spirits went out of them.*

Often, we can look at these events and excuse it away as a 'special' minister being anointed, but it is primarily the result of coming into contact with the presence of God. This presence is not some vague power but the presence of the Holy Spirit, God on Earth, who continues the ministry of Jesus today.

We can pursue being in His presence and align ourselves with Him, so that God's presence remains on us and has its effect through us. When the disciples, untrained in the law, spoke boldly in front of the religious leaders, having just prayed for a lame man to receive his healing, it was noted that they had been with Jesus. They had walked and talked with Jesus, learned from Him, aligned their lives with Him and now the Holy Spirit was manifesting Jesus' life through them.

> **Acts 4:13** *Now when they saw the boldness of Peter and John, and perceived that they were uneducated and untrained men, they marvelled. And they realized that they had been with Jesus.*

We all need to keep being filled with the Holy Spirit - not just relying on someone to lay hands on us for this, but us, praying, worshipping and seeking God with all of our hearts.

> **Ephesians 5:18-21** [18] *And do not be drunk with wine, in which is dissipation; but be filled with the Spirit,* [19] *speaking to one another in psalms and hymns and spiritual songs, singing and making melody in your heart to the Lord,* [20] *giving thanks*

> *always for all things to God the Father in the name of our Lord Jesus Christ,* [21] *submitting to one another in the fear of God.*

So, if you have received the power of the Holy Spirit, when you are praying and laying hands on a person, He is there with you, ministering to them. In this we have our confidence, along with the secured and full provision of the Cross and the authority in Jesus' name to release His finished work. Are you getting a sense that you have been given enough 'sufficiency' from God (2 Corinthians 3:5) to see healings and miracles happen?

Thirdly, after our positioning in Christ and receiving of His power, we need His perspective.

> **John 14:10** *"…The words that I speak to you I do not speak on My own authority;…"*

It amazes me that even Jesus Himself, didn't just speak of His own will, but He aligned Himself perfectly with the words of the Father. Now, I know He is still God in His earthly ministry, but He is constantly giving us the example of how to live and how to minister. There are boundaries around ministering in the Holy Spirit. We can't just speak whatever we want. We aren't to be talking about the problem, when we see Jesus always avoiding doing that. Like Jesus, we are to speak in alignment with God's Word and God's perspective of the situation.

In prayer, don't pray according to the person's problem but according to the finished work of the Cross. We are not praying from the earthly problem and presenting it up to Heaven but rather, realigning ourselves to being positioned in Heaven's perspective, we pray or declare God's answer to the problem – for God's will to be done on Earth as it is in Heaven. Don't get too deep into discussing the problem but declare God's perspective if you want the power of God to operate.

We are to use the Name of Jesus to declare the things that God has already given us, by grace, to take effect in our and others' lives and not just ask Him to do it for us. We are not commanding God, but declaring the release of His will; what He said He has already given us; what He is waiting for us to release. God didn't need us to do His works, but He still ordained that ministry would be worked out through His children as we align with and co-operate with Him.

> **John 14:10** *"....but the Father who dwells in Me does the works".*

For Jesus, the Father did the works through Him as He released His Father's will. For us, the Holy Spirit does the works through us. So, as we pray or declare God's will, we need to 'release' the Holy Spirit through us. This is in no way saying we control how He moves, but rather, it is an expression that describes our aligning with Him and cooperation with what He wants to do.

Be sensitive to the leading of the Holy Spirit. You sense Him and release the power of God from your spirit and not your mind. Practice being sensitive to how the Holy Spirit wants to move through you. The Holy Spirit brings healing through any of His gifts and not just the gifts of healings and working of miracles.

I would sense the gifts of healing being in manifestation with the feeling of the anointing moving down my right arm and intense heat in the palms of my hands, like a ball of hot coal in my hands. So, when I sense that, I am ready to move with the Holy Spirit to minister healing.

I can sometimes feel what is like bubbles on the inside of my spirit that I just have to release in prayer, and for me, this is when I know that God is releasing a miracle.

This awareness also lifts my faith as I can sense the Holy Spirit working His gift.

The gift of faith feels like an absolute conviction that something will happen, usually in a circumstance that may lie beyond my personal level of faith. I just know that it will absolutely happen and the Holy Spirit moves on that heightened faith to bring the miraculous to pass. He does it according to His will and it's not something 'hyped up' by me, or you.

You may sense a prophetic word. Remember that it must be kept within the bounds of Scripture, aligned with the Word of God and that it is for exhortation, encouragement and comfort. It is never harsh, exposing, negative, manipulative or controlling. Keep within the boundaries of grace given to you.

> **1 Corinthians 14:3** *But he who prophesies speaks edification and exhortation and comfort to men.*

You might get a word of knowledge where the Holy Spirit highlights something to you that may be at the root of what someone is struggling with. Just gently say, "I am sensing this; take it or leave it but does it mean anything to you?" If it does, go with it and pray from that revelation.

As you pray, sense a release from your spirit. Sometimes you can do something in the 'natural' that, in and of itself is not accomplishing anything, but partnered with what you are intending 'in the spirit', assists you to step into that place of 'releasing' the Holy Spirit. So, in the natural you can feel yourself releasing something from your spirit with a forward movement (not obvious to others), transferring something from your spirit to the other person; and at the same time being focused on the Holy Spirit and what He is doing.

That may sound a bit confusing for you but the best thing to do is to practise in prayer. How do you feel God's presence? Does His presence or the anointing feel different when you pray for different scenarios? What does it feel like? Practise praying from your spirit and how you would sense a release from your spirit if you were to be ministering to someone. Pray healing for someone in your prayer time as if you were standing in front of them ministering to them. Sense the leading of the Holy Spirit and minister and pray according to that leading.

1 Peter 4:10 *As each one has received a gift. Minister it to one another, as good stewards of the manifold grace of God.*

Reading:

- John 14
- John 15

Thought for the day: The works that Jesus did, you will do also (from John 14:12).

Reflection: Write down any insights or revelations that you have had as you reflect on Jesus' teaching on ministry in John chapters 14 and 15. Write down any Scriptures that speak to you in these chapters.

_____
_____
_____
_____
_____
_____
_____
_____
_____
_____
_____
_____
_____
_____
_____
_____
_____
_____
_____
_____
_____
_____

38

MINISTERING HEALING

Mark 7:37 *And they were astonished beyond measure, saying, "He has done all things well. He makes both the deaf to hear and the mute to speak."*

Mark 7:31-37 [31] *Again, departing from the region of Tyre and Sidon, He came through the midst of the region of Decapolis to the Sea of Galilee.* [32] *Then they brought to Him one who was deaf and had an impediment in his speech, and they begged Him to put His hand on him.* [33] *And He took him aside from the multitude, and put His fingers in his ears, and He spat and touched his tongue.* [34] *Then, looking up to heaven, He sighed, and said to him, "Ephphatha," that is, "Be opened."* [35] *Immediately his ears were opened, and the impediment of his tongue was loosed, and he spoke plainly.* [36] *Then He commanded them that they should tell no one; but the more He commanded them, the more widely they proclaimed it.* [37] *And they were astonished beyond measure, saying, "He has* *done all things well. He makes both the deaf to hear and the mute to speak."*

Jesus didn't minister to make Himself celebrated or famous. His motivation was purely compassion for the sick and suffering, making His Father known and to bring the revelation of God and His holistic salvation.

In the above story, Jesus removes the man from the crowd and gets his attention to engage him in the process. Being deaf and mute, perhaps this poor man is overwhelmed and confused with a crowd around him and not knowing what is going on. Nothing is known of his story prior to this, but he would probably have experienced isolation, prejudice and judgement (as seen with the blind man healed at the Pool of Siloam). He wouldn't have heard the message of Jesus nor others' discussion of it.

Jesus didn't use him as a performance but was motivated to demonstrate God's kindness to the man. So respectfully, He takes the man apart; He communicates by His actions what He is about to do with putting His fingers in his ears, putting spittle on the tongue and looking to heaven. He has communicated that God is going to open his ears and unloose his tongue. This also shows that Jesus looks to have some element of faith and engagement from the man himself. The man is not someone to impose ministry on, but respected and valued. In ministry, we are to connect people to God and communicate what is happening and encourage a response of faith to God.

We find some keys here, for when we too, minister God's kindness and healing grace to others. Jesus made the man feel safe, communicated what God was going to do, showing that He wanted the man to engage with God and the process - and then He ministered healing. We are not the Healer but rather, a facilitator between God and the person receiving healing. We are connecting the person to God and then we are to take a step back. Don't get in the way - we are often so full of ourselves, our call and our ministry that we can stay in the centre of the process, but it's not about us. Be sensitive to the Holy Spirit and communicate to the person what He wants to do, so that they can respond to Him.

Below are just some practical instructions on how to pray for someone. Remember that this is from a foundational faith in God's character as the Healer; in the Word of God and Jesus' finished work of the Cross; and being positioned in God's perspective as you pray.

- Memorise some passages of Scripture to pray and to encourage those you are praying for.
- Ask the person what their need is and try and phrase it in such a way that they can respond with a positive statement of faith. For example, "What are you believing God to do for you today?" rather than "What do you want prayer for?". This is to limit the detail of the problem that the person may then be inclined to share.

  Do not let the person go into long detail about the problem because as a person is discussing the problem at length, you can perceptibly feel the anointing level drop. Their faith is dropping at the same time as they refocus on the size of their problem and then you can be distracted by the problem when your eyes should be on Jesus.

  So, there is a time to discuss issues over a coffee or in pastoral counselling but in a moment where you want the power of God to move, it is a hindrance to have more than a brief explanation. Gently try and rein it in, if the person is going into prolonged detail, assuring them that God knows what they are going through. Assure them of His promises and redirect them to faith (even if it's a mustard seed size) and a focus on Jesus and the finished work of the Cross.

This is not a lack of compassion to not accommodate, in that moment, a long presentation of an issue. We want the person to receive their healing and so compassion demands that we do everything we can to help them do just that. If the tangible anointing diminishes in a long discussion of a problem, then compassion demands that we limit the talk of the problem and go to faith.

- Next you lay hands on the person. Hebrews 6:1,2 lists the fundamental doctrines of Christ, and it is amazing that the laying on of hands is one of these basic doctrines. The laying on of hands has always been used to impart, or transfer, from one to another. Through the laying on of hands by Moses, wisdom was transferred to Joshua (Deuteronomy 34:9). In Matthew 19:13-15, Jesus laid hands on children to impart His blessing to them. In Acts 19:6, Paul laid hands on some believers to receive the Baptism in the Holy Spirit. Many times, in Jesus' own ministry He laid hands on a person to transfer the power of God directly to them, bringing healing.
- If the person is of other gender or older you should ask their permission if you can lay hands on them. Never touch a person in a way that may seem inappropriate to them. If it's a child I ask the parent's permission - however, it's usually the parent who has brought them for prayer, and so then, I get down to the child's level and ask them. If they seem shy or confused, then get the parent to just put their arm around them and then you, lay a hand on the parent. We don't want a child to be afraid, confused or feel unsafe.
- The need to feel safe goes for everyone. So, don't pray in a way that makes a person feel embarrassed, unsafe or uncomfortable in

any way. If they are focused on how uncomfortable they are feeling, they are not opening their hearts to receive prayer and yielding themselves to Jesus in that moment. So, this can prevent them receiving His healing grace in that moment.

- If you pray for someone in hospital, don't go in praying loudly and embarrassing them. Pray beforehand and then a very simple laying on of your hand and "be healed in Jesus' name" is enough to release what you have already laid hold of in prayer beforehand.
- Don't push people, rock them or lay your hands too heavily on them - many ministers want people to fall over for their ego's sake. The person who falls 'under the power of the Spirit' doesn't necessarily receive more than the one who doesn't. We are seeking to have a person receive the power of God to bring healing and miracles into their life. Equally, I have seen people dramatically fall and receive nothing - because it was all in the flesh. We can't make something of the Spirit happen in the flesh.

Now, falling under the power of the Holy Spirit is a very real phenomena as people encounter the power of God, but it's just not the end that we seek. I intentionally lay my hand lightly on someone's shoulder or head, so that if they fall, it was of God and not of me. No amount of trying to make something happen in the flesh will bring the power of God. In fact, it often hinders the person receiving God's grace because the person is so 'unnerved' by the experience that they lose their own focus on Jesus.

- Never be weird, loud or harsh. It is good to remember that Jesus was supremely powerful but never weird and He didn't humiliate or embarrass people. If the power of the Spirit is not evident, then, one needs to draw aside and fast and pray, with meditating on the Word, until it is there.

- As you pray, focus on Jesus, the finished work of the Cross and what God's Word says.
- Use your authority in the Name of Jesus and speak God's Word or the prophetic leading of the Holy Spirit. Remember that any prophetic utterance must align with Scriptural guidelines - that it is to be consistent with written Scripture, and brings edification, exhortation and comfort (1 Cor 14:3). It is never negative, demeaning, exposing nor used to manipulate behaviour.
- I will often pray according to the understanding of the Centurion in Matthew 8:9. The Centurion understood the way authority worked and noting, that because He was under Caesar, he just had to tell someone to go and they would go; another come and they would come and another do this and they would do it. Hence, seeing that Jesus was under the Father, he said that Jesus just needed to say a word and his servant, who was elsewhere, would be healed.

   So, in the name of Jesus I command whatever is not of God to go. I tell sickness, confusion of mind, oppression, demonic spirits if they are present, to go. I command healing to come. I am not commanding God but the release of what is already His will (and that He is waiting for the church to release) to be done on Earth as it is in Heaven. If there is, for example, scoliosis I would command the spine to be realigned to how God intended it to be.
- If a person starts to demonstrate awkward jerky movements, a rolling head, groaning or pain that moves from one part of the body to another, then you are dealing with an unclean spirit. Use your authority in the name of Jesus to tell it clearly and firmly to depart and command it to do so without causing any distress to the person, or any noise or disruption, if you are in a service.

- If it looks like something you aren't ready for, call pastoral support or the elders of the church to help. The person may be prayed for in private, as we don't want anyone to feel distressed, uncomfortable or embarrassed.
- If a spirit won't depart, then the reason is, usually, a sin that hasn't been repented of, forgiveness that hasn't been released, a generational or word curse that needs to be broken (by the blood of Jesus and in the name of Jesus) or a practice (e.g., occult; New Age; many alternative healing therapists have a spiritual entity attached to their practice however reasonable they may sound in theory; or other religious backgrounds) that still needs to be renounced and turned away from. Once this area has been ministered to, then deliverance and healing are released, usually quickly and with ease.
- Help them to stand in faith and not succumb to discouragement if the healing isn't instantaneous. Many are healed as they 'go their way'.
- Be sensitive to the Holy Spirit - what He would have you say or do. Does He want you to directly lay hands on the affected area? Ask their permission first and if it's a more sensitive area, they can lay their own hand on the area and you lay your hand on their shoulder. Does He want you to anoint them with oil? Does He want you speak a certain word of healing and life over them?
- When someone is healed encourage them to have a response of gratitude to God. For example, when Jesus laid hands on Peter's mother-in-law and she received healing, she got up and started to serve Jesus and the team. The response of gratitude may take many forms, but it is important.

> **Matthew 8:14,15** *14 Now when Jesus had come into Peter's house, He saw his wife's mother lying sick with a fever. 15 So He touched her hand, and the fever left her. And she arose and served them.*

Creating a place for people to encounter God's healing power

If you happen to have a healing focused meeting or service, the following are some helpful elements that we fostered in the healing services that we ran, which optimised the receiving of healing.

First of all is to create an atmosphere of faith, not only in the team but in the congregation. More healings are seen when there is a corporate faith and understanding, and not just that in the individual minister or person receiving healing. We are part of the Body of Christ and what happens in the Body impacts all. It is much more difficult for a minister to impart healing, or for a person to receive it, when in an atmosphere that doesn't embrace healing and faith. Healing doesn't just happen because you declare it but also involves taking time to impart faith and understanding into people.

The Holy Spirit moves on the Word of God and the revelation of Jesus and so, bring God's Word on healing and bring revelation of Jesus and what He has done into that meeting or service and the Holy Spirit will confirm that Word with signs and wonders following.

Then you need anointed worship, preferably with a team that knows how to respond to the Holy Spirit. It is not just having uplifting songs in worship, but a moving with the Holy Spirit and our worship team would minister in a way that would flow with the prayer ministry team. It is a holistic team ministry in bringing healing to a person in those moments.

Then we would have intercessory prayer by anointed prayer ministers before and during each service. The team were full of faith for healing, full of the Holy Spirit and the Word, insightful and could pray according to Scripture, led by the Holy Spirit and with a boldness and authority to see breakthroughs for others. They foresaw and prayed through challenges that people were facing. Some during the service would pray quietly up the back when moved by the Holy Spirit for a particular person or they would sit with a person and continue praying after the minister had moved onto the next person in the prayer line.

We then had prayer ministry by ministers full of faith and the Holy Spirit. Interestingly, they were all also in the intercessory prayer team who prayed prior to the services. Sometimes the prayer ministry for healing is slower than just quickly laying hands on someone. So, make time and the creation of a safe place, with not too loud a volume of worship, for people to receive ministry.

The final aspect was having a unified team. The Holy Spirit falls where there is unity and we were so grateful to be blessed with a beautiful team who all worked together in unity, bringing all of the above elements as a team and not just as individuals. We carefully cultivated this unity and resisted having team members who wouldn't flow with this, even if they were gifted. Unity matters and for that, team members need to be humble, not focused on their ministry or appearance, and to be able to work together for God's great purpose.

Four frequently asked questions.

1. How do I pray for someone who has cancer or some serious disease?

Without minimising the immense challenge for the suffering person, the foundation and provision of healing from God's perspective is the same for cancer as it is for a more minor complaint - it has been laid upon Jesus with healing made fully available. However, we can get intimidated by the problem, losing this perspective and that shuts down the power of God. We have to stay strong in the Truth, maintaining God's perspective.

So, God's perspective and the provision of healing is the same; the authority and position given to the believer to minister healing is the same, but a difference can be seen with the power level required. The minister of healing needs to keep full of the Word of God, faith and the Holy Spirit and there may be the need to seek God at a deeper level; to fast and pray, in order to see a greater level of power.

2. **How do I pray for something that I don't feel I have the faith for? i.e., someone is requesting prayer for something that you aren't sure is going to happen.**

Jesus often asked people "Do you believe I can do this?" Even though the prayer request may seem out of reach to us, we do serve a God with whom nothing is impossible and so, rather than limit people to our own faith or what we think is possible, leave room for God to do the impossible and ask them "What do you believe?". Then pray "Lord let it be done according to their faith".

> **Matthew 9:28,29** [28] *And when He had come into the house, the blind men came to Him. And Jesus said to them, "Do you believe that I am able to do this?" They said to Him, "Yes, Lord."* [29] *Then He touched their eyes, saying, "According to your faith let it be to you."*

If, however, someone requests prayer for something that is clearly not God's will i.e., contrary to His Word, then you cannot proceed with prayer for that.

3. **What if someone isn't healed? How do I support them moving forward?**

Some breakthroughs and healings happen immediately; most will be worked out through prayer and application of the Word of God and a few, despite the power of Christ's sacrifice and the person's faith, linger. However, the more we press in and engage with God, allow Him to change us, get revelation of His Word and apply it, the more the power of God is outworked in our lives.

So, encourage the person to keep pursuing God and keep believing whilst understanding the juggle that exists between what has been promised and what we experience. We are always encouraging people towards God and His promises and not making them feel 'lesser' if they are not currently experiencing healing. Never make someone feel at fault or accuse them of not having enough faith. Keep praying for them; keep declaring the Scriptures over them and help them to navigate the common doubts, disappointment or discouragement that come with these challenges.

4. **How do I build resilience to not go to disappointment, doubt or discouragement if I don't see someone healed after I have prayed for them?**

Stay in the Scriptures knowing that God's character and provision in Christ are not dictated by our circumstances. Our life's journey in Christ requires that we are able to step over many hurdles and move on. Not everything can be processed, resolved and understood and God doesn't give us detailed explanations about what happened (or didn't happen). We need to intentionally step over disappointment, what didn't happen and believe again.

We need to be aware that discouragement and disappointment are very effective and well-used weapons of the enemy that prevent us moving in the power of the Spirit. We need to be conscious of not embracing that which is meant for our destruction. Put the enemy's weapons down; embrace God's truth and believe again - believing releases the power of the Holy Spirit.

Reading:

- Matthew 8:14,15
- Luke 4:38-40
- Acts 28:8,9
- Luke 22:51
- Mark 6:13
- Acts 8:5-8

Thought for the day: And these signs will follow those who believe: In My name…. they will lay hands on the sick and they will recover (from Mark 16:17-18).

Reflection: Write down any insights or revelations that you have had as you reflect on how you will step out and pray for someone who is sick. How will you build and maintain faith to do this? How will you stay filled with the Holy Spirit and minister from God's perspective?

_____
_____
_____
_____
_____
_____
_____
_____
_____
_____
_____
_____
_____
_____

CONCLUSION

Thank you for coming on this journey of studying the Scriptures on healing and it is my hope that you have found some encouragement, wisdom and faith in this study to help navigate any healing battle. God has declared your completed healing in Christ and, even if your reality looks very different to that right now, can I encourage you to believe and trust Him with the truth that He speaks? For, in so doing, you connect to the power of God that is essential in taking you to experience His healing grace.

I know it can be challenging but keep believing, keep seeking His face and keep declaring His Word of power. God's favour is toward you and His intent is to do you good in the end. So, don't give up and don't lose heart.

> **Psalm 27:13** *I would have lost heart, unless I had believed That I would see the goodness of the Lord In the land of the living.*

My prayer for you is that God's blessing and favour rest upon you always as you walk with Him. I pray that you will know and experience His great and precious promises for healing and freedom and that you will have a great testimony of what the Lord has done for you.

THE LORD WHO HEALS YOU

Numbers 6:24-26

> ^{24} "The Lord bless you and keep you; ^{25} The Lord make His face shine upon you, And be gracious to you; ^{26} The Lord lift up His countenance upon you, And give you peace." '

Bless you

Kate Forsyth

REFERENCES

1. New Spirit Filled Life Bible, New King James version, Jack Hayford, executive editor. Published by Thomas Nelson Inc, Nashville, USA 2002. Used for all scriptural references unless specified otherwise.
2. New International Version of the Bible, International Bible Society, Colorado Springs, USA, 1973.
3. Strong's Concordance / Greek and Hebrew dictionary, James Strong. WORDsearch Corp.
4. Message Bible, Eugene H. Peterson. Navpress, Colorado Springs, Colorado, 1993.
5. New Living Translation Bible, 2nd edition, Tyndale House Publishers, Inc, Carol Stream, Illinois, 1996.
6. Young's Analytical Concordance to the Holy Bible, by Robert Young, LL.D. Eighth edition. Published by Luterworth Press, Guildford and London, 1975.
7. Young's Literal Translation of the Bible, verses sourced from Biblegateway.com.
8. The Amplified Bible, Zondervan Publishing House, Grand Rapids, Michigan, 1987.
9. A Picture of Health by Kate Forsyth. Published by Ark House Press, 2012.

10. English Standard Version Bible (ESV). Published by Crossway, a publishing ministry of Good News Publishers. Wheaton, Illinois, 2001.
11. Google's English dictionary provided by Oxford Languages.
12. Vine's Complete Expository Dictionary of Old and New Testament Words. Thomas Nelson Inc, publishers, Nashville, Tennesee, 1985.
13. MacMillan Dictionary - used by Google search for 'renounce'.
14. Collins Dictionary - used by Google search for 'renounce'.

ABOUT THE AUTHOR

Kate Forsyth is a pastor and pastoral trainer at C3SYD church and has been teaching and ministering healing since 1993. In that time, she taught a healing course under C3 Bible College, seeing many trained and ministering healing for themselves. Between 2014 and 2024 she ran a monthly healing service, with her husband Richard, at C3SYD Oxford Falls location on the Northern Beaches of Sydney and, over the years, they have had the privilege of seeing many healings and miracles through Jesus' miraculous power.

In 2014, she released her first book '*A Picture of Health*' which presented the Scriptural truths around healing, and the key that the Lord revealed to her in taking people from believing about healing to experiencing it. Many people experienced healing in discovering the Scriptures and how to apply them. In 2019, Kate authored a 21-day healing devotional on the YouVersion Bible App titled 'The Lord who heals you' which, at the time of writing, more than 25,000 people have accessed. This much expanded version of that carries the same name.

Kate is also a Pharmacist in the area of immunotherapy clinical trials. Kate and Richard have two miracle children, now adults, Annalise and Michael and a beautiful daughter-in-law, Tonia.

Kate's passion is for people to see the enormity of what Jesus has done for us, particularly in the area of healing, and to bring people into experiencing that. The desire is to see people healed but also, that Jesus will receive the due honour and praise for what He has done. She loves to take the truths of the Bible and make them practical and applicable to everyday life so that people can experience the promises of God.

Kate is available for speaking engagements.

www.ingramcontent.com/pod-product-compliance
Lightning Source LLC
Chambersburg PA
CBHW060109170426
43198CB00010B/823